Ramses

VOLUME 1

The Son of the Light

Ramses

VOLUME 1

The Son of the Light

Christian Jacq

Translated by Mary Feeney

SIMON & SCHUSTER

A VIACOM COMPANY

First published in Great Britain by Simon & Schuster Ltd, 1997
A Viacom Company

Simon & Schuster Ltd
West Garden Place
Kendal Street
London W2 2AQ

Simon & Schuster Australia
Sydney

A CIP catalogue record for this book is available
from the British Library

ISBN 0-684-82136-2

Typeset in Times 12/14pt by
Palimpsest Book Production Limited, Polmont, Stirlingshire
Printed and bound in Great Britain by
The Bath Press, Bath

Foreword

'Ramses, the greatest of conquerors, the Sun King guardian of truth.' In those terms Jean-Francois Champoillon, who deciphered the Rosetta Stone, unlocking the secrets of Egypt, described his idol, Pharaoh Ramses II.

Ramses's fame has endured for centuries. His name is synonymous with the power and glory of Ancient Egypt, the spiritual mother of Western civilization. For 67 years, from 1279 to 1212 BC, Ramses, 'Son of Light', guided the country to its peak of political power and cultural influence.

Travellers to Egypt still encounter Ramses at every turn. He left his imprint on the countless monuments he built, as well as those enlarged or restored during his reign. There are the two temples at Abu Simel, where Ramses is enshrined for ever as a god with his beloved consort, Nefertari: the vast colonnade at Karnak, and the giant statue, seated and smiling, at the temple of Luxor.

Ramses would not fit into one book. His life is an epic journey, from his initiation into the art of kingship under the guidance of his father, Seti (as impressive a figure as his son), to the final days of a long and evenful reign. That is why I chose to write a series of five novels, reflecting the breadth of an extraordinary destiny, marked by unforgettable characters such as Seti, his wife Tuya, the sublime Nefertari,

Christian Jacq

Iset the Fair, the poet Homer, the snake charmer Setau, Moses the Hebrew, and a host of others.

Ramses's mummy is preserved in the Cairo museum, his aged face still regal. Many visitors say he looks as if he might awake any moment. While death has robbed him of that power, the magic of the novel can restore it to him. Thanks to fiction and Egyptology, it is possible to share his hopes and fears, experience his failures and successes, meet the women he loved, suffer his betrayals and value his faithful friends, fight the forces of evil and seek the light from which everything originates and to which everything returns.

Ramses the Great — what a traveling companion for a writer! From the initial showdown with a wild bull to the soothing shade of the Western acacia, he was a legendary leader in a fabled country. The gods smiled on Egypt, a land of water and sunlight, where the words rectitude, justice, and beauty had meaning and penneated everyday life. A land where the Great Beyond connected with the here and now, where life could overcome death, where the invisible had a palpable presence, where the love of life and undying values made glad the hearts of men.

In truth, the Egypt of Ramses.

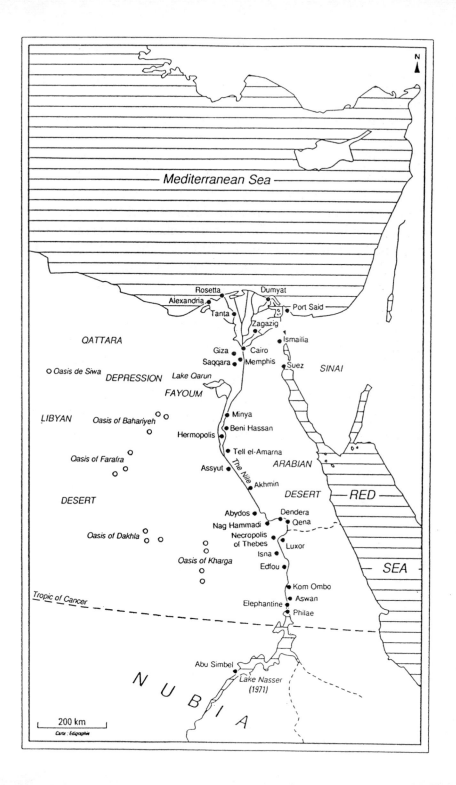

N

Mediterranean Sea

Rosetta
Dumyat
Alexandria
Port Said
Tanta
Zagazig
Ismailia

QATTARA

Giza • Cairo
○ Oasis de Siwa
Saqqara • Memphis
DEPRESSION
Suez
SINAI
Lake Qarun

FAYOUM

LIBYAN
Minya
Oasis of Bahariyeh
Beni Hassan
Hermopolis
Tell el-Amarna
ARABIAN
Oasis of Farafra
Assyut
Akhmin

DESERT
DESERT
RED
Abydos •
Dendera
Nag Hammadi
Qena
Oasis of Dakhla
Necropolis
of Thebes
Luxor
Oasis of Kharga
Isna
SEA
Edfou

Tropic of Cancer
Kom Ombo
Elephantine
Aswan
Philae

Abu Simbel
Lake Nasser
(1971)

N U B I A

200 km
Carte : Edigraphie

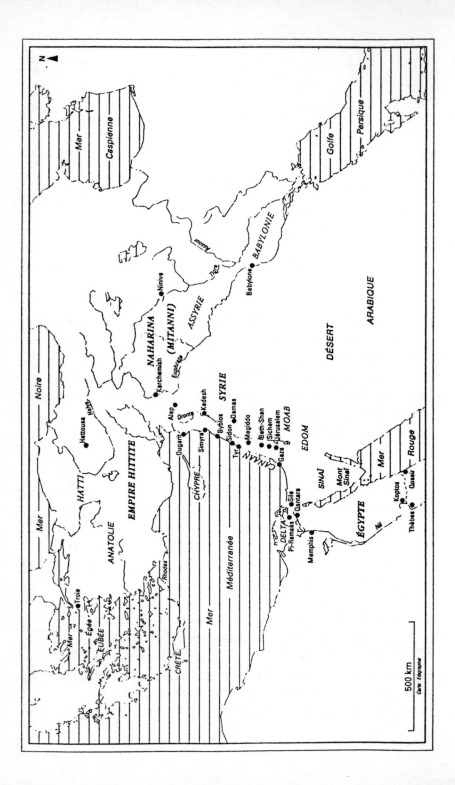

1

The wild bull froze, staring at young Ramses.

The animal was huge and dark, with legs thick as pillars, drooping ears, a stiff pointed beard. It had just sensed the young man's presence.

Ramses was fascinated by the horns, broad and almost joined at the base, then flaring out and upward in a helmet shape, tipped with two lethal points.

In all his fourteen years, Ramses had never seen such an enormous bull.

Even the ablest hunters steered clear of this particular breed. Calm in his own surroundings, protective of the sick and wounded, a watchful parent, the dominant male instantly transformed into a terrifying warrior when his territory was invaded. The slightest provocation could send him charging furiously and with amazing swiftness, retreating only when his opponent was trampled.

Ramses took a step backward.

The bull's tail swished as he kept a fierce eye on this intruder into his marshy domain. By the tall reeds, a cow was calving, her sisters in a ring around her. In this solitary backwater of the Nile, the huge male reigned over his herd and permitted no challenge to his authority.

The young man had hoped the thick grass would hide him,

but the bull's brown eyes, deep in their sockets, were trained on him. Ramses knew there was no escape.

Ashen, he turned slowly towards his father.

Seti, Pharaoh of Egypt, stood a few feet behind his son. 'Victorious Bull', they called him: his mere presence was said to paralyse his enemies. His mind, sharp as a falcon's beak, flew everywhere; there was nothing he did not know. Slender, stern-faced, with a high forehead, hooked nose, jutting cheekbones, Seti was authority incarnate. Worshipped and feared, the monarch had restored Egypt to her past glory.

Ramses had just met his father for the first time.

Until now, he had been in the care of royal guardians, who taught him all a king's son must know in preparation for a high government position. But this morning Seti had pulled the boy away from his hieroglyph class and driven him deep into the country. Not a word had yet passed between them.

When the vegetation had grown too dense, the two had abandoned their two-horse chariot and waded into the tall grass. Once clear, they had entered the realm of the bull.

Which was more frightening, the wild beast or Pharaoh? Ramses felt unequal to the power each of them radiated. In legend, the bull was a celestial animal, burning with the fire of the other world, and Pharaoh walked among the gods. Even though he was taller than most grown men, robust and naturally brave, Ramses felt trapped between two almost conspiring forces.

'He spotted me,' the boy said, trying to sound assured.

'Good.'

The first word his father spoke to him rang like a death sentence.

'He's so big, he—'

'And you, who are you?'

The question threw Ramses off guard. The bull pawed the ground with his left front hoof, faster and faster; egrets and herons flew off, as if clearing the battlefield.

2

'Are you a coward or a king's son?' Seti's gaze pierced his soul.

'I like a fight, but—'

'A real man goes to the limit of his strength. A king goes beyond it. If that is not in you, you are not meant to rule and we will never see each other again. No test should daunt you. Leave, if you wish; otherwise, catch the bull.'

Ramses dared to raise his eyes and hold his father's gaze.

'It's certain death.'

'My own father told me, 'Take for yourself the power of a bull, forever young, with a stout heart and sharp horns, stronger than any enemy.' Ramses, you came out of your mother's womb like a bull calf. You must become the light of your people, shining like the sun. You were hidden in my hand like a star; today I am setting you free. To shine – or to vanish.'

The bull snorted, irritated by the sound of their voices. All around them, a hush fell over the countryside; from burrower to bird in flight, every creature sensed conflict brewing.

Ramses turned towards the bull.

In hand-to-hand combat, he had already beaten opponents bigger and stronger than himself, thanks to holds learned from his trainer. But what strategy would work against a monster this size?

Seti handed his son a long rope with a slip knot. 'His strength is in his head. Catch him by the horns and you will have him.'

The young man saw a glimmer of hope. In mock water battles on the palace lake, he had done a great deal of roping.

'Once the bull hears the lasso, he'll charge,' warned the Pharaoh. 'Don't miss, for you won't get a second chance.'

Ramses rehearsed in his mind, silently working up courage. He had the muscular build of an all-around athlete, and chafed at having to wear his red-gold hair in the ritual style of childhood, pulled to one side and anchored in place above his ear. As soon as he was appointed to a court position, he would be allowed to change — if fate let him live to see the day.

Young and full of himself, he had been longing for the chance to prove his worth. Yet never did he imagine that Pharaoh in person would translate his dreams into brutal reality.

Riled by the human scent, the bull grew impatient. Ramses gripped the lasso; once the bull was roped, holding him would take the strength of a giant, a strength he did not have. So he would have to surpass himself, even if his heart burst.

No, he would not disappoint Pharaoh.

Ramses twirled the lasso; the bull ran at him, horns lowered.

Surprised by the animal's speed, the young man stepped quickly aside, snapped his arm and tossed the rope. It snaked through the air, landing on the bull's back. Recoiling, Ramses stumbled on the damp soil and fell just as the bull's horns were about to gore him. Even as they grazed his chest, he kept his eyes open. He wanted to look death in the face.

The angry bull raced to the edge of the reeds, then swung round menacingly and lunged towards him. Ramses, back on his feet, looked the monster straight in the eye. He would stand up to the beast until the very end. He would show Seti that a king's son knows how to die.

Then the bull stopped in his tracks. Pharaoh had roped him tight around the horns. Tossing his head until he nearly strangled, the raging beast struggled to break free. Seti grappled wildly and flipped the animal.

'Cut off the tail!' he ordered his son.

Ramses ran over and grabbed the smooth, tasselled tail, like the one in the waistband of Seti's kilt, proof he was master of the bull's power.

Beaten, the beast relaxed into panting and groaning. The

king released the animal after signalling Ramses to get behind him.

'The male of this breed can't be broken,' he told the boy. 'It will run through fire and water, even launch a surprise attack from behind a tree.'

The bull stole a sidelong glance at his opponent. Knowing he was powerless against the Pharaoh, he lumbered off towards his herd.

'You beat him!' said Ramses.

'No, we reached an agreement.' Then Seti unsheathed his dagger and with a single quick stroke severed the side lock in his son's hair.

'Father . . .'

'Your childhood is over. Tomorrow your life begins, Ramses.'

'I didn't beat the bull.'

'You conquered your fear, the first enemy on the path to wisdom.'

'Are there many others?'

'More than there are grains of sand in the desert.'

The question burned on the young prince's lips. 'Am I to understand . . . that you've chosen me to succeed you?'

'Do you think courage is all it takes to govern men?'

2

Sary, Ramses's guardian and teacher, scoured the palace for his pupil. It was not the first time the young man had skipped his mathematics lesson and headed for the stables or an impromptu swimming race with his pack of idle, unruly friends.

Paunchy, affable, detesting exercise, Sary constantly cursed his disciple but fretted over the boy's slightest escapade. His marriage to Ramses's older sister Dolora had won him the coveted post of royal guardian. Coveted, at least, by those who had never dealt with Seti's strong-willed son.

Sary was blessed with patience and was stubbornly determined to open the boy's mind, or he would have given up long ago on the insolent, overconfident prince. In keeping with tradition, the pharaoh was not involved in his children's upbringing. He waited until they were on the brink of adulthood to meet and test them, to see whether they might be fit to rule. In the present case, the decision had been made some time ago: Shaanar, Ramses's older brother, would mount the throne. Still, the younger son's high spirits must be channelled. At best, he could be molded into a good general, at worst a court fixture.

Well into his thirties, Sary would gladly have spent his time lounging by the pond behind his mansion, his bride of twenty at his side. But that might grow boring. Thanks to Ramses, no two days were alike. With his insatiable craving for life, his boundless imagination, he had run through several guardians before settling on Sary. Despite their frequent clashes, he was achieving his goal as a teacher: to educate the young man as a scribe, with all a scribe's knowledge and technique. Secretly, Sary took real pleasure in moulding his pupil's acute intelligence, his sometimes exceptional insight.

Now Ramses was changing. The boy who could not sit still for a minute had started to pore over the old sage Ptah-hotep's *Maxims*. Sary had even seen him dreamily watching the swallows dart through the early-morning sky. The maturation process had begun; many young men never completed it. The teacher wondered what manner of man Ramses would be if his youthful fires could be banked, burning more steadily but still as strong.

Such gifts did not come without a price, of course. At the royal court, as at every level of society, mediocrity was the rule, and mediocre people, hating to be shown up, instinctively shun stronger personalities. Although Seti's succession was established and Ramses need not fear plots and intrigues, his future might be less sunny than his birth would dictate. Some, including his own brother, were already making plans to exclude him. How would he do, exiled in some dusty provincial capital? Would he adapt to a simple country life, in tune with the seasons?

Sary had not confided these worries to his wife – she kept nothing to herself. As for approaching Seti, that was impossible. Immersed in managing affairs of state in his flourishing kingdom, he was far too busy to be burdened with a royal guardian's vague concerns. It was good that the father and son had no contact. A character as strong as Seti's would leave Ramses only two options: rebel or be crushed. Appointing guardians was definitely a sensible tradition: fathers did not always know best.

Ramses's mother, Tuya, the Great Royal Wife, was another

matter entirely. Sary was among the few who were privy to her strong attachment to her younger son. Cultured, refined, Tuya gauged the strengths and weaknesses of each royal courtier. She reigned supreme over the royal household, demanding strict adherence to etiquette and commanding the respect of nobles and commoners alike. But Sary was in awe of Tuya; troubling her with his little worries might discredit him. The queen disliked loose talk: in her eyes, an unfounded accusation was as serious as an intentional lie. No, it was better to keep quiet than to be a bearer of bad tidings.

Reluctantly, Sary headed for the stables. He was terrified of bucking horses, hated being around the grooms or, even worse, the royal horsemen bragging of their ludicrous exploits. Ignoring the jokes they made at his expense, the guardian continued his investigation. No one had seen Ramses for two days, which was most unusual.

Sary searched on for hours, forgetting his lunch. Exhausted, grimy, he straggled back to the palace as night fell. Soon, he would have to report his pupil's disappearance and prove he had played no part in it. And how could he face his wife?

He was too glum to return the greetings of his fellow teachers leaving the royal academy. In the morning, he would question Ramses's closest friends. If this proved fruitless, he would have to acknowledge the awful truth.

What had he done to bring the wrath of the gods down on his head? His career would be unjustly shattered, he would be banished from court, his wife would renounce him, he would end up as a washerman by the Nile. Horrified at the prospect of his own decline, Sary found his usual spot and settled in the classic cross-legged position of a scribe.

Ramses was supposed to be seated across from him, sometimes attentive, sometimes in the clouds, but always ready with an unexpected answer. At the age of eight, he had been able to draw beautiful hieroglyphs and could calculate

a pyramid's slope to the nearest degree — but only because
he enjoyed it.

The royal guardian closed his eyes, picturing the happier
moments of his rise through the ranks.

'Feeling all right, Sary?'

That voice — already so deep and commanding!

'Is it really you?'

'Take a look, if you're not too tired.' Sary saw that it really
was Ramses, dishevelled, but with a gleam in his eye. 'We
both need a wash, teacher. Where did you get so dirty?'

'In the stables, among other unsavory places.'

'Searching for me?'

Dumbfounded, Sary rose and inspected Ramses.

'What have you done to your hair?'

'My father cut the side lock off himself.'

'That can't be! The correct ritual—'

'Do you doubt my word?'

'Forgive me.'

'Sit down, guardian, and listen.'

The prince's tone had no trace of the child in it. Sary did
as he was told.

'My father tested me: the wild bull.'

'What in the world—?'

'I didn't beat it, but I faced it. And I think . . . I think my
father has chosen me to rule.'

'No, my prince. Your brother has already been named
successor.'

'But has Pharaoh tested him?'

'Your father simply wanted to see you react to danger. He
knows your reputation.'

'Why would he waste his time on that? No, I'm sure it
was a summons.'

'Don't get carried away, Ramses. This is madness!'

'Why?'

'The court is full of influential people with no use for you.'

'What have I done to them?'

'It's nothing you've done: it's who you are.'

'Are you telling me I should blend in with the crowd?'

'Listen to reason.'

'A bull makes a stronger argument.'

'Ramses, you have no idea how vicious power politics can be. It takes more than bullfights to come out on top.'

'Then you can help me.'

'I beg your pardon?'

'You know how the court works. Tell me who my friends are, and my enemies; be my secret adviser.'

'Don't ask too much of me. I'm only your guardian'

'Are you forgetting that my childhood is officially over? Now you become my tutor, or we go our separate ways.'

'It isn't fair. You want me to take uncalculated risks when you're not even first in line for the throne. Your older brother has been groomed for it. Go against him, Ramses, and he'll destroy you.'

3

The big night was finally here.

With only a new moon, it was deliciously dark out. Ramses had dared his classmates from the royal academy to sneak out and meet him in town. There they could discuss what really mattered, the question foremost in their minds, until now unspoken.

Ramses lowered himself out of his second-storey window and let go. The loose soil of the garden below softened the impact, and the young man crept along the wall. The palace guards posed no problem: some were sleeping, others played dice. If he happened on one who was actually alert, Ramses planned either to talk his way around him or knock him out.

In his excitement, he hadn't reckoned with one conscientious sentinel: a golden-haired dog, medium-sized, sturdy and muscular, with long ears and a curlicue tail. He made no sound, but stood resolutely in Ramses's path.

Instinctively, the prince made eye contact. The animal sat, his tail wagging rhythmically. Ramses went up and petted him; they were instant friends. The red leather collar was inscribed with the name 'Wideawake'.

'Want to come, boy?'

With a jerk of his short, black muzzle, Wideawake led his new master towards the gate of the royal academy.

Late as it was, people still strolled the streets of Memphis, the country's ancient capital. The southern city of Thebes might be wealthy, but Memphis remained the home of the great universities, the place where royal offspring and others earmarked for a high government posts received a thorough and rigorous education. Admission the *Kap*, 'the closed, protected, nourishing place', was a highly sought prize, but Ramses, like others who had spent their whole lives within its walls, longed only to escape.

A short-sleeved tunic of ordinary weave helped him blend into the crowd. It was an easy walk to the famous House of Beer near the medical school, where healers in training liked to unwind after long hours of study. With Wideawake still trailing him, the prince went into the tavern. School rules stated that academy students must never set foot here. But Ramses was no longer a child and was finally out of his gilded cage.

The main room of the House of Beer had whitewashed walls, mats and stools where loud groups of patrons crowded to enjoy strong beer, wine and palm liquor. The owner freely displayed his wares in amphorae from the delta, the oasis regions, or Greece, vaunting their quality. Ramses found a quiet spot and watched the door.

'What will it be?' asked a server.

'Nothing right now.'

'Strangers pay in advance.'

The prince handed over a carnelian bracelet.

'Will this cover it?'

'I suppose. Wine or beer?'

'Your best beer.'

'How many?'

'I'm not sure yet.'

'I'll bring the jar. When you're ready, you'll get the cups.'

Ramses realized he had no idea what things cost; he was

probably being robbed. It was high time for him to leave school. He had been too sheltered from the outside world.

With Wideawake curled at his feet, he watched for new arrivals. Would any of his classmates make it? He weighed his bets, eliminating the overcautious, the career-minded, until his list was whittled down to three names. He knew the danger would not deter them.

He smiled when Setau crossed the threshold. Swarthy, well built and masculine, Setau was the son of a sailor and his Nubian wife. His unflagging energy, as well as his gifts for chemistry and plant lore, had singled him out in his village school; he had done just as well at the *Kap*.

Setau was not a big talker, which was just as well. He had barely sat down when they were joined by Ahmeni.

Short, slight and pale, with wispy hair, Ahmeni was not cut out for sports or heavy lifting, but he was a tireless worker, sleeping only three or four hours a night. He was at the top of his class in hieroglyphs; he already knew more about literature than his teachers. The son of a plasterer, he was his family's pride and joy.

'I bribed a guard with my dinner,' he announced proudly.

He was on Ramses's short list. He had counted on Setau to use force, if necessary, and Ahmeni to rely on his wits.

The next arrival took him by surprise. He never would have expected pampered young Ahsha to take such a risk. He was the only son of wealthy nobles, and for him the *Kap* was just a necessary rung on the ladder to a high government post. Slim and elegant, he had a long face with a thin moustache and often wore a haughty expression, yet won people over with his smooth voice and sparkling, intelligent eyes.

He sat across from the trio of friends.

'Surprised, Ramses?'

'I have to admit I am.'

'Slumming with you sounded rather fun. Life has been dull lately.'

'It won't be much fun if we're caught.'

'That adds a bit of spice to the evening. Are the gang all here?'

'Not yet.'

'Your best friend wouldn't let you down, would he, old fellow?'

'He'll be here.'

'Of course.'

Ahsha called for the beer, but Ramses could not touch a drop, his throat tight with anxiety and disappointment. Could he have been so badly mistaken?

'Here he comes!' cried Ahmeni.

Tall, broad-shouldered, with long, thick hair and a beard outlining his jaw, Moses looked much older than fifteen. Descended from several generations of Hebrew immigrant workers, Moses had such remarkable intellectual gifts that he was singled out for the *Kap* as a very young child. He was as strong as Ramses physically, and the two had initially clashed, then had come to terms and joined forces against their teachers.

'A guard tried to stop me. He was too old to hit, so I had to reason with him.'

They drank a congratulatory round, enjoying the inimitable flavour of forbidden fruit.

At length Ramses spoke. 'Let's tackle the only important question,' he said bluntly. 'How do you find true power?'

'Reading and writing hieroglyphs,' Ahmeni said instantly. 'The language of the gods, the tool our sages used to hand down their precepts. "Do as your ancestors did," it is written, "for they knew life before you. Knowledge is power, and only writing immortalizes."'

'Spoken like a writer,' objected Setau.

Ahmeni coloured. 'Are you denying that a scribe holds the key to power? Good conduct, manners, fairness, trust, honesty, self-control, freedom from envy – those are the

14

things I want. And enough silence to surround the writing. Writing comes first.'

'I disagree,' said Ahsha. 'Diplomacy is the route to power. That's why I plan to go abroad, study the languages of friend and foe alike, understand how international trade works, learn the true intentions of other leaders, so that they can be manipulated.'

'I can tell you were born and raised in the city,' moaned Setau. 'You've completely lost contact with nature. The city is our greatest danger.'

'Then where are you going to find power?' asked Ahsha pointedly.

'There's only one way to find a combination of life and death, beauty and horror, poison and antidote: follow the snake.'

'You must be joking.'

'Where are snakes found? In the desert, in the fields, in swamps, by the Nile and the canals, on threshing floors, in shepherds' huts, cattle pens, even the cool dark recesses of houses! Snakes are everywhere, and in them lies the secret of creation. I plan to devote my life to learning it.'

No one attempted to argue. Setau had obviously made up his mind.

'What about you, Moses?'

The young giant hesitated. 'I envy you, my friends, because I have no answer. Strange thoughts trouble me, my mind drifts, but my destiny remains unclear. I'm probably going to be offered an important post in a great harem*, and I plan to take it, until something more exciting comes along.'

---

* In ancient Egypt, a harem was not merely a household for the Pharaoh's lesser wives, but also an important economic and cultural institution.

Now all four young men looked Ramses deep in the eye.

'Only one true power exists,' the prince declared. 'To be pharaoh.'

4

'Just what we thought you'd say,' complained Ahsha.

'My father took me to face a wild bull,' Ramses revealed. 'Why would he do that unless he wants me to be Pharaoh?'

His four classmates were stunned. Ahsha was the first to regain his composure.

'Didn't Seti already name your brother to succeed him?'

'Then why wasn't he put to the test?'

Ahmeni was radiant. 'That's wonderful, Ramses. I never expected to be friends with a future pharaoh!'

'Don't get carried away,' Moses advised. 'Maybe Seti is still deciding.'

'Are you with me or against me?' Ramses asked.

'With you, for life!' answered Ahmeni.

Moses nodded his agreement.

'Two sides to everything,' Ahsha opined. 'If I see you gaining the upper hand, I'll gradually lose confidence in your brother. If it's the other way around, I won't go with the loser.'

Ahmeni raised his fists. 'I ought to—'

'Perhaps I'm simply the most truthful of us all,' the future diplomat ventured.

'That would amaze me,' said Setau. 'I think my outlook is more realistic.'

'Pray tell.'

'I'm not interested in pretty speeches. Only actions count. A future king must be able to deal with reptiles. The night of the next full moon, when the snakes come out to hunt, I'll take Ramses out with me. We'll see how he measures up.'

'Don't go!' begged Ahmeni.

'You're on,' said Ramses.

The scandal shook the *Kap* to its ancient foundations. Never had the top of the graduating class so flagrantly broken school rules. Sary was given the unwelcome task of calling in the culprits and reading them their penalties. A few days before summer recess, the task seemed even more daunting in that all five young men had just been given government appointments in recognition of their gifts and academic accomplishments. For them, the gates of the *Kap* should be opening on a promising career.

He found Ramses playing with the dog that had quickly adapted to sharing his master's diet. Sary soon had enough of watching the dog lunge and chase after a rag ball, but the prince insisted on working with his pet, to make up for the former owner's supposed neglect.

Exhausted, panting, his tongue lolling, Wideawake lapped water from an earthenware bowl.

'You're in trouble, Ramses,' Sary began.

'What for?'

'That sordid little episode in the tavern, of course.'

'Come on, Sary, we weren't even drunk.'

'No, but you were stupid, especially considering the appointments you all would have had.'

Ramses grabbed his guardian by the shoulders.

'Do you have news? Tell me!'

'Your punishment—'

'That can wait. What about Moses?'

'Assistant director of operations at Merur, the great harem

in Faiyum.* Quite a responsibility for one so young.'

'He'll shake things up. It will be good for them. And Ahmeni?'

'A palace scribe.'

'Perfect! Tell me about Setau?'

'Certified as a healer and snake hunter. He'll harvest venom to serve as an antidote. Except that—'

'Ahsha? You forgot Ahsha.'

'Advanced courses in Libyan, Syrian and Hittite. Then he'll serve as an interpreter in Bylbos. Except that . . . What I've been trying to say is that all of your appointments are being held up.'

'But how?'

'By vote of the dean and the faculty, including me. Your behaviour was quite unacceptable.'

Ramses thought a moment. If he and his friends protested and the situation soured, news would be sure to reach the vizier, then Seti. Just the way to make the pharaoh furious!

'I seem to remember, Sary, that the *Kap*'s teaching is always to seek the just course.'

'Correct.'

'Then only the guilty party should be punished, namely me.'

'But—'

'The whole thing was my idea. I set the time and the place, I talked my friends into meeting me. If it had been anyone else, they'd never have tried it.'

'Probably, but—'

'Give them the good news about their appointments and let me serve their punishment. And now that we've settled things, I need to get back to that poor dog.'

Sary gave thanks to the gods. Ramses's plan gave him a graceful way out of a delicate situation. The prince, no favourite

* Some sixty miles southwest of present-day Cairo.

with the faculty, would stay on in-house suspension, receiving extra tutoring in mathematics and literature during the New Year festivities, which marked the return of the Nile's annual flooding. When Pharaoh presided at the festivities, Shaanar would appear at this side. Ramses's absence would attest to his insignificance.

Before serving his sentence, the prince was allowed to say goodbye to his classmates.

Ahmeni was warm and encouraging. With his job nearby at the palace, he would think of Ramses constantly and find some means of communication. As soon as they let him out, the sky was the limit.

Moses embraced him. Leaving Memphis would be a difficult adjustment. He was plagued by dreams, but telling his friend about them could wait until Ramses was free.

Ahsha was cold and distant. He thanked the prince for doing him such a favour and promised to pay it back if ever he had a chance, which was doubtful, since their paths were unlikely to cross in the future.

Setau reminded Ramses about their date and told him a promise was a promise. While Ramses was under house arrest, Setau would be scouting locales for their snake hunt. He was clearly delighted to be leaving the city and looking forward to daily contact with his true source of power.

To Sary's surprise, Ramses bore his confinement stoically. While others of his age dipped into all the pleasures of the season, the prince studied theorems and classical authors, breaking only to walk his dog in the campus gardens. Their tutorials ranged over the most serious subjects. Ramses showed astonishing powers of concentration, reinforced by an exceptional memory. In the space of a few weeks, the boy had become a man. Soon his former guardian would have little left to teach.

Ramses treated his suspension like a hard-fought wrestling match in which the opponent was none other than himself. Since his encounter with the wild bull, he had been struggling with another monster: a self-important adolescent, overconfident, impatient and disorderly. It was no less diffi- cult a fight.

His father was never far from his mind.

Perhaps they would never meet again and he would have to make do with his memories and the image of a peerless pharaoh. After Seti had released the bull, he had let his son take charge of the chariot, then after a few seconds had yanked the reins away without a word. Ramses had not dared question him. Spending time with Seti, no matter how brief, was a privilege.

Becoming pharaoh? The question seemed pointless now. He had let his imagination run away with him, as usual.

Still, Seti had made him face the bull, an ancient rite of passage now fallen into disuse. And Seti did not take such things lightly.

Instead of giving in to idle conjecture, Ramses had decided to fill the gaps in his knowledge and try to emulate Ahmeni's. No matter what work he did in the future, it would require more than courage and spirit. Seti, like all the pharaohs, had first been trained as a scribe.

Pharaoh! He could not get the thought out of his mind, no matter how he tried.

Sary informed him that his name was hardly mentioned in court circles, even negatively. He was beneath notice now that rumour had him heading for a plush exile in some provincial capital.

Ramses made no comment. He steered the subject back towards the sacred triangle used for temple walls or the correct proportions for a building based on the law of Ma'at, the frail and marvellous goddess of harmony and truth.

The boy who loved to ride, swim and fight forgot about the world outside as a delighted Sary moulded him into a scholar. In a few more years this former truant would make a learned professor! Ramses's crime and his punishment had finally set him straight.

On the final evening of his house arrest, the prince and Sary dined on the schoolhouse roof. Seated on reed mats, they drank cool beer, ate dried fish and spicy beans.

'Ramses, congratulations. You've made remarkable progress.'

'Yes, but do I have a job?'

The tutor shifted uneasily.

'Well . . . you've worked like a demon. You must need to give your mind a rest.'

'Are you trying to tell me something?'

'How can I put it? You have your position as a member of the royal family.'

'Can't I also have a post with the government?'

Sary avoided the prince's eyes.

'For the moment, no.'

'Who says so this time?'

'Your father, King Seti.'

5

'A promise is a promise,' said Setau.

'Is it really you?'

Setau looked different. Unshaven, without a wig, dressed in an antelope-skin tunic covered with pockets, he bore little resemblance to an accomplished university graduate. He had almost been turned away from the palace before one of the guards finally recognized him.

'What's happened to you?'

'I'm doing my job and I'm keeping my word.'

'Where are you taking me?'

'You'll see – unless you're too scared. You can always back out of your promise, you know.'

Ramses's eyes blazed. 'Let's go.'

Perched on donkeys, they made their way through the city, rode south along a canal, then branched out into the desert and headed towards an old burial ground. It was Ramses's first trip outside the lush valley and into this disturbing world where the laws of man held no sway.

'Tonight's the full moon!' said Setau, his eyes dancing eagerly. 'All the snakes will come out.'

The donkeys were following a path the prince would never have been able to pick out. At a steady, sure-footed pace, they headed deep into the deserted cemetery.

They had left behind the blue Nile, the green fields; here,

as far as the eye could see, stretched sand, silence and wind. Ramses felt in his bones why in the language of the temple the desert was 'Set's red land'. Set, the god of thunder and cosmic fire, had burned this desolate soil, but had also cleansed the human race of time and corruption. He had inspired the eternal dwelling places where mummies never decomposed.

Ramses took a breath of the bracing air. Pharaoh was the master of this red land just as he ruled the rich alluvial 'black land'. He must know the desert's secrets, use its strength, channel its power.

'We could still turn back, if you want to,' Setau told him.

'I can't wait for dark,' said Ramses.

A snake with a reddish back-and-yellow belly darted past Ramses and slithered between two rocks.

'Harmless,' Setau said. 'Hundreds of them live around deserted tombs. In the daytime, they sleep inside. Follow me.'

The young friends went down a steep slope with a ruined monument at the bottom. Ramses hung back.

'No mummies in here; it's cool and dry inside, you'll see. Nothing to be afraid of.'

Setau lit an oil lamp. Ramses found himself in a sort of grotto with rough-hewn walls and ceiling; perhaps the tomb had never been occupied. The snake charmer had brought in several low tables where he had arranged a whetstone, bronze razor, wooden comb, gourd, writing boards, scribe's kit and pot after pot of creams and unguents. Jars held ingredients used in remedies: asphalt, brass filings, lead oxide, red ochre, alum, clay and a variety of dried plants, including bryony, white sweet clover, castor oil, valerian.

In the gathering dusk, the sun turned orange. The desert was a sea of gold rippling with veils of sand that skipped from dune to dune.

'Take off your clothes,' Setau demanded. When the prince

had stripped, his friend coated him with a thick purée of onions and water. 'Snakes can't stand the smell,' he explained. 'By the way, did you mention where you're going to be working?'

'Nowhere.'

'A prince without a job? Must be another favour from Sary.'

'No, an order from my father.'

'So he wasn't impressed with the way you handled that bull.'

Ramses had tried to deny the obvious, although it would explain why he was being shunted aside.

'Forget the court, the political deals and back-stabbing. Come out here and work with me. Snakes can be dangerous, but at least they never lie.'

Ramses was shaken. Why hadn't his father told him the truth? It had all been a sham, leaving him without another chance to prove himself.

'Now for the real test, Ramses. To be immune to snakebite, you have to drink a nasty and toxic mixture made from nettle tubers. It slows the circulation, sometimes even shuts it down. If you vomit, you're dead. I wouldn't try this on Ahmeni, but you should be strong enough to handle it. Then most snake venom won't do a thing to you.'

'Most? You mean not all?'

'Venom from the biggest species requires a daily injection of a small amount of cobra blood. If you turn professional, you'll have to try it. Here, drink this.'

The taste was horrible. His blood ran cold and a wave of nausea hit him.

'Hold on now.'

But the nansia was overwhelming. He must get rid of the pain in his stomach, get rid of it, lie down and sleep . . .

Setau was gripping his wrist. 'Hold on now, open your eyes!'

Ramses fought the feeling. His stomach calmed, the cold sensation abated.

'You're strong all right, but you'll never make a king.'

'Why not?'

'Because you trusted me. I could have poisoned you.'

'You're my friend.'

'Can you be sure?'

'I know it.'

'I only trust snakes. They never betray their nature. With men, it's different. They spend their lives cheating and trying to get away with it.'

'Do you?'

'I chose the desert.'

'If I'd really been in danger, you would have saved me.'

'Put on your tunic and let's get going. You're not as stupid as you seem.'

Night in the desert was a feast, so full of wonders that not even the sinister laughter of hyenas, the howling of jackals, the thousand and one eerie sounds could trouble Ramses. Set's red land was full of the ghostly voices. The valley had its own enchantments, but here he sensed the power of the other world.

True power – it might after all lie deep in the haunted solitude of Setau's desert home.

Around them, the air was sibilant. Setau was in the lead, striking the ground with a long staff. He walked towards a heap of stones the bright moonlight transformed into a spirit fortress. Following his guide, Ramses had no sense of danger; besides, he had the little pouches of first-aid remedies that Setau had strung on his belt.

He stopped at the foot of the stone heap.

'My master lives here,' Setau revealed. 'He may not come out; he's afraid of strangers. Let's wait a while and pray.'

The young men sat cross-legged, the classic scribe's position. The prince felt light, almost airborne, inhaling the sweet desert darkness. The star-studded night was his classroom now.

A lithe and elegant outline appeared in the centre of stone heap. A gleaming black cobra, almost as long as a man, came out of its lair and reared majestically, wreathed in a silvery aura of moonlight. Its head shook rhythmically, ready to strike.

Setau stepped forward. The black cobra hissed. The snake charmer motioned Ramses to move closer.

Intrigued, the reptile swayed from side to side. Which intruder to strike first?

Taking two steps forward, Setau was only a few feet from the cobra. Ramses followed.

'You are the master of the night. You make the earth bear fruit,' Setau intoned slowly, enunciating each syllable. He repeated the chant at least ten times, urging Ramses to do the same. The melodic words seemed to calm the snake. Twice it reared up to strike but stopped short of Setau's face. When he put his hand on the snake's head, it froze. Ramses thought he could see the eyes glint red.

'Your turn, Prince.'

He reached out. The cobra struck.

Ramses felt the touch of the fangs. Repelled by the onion mixture, the snake did not bite down.

'Put your hand on his head.'

He held it there without flinching. The cobra seemed to back down. His outstretched fingers touched the black snake's hood. For a few moments, the master of the night submitted to the king's son.

Setau pulled Ramses backward. The cobra strike faded in the distance.

'You should have ended it sooner, friend. Don't forget that the forces of darkness are never vanquished. You've seen the uraeus on Pharaoh's crown, the sign of the cobra protecting Egypt. If the snake had struck again, then where would we be?'

Ramses let out a long breath and gazed at the stars.

'You're not careful, but you're lucky,' Setau told him. 'There's no known cure for a cobra bite.'

6

Ramses scrambled up on the fragile raft of lashed papyrus sheaves. It would never last the whole slate of ten swimming races he had organized. His name had attracted a small battalion of challengers, all the more eager to beat him since a bevy of Memphis beauties cheered from the canal banks. For luck, the contestants wore amulets around their necks: a frog, an ox leg, a magic eye. Ramses was naked, with no talisman, yet he outswam them all.

Most of the swimmers raced with a lady in mind. Seti's younger son competed only for himself, to prove could still reach beyond the limit of his strength and be first to touch the opposite bank.

Ramses finished five lengths in front of his nearest competitor. He felt not the least bit tired and could have kept swimming for hours. Smouldering, the other swimmers murmured congratulations. They watched their step around the prince. Life was not easy for a second son, soon to be packed off to a token post in the south.

A pretty brunette, about his age but mature in appearance, approached to offer him a strip of cloth.

'The wind is cool. Use this to dry yourself.'

'I don't need to.'

Inviting green eyes lit her oval face, with a small, straight nose and curving lips. Graceful, lively and poised, she wore an expression of mischief along with a filmy linen dress of the finest quality. In her headband, a lotus flower.

'You ought to. No matter how strong you are, it's easy to catch cold.'

'I've never been sick a day in my life.'

'My name is Iset,' she continued. 'I'm having a few friends over tonight. Would you care to join us?'

'Certainly not.'

'Well, if you change your mind, the invitation's open.' Smiling, she walked away without a backward glance.

Sary dozed beneath the tall sycamore shading his garden. Ramses paced in front of his sister Dolora, who also reclined on a lounge chair. She was an unattractive woman interested only in the creature comforts afforded her by her position in society. Her husband's prospects would guarantee her a life of ease, free from everyday concerns. Tall and ungainly, perpetually exhausted, endlessly pampering her bad complexion, Ramses's older sister prided herself on knowing all there was to know about life at court.

'You really should stop by more often, brother dear.'

'I've been busy.'

'Oh? That's not what I heard.'

'Ask your husband.'

'You certainly haven't come here just to flatter me.'

'No. I need some advice.'

Dolora was delighted, knowing how Ramses hated to ask for help.

'Ask away. I'll answer if it's within my power.'

'Do you know a girl named Iset?'

'Describe her.' Ramses complied. 'Iset the Fair!' said his sister, and frowned. 'Quite the temptress. Only fifteen, and beating admirers away from her door. The most beautiful woman in Memphis, some people claim.'

'Her parents?'

'Rich and socially prominent, palace connections that go back generations. So you're Iset's latest catch?'

'She only asked me to a party.'

'Join the crowd. Every night is a party for Iset. Are you going?'

'She has some nerve.'

'Because she took the initiative? Don't be old-fashioned, brother dear. Iset the Fair finds you to her liking – it's as simple as that.'

'A young unmarried woman shouldn't—'

'Why not? This is Egypt. We're not some backward barbarians. I wouldn't recommend Iset as a wife, but—'

'Quiet, Dolores.'

'Wouldn't you like to hear more about her?'

'Thank you, dear sister. I've had quite enough of your expert advice.'

'Just one more thing. It's time you got out of Memphis.'

'Why the warning?'

'You no longer count here. Stay much longer and you'll wither on the vine. In the provinces, though, they'll respect you. Don't plan on taking Iset the Fair along for company – she doesn't care for underdogs. I've been told that our brother finds her quite attractive. And he in the future king of Egypt. So get as far away from her as you can – and stay away, unless you plan to die young.'

It was no ordinary gathering. Several well-bred young ladies were giving a dance recital. Their wealthy parents had under-written years of professional lessons. Ramses came late, not wishing to dine. Now he somehow found himself in the front row of the sizeable audience.

The twelve dancers had chosen a vast lotus pond as their torchlit backdrop. Wearing pearl-studded netting beneath short tunics, triple-braided wigs, strands of beads and lapis

31

lazuli bracelets, the young women swayed suggestively. Supple and moving in unison to a delectably languid beat, they bent to embrace invisible partners. No one in the audience moved a muscle.

Suddenly, the dancers discarded their wigs, tunics and netting. Hair in a strict chignon, bare-breasted, clad in a wisp of kilt, they each tapped their right foot, then executed a breathtaking back flip, perfectly timed. Arching and bowing gracefully, they performed more acrobatic feats, all just as spectacular.

Four young women came forward, as the others sang and clapped to the beat. To the timeless melody, the soloists depicted the four winds. Iset the Fair was the north wind, bringing sweet relief on torrid summer nights. She outshone her partners, obviously satisfied to be the centre of attention.

Ramses could not take his eyes off her. Yes, she was beautiful, the most beautiful. She played her body like an instrument, moving with a sort of detachment, as if watching herself, unashamedly. For the first time, Ramses felt the need to take a woman in his arms.

As soon as the recital was over, he made his way through the crowd to the back of the garden and sat near the donkey pen.

Iset the Fair was toying with him, he mused, intending all along to marry his brother. She was only tempting him with what he would never have. For all his dreams of grandeur, he was sinking lower and lower. He must stop the downward spiral, sweep his demons out of the way. The provinces? Fine. He would find some way, any way, to prove his worth. If he failed, he could always work with Setau, handling the most dangerous snakes.

'Is something troubling you?' Iset the Fair had approached without a sound and now stood smiling at him.

'Just thinking.'

'You must think deep thoughts. All the guests have left; my parents and the servants have retired for the night.'

Ramses had lost track of time. Flustered, he rose. 'Please forgive me. I'll leave at once.'

'No need,' said Iset. 'You add something to the garden.'

Her hair loose, her breasts still exposed, her green eyes filling him with a disturbing warmth, she blocked his exit.

'Aren't you engaged to my brother?'

'Do princes believe everything they hear? I plan to choose for myself, and it won't be your brother. It's you I want, here and now.'

'I'm not sure I qualify as a prince.'

'Make love to me.'

Together, they undid their flimsy garments.

'I worship beauty, Ramses. I didn't know a man could be so beautiful.'

His hands caressed her all over, taking command. He wanted to give, to take nothing, to warm this young woman with the fire that consumed him. Iset was more than willing. Instinctively, with a sureness that amazed him, Ramses found every hiding place of her pleasure, lingering tenderly despite his growing urgency.

She was a virgin. So was he. They gave themselves to each other like a gift, their wild desire rekindling all through the balmy night.

7

Wideawake was hungry. He licked his sleeping master's face insistently: Rise and shine!

Ramses sat bolt upright, still in a dream where he lay with a woman, a passionate woman with breasts like delicious apples, lips like reed candy, legs wrapped around him like climbing vines.

But it was no dream. There was a such a woman. Her name was Iset the Fair. They had lain together and learned the meaning of pleasure.

The dog couldn't wait for the prince's head to clear. He yipped and whimpered until Ramses finally got the message and walked him to the palace kitchens. After Wideawake had cleaned his dish, they went out for a walk.

The royal stables were kept immaculately clean. The magnificent horses housed there were cared for and trained expertly. Wideawake didn't trust the oversized and unpredictable quadrupeds; he trotted warily at his master's heels.

They met a gang of grooms harassing a stable boy who struggled under a basket load of manure. One of them tripped the scapegoat, sending the boy, the basket and its contents tumbling.

'Clean it up,' ordered the perpetrator, a thick-faced fellow of fifty.

The wretched boy turned around and Ramses gasped,

'Ahmeni!' The prince jumped forward, shoved the groom aside, and helped his quivering friend to his feet. 'What are you doing here?'

Shaken, his former classmate could only stammer an answer. A rough hand grasped Ramses's shoulder.

'Hey! What makes you think you can mess with us?'

Elbowing the man's chest, Ramses sent him sprawling. Furious at losing face, grimacing, the groom rallied his gang.

'Let's teach these naughty boys some manners!'

The yellow dog growled and bared his teeth.

'Run,' Ramses ordered his friend. Ahmeni sat frozen.

Six against one: Ramses knew the odds were against him, but, as long as the grooms thought he didn't have a chance, there was a very slight possibility he could fight his way out of this predicament. The biggest one rushed him. Ramses ducked his punch, and before the groom knew what was happening he was flat on his back. Two more of the assailants also went down with a thud.

Ramses was glad he had worked so hard with the palace trainers. These men did were completely lacking in tactics, relying on brute strength to give them a quick win. Wideawake seconded his master, nipping at the fourth groom's ankles, then darting out of his way. Ahmeni's eyes were closed, tears streaming down his face.

The grooms regrouped, less confident. Only a nobleman would know such professional moves.

'You cheater,' the leader growled.

'Six to one isn't safe enough?' the prince countered.

The groom flashed a knife at him, snickering.

'An accident could spoil that pretty face.' Ramses had never fought an armed opponent. 'An accident with witnesses – even your little friend here would back us up, to save his hide.'

The prince kept his eyes glued to the short-bladed knife as

the groom traced threatening circles, toying with his victim. Ramses stood still, letting the man dance around him. The dog danced too.

'Down, boy.'

'You love the disgusting beast? A dog that ugly doesn't deserve to live.'

'Pick on someone your own size.'

'Meaning you? You're dreaming.'

The blade brushed Ramses's cheek. He tried to kick the knife out of the groom's hand, but only managed to swipe his wrist.

'You're tough, all right. But there's only one of you.' The other grooms pulled out their knives.

Ramses felt no fear. These cowardly bullies had stirred an untapped strength in him, a rage against injustice.

Before the grooms had time to orchestrate their attack, he knocked two of them down, narrowly missing the avenging blades.

'Stop, men!' cried one of the pack.

A sedan chair had just come into sight beneath the stable porch. Such a splendid vehicle could only be carrying an important personage, and indeed, snug against the tall backrest, feet on a footrest, forearms on armrests, head in the shade of a parasol, sat a man of twenty, pressing a scented cloth to his forehead. He had a round, almost moon-shaped face, pudgy cheeks, small brown eyes and thick greedy lips. Overfed, out of shape, the young lord made a heavy burden for his twelve highly paid professional bearers.

The grooms scattered. Ramses turned towards the sedan chair, while his dog licked Ahmeni's leg comfortingly.

'Ramses! In the stables again – but then animals *are* the best company for you.'

'And what brings you here, Shaanar, if you find it so distasteful?'

'Inspecting the premises, at Pharaoh's request. A future ruler needs detailed knowledge of his domain.'

'Thank heaven you came.'

'Really?'

'There's matter that needs your attention.'

'Yes?'

'Ahmeni, one of the palace scribes, was dragged out here and bullied by six grooms.'

Shaanar smiled. 'Poor Ramses, you never know what's happening! Hasn't your friend explained that he works here now?'

Dumbstruck, the prince turned towards Ahmeni.

'As an entry-level scribe, he found a mistake in a superior's text, then went over his head to correct it. When the senior scribe brought a complaint, I decided that an apprenticeship in the stables might be just the thing for this little snip. Hauling manure and fodder will shape him up in no time.'

'He doesn't have the strength for it.'

Shaanar ordered the his chair lowered to the ground. His sandal-bearer, the chief body servant, instantly produced a stepladder, slipped sandals on his master's feet and helped him down.

'Let's take a walk. I need to speak to you in private.' Ramses left his watchdog with Ahmeni.

The two brothers paced the roofed walkway of a paved inner courtyard. Shaanar hated exposing his fair complexion to the sun.

How could two men be less alike? Shaanar was short, squat, fleshy, already resembling a dignitary who has spent a little too long on the banquet circuit. Ramses was tall, lithe and muscular, glowing with youthful energy. The older brother's voice trilled and gushed, while the younger's was low and clear. They had nothing in common except for being Pharaoh's sons.

'Reinstate Ahmeni,' Ramses demanded.

'Forget your little friend. We have more urgent matters to discuss. As I understand it, you were supposed to leave town.'

'No one told me that.'

'Consider yourself told.'

'Since when do you give me orders?'

'You must be forgetting who's next in line to the throne.'

'Thanks for the reminder.'

'Don't be impudent with me, Ramses. Save your energy for wrestling. One day my father and I may find you an active command in the army; defending your country's interests is a worthy cause. But Memphis is no place for someone like you.'

'I was just beginning to like it.'

'If I have to go to our father, I will. You're only making it harder on yourself. Why not go quietly? I can have everything ready in two or three weeks.'

'Where does that leave Ahmeni?'

'I told you to forget the little snitch. Don't make me say it again! One last thing: leave Iset the Fair alone. She won't settle for second best.'

8

Queen Tuya's day had been trying. With her husband off on an inspection tour of the north-eastern border's defences, she had granted audiences to the vizier, the exchequer, two provincial leaders and a scribe from the royal archives. So many pressing problems to attend to, and each deserved her attention.

Seti was increasingly concerned about disturbances the Hittites were stirring up in some of his Asian and Syro-Palestinian territories. Usually the local rulers simply needed to air their grievances, and a state visit from Pharaoh was enough to smooth ruffled feathers.

Tuya, the daughter of a charioteer, had neither of royal lineage nor noble ancestry, yet her qualities were such that she quickly won the devotion of court and country. Naturally elegant, her lofty bearing enhanced a slender figure, a face with huge almond eyes, intent and piercing, a thin, straight nose. Like her spouse, she commanded respect and did not tolerate overfamiliarity. Her mission was to maintain and increase the influence of the Egyptian court. Carrying out her duties was crucial to the country's stature and the people's welfare.

At the thought of her next interview, the queen's fatigue vanished. Ramses, her favourite son, was coming to lunch with her. Although she had chosen the palace pleasure garden as their setting, she still wore her long, gold-hemmed linen robes, a short pleated cape, a necklace with six strands of amethysts, a wig with neatly spaced twists of hair. How she loved to stroll beneath the acacias, willows and pomegranate trees, along the borders of cornflowers, daisies and larkspur! There was no more heavenly creation than a garden, where every plant, in every season, sang glory to God. Morning and evening, before she turned to her royal duties, Tuya allowed herself a few minutes in this earthly paradise.

When Ramses arrived at her side, the queen was astonished. In just a few months, he had grown strikingly handsome. He gave an impression of power. A hint of the adolescent remained, of course, but the carefree child was gone.

Ramses bowed to his mother.

'Is a kiss against protocol?' she enquired. He clasped her briefly, amazed at how fragile she seemed. 'Remember the sycamore you planted when you were three? Come, see how it's flourished.'

Within moments Tuya realized that the muted anger she felt in her son would not be easily soothed. He was a stranger to this garden, where he had spent countless hours tending the trees.

'The last few months have been hard for you,' she said.

'Do you mean my house arrest, or have you heard how I didn't rope the bull? But none of that matters, really. What bothers me is losing the fight for justice.'

'You have an official complaint to make, then?'

'My friend Ahmeni has been falsely accused of insubordination. My brother had him dismissed as a palace scribe and sentenced to menial labour in the stables. He's not strong enough for the work. It's going to kill him.'

'That's a serious accusation. You know I won't deal with unsubstantiated rumours.'

'Ahmeni wouldn't lie to me. There's no one more truthful.

Does he have to die because he's my friend and Shaanar couldn't make him grovel?'

'Do you hate your brother?'

'I don't even know him.'

'Do you know he's afraid of you?'

'Then how did he have the gall to tell me I have to leave Memphis?'

'He must not be happy to hear that you and Iset are lovers.'

Ramses stammered 'You've already heard?'

'It's my job to keep track of you.'

'I'm not allowed any privacy?'

'In the first place, you're Pharaoh's son. And then, Iset may be fair, but she's not discreet.'

'Why would she brag about choosing not to be queen?'

'Probably because she believes in you.'

'It's just an affair. My brother can never have her first now.'

'Is it that simple, Ramses, or do you love the girl?'

The young man hesitated. 'Physically, yes. I want to keep seeing her, but—'

'Are you thinking of marriage?'

'Marriage!'

'That's where it leads, my son.'

'Not yet.'

'Iset the Fair is a very determined young woman. Now that she's chosen you, she won't let go easily.'

'Wouldn't Shaanar make a better match for her?'

'You don't seem to think so.'

'Maybe she plans to compare us.'

'You must think women are ruthless.'

'After what happened to Ahmeni, how can I trust anyone?'

'Not even me?'

Ramses took his mother's right hand. 'I know you will never betray me.'

'As for your friend, I can think of one solution.'

'What's that?'

'Become a royal scribe. Then you can appoint your own secretary.'

Ramses could not help but admire Ahmeni's obstinate refusal to crumble under the physical strain of his punishment. The grooms knew who Ramses was now, and fearing further reprisals they left Ahmeni in peace. One of them even stopped heaping his baskets so full and lent him a hand now and then. Still, Ahmeni grew weaker by the day.

Royal scribes were chosen by means of a competitive examination, and Ramses had not had time to prepare for it. The test was administered in a courtyard outside the vizier's offices. Carpenters had been called in to erect wooden posts and drape them with cloth as sunshades.

Ramses was given no special consideration. Requesting it would be in violation of the law of Ma'at. Ahmeni should have been the one to take the exam. Ahmeni would be better qualified for the job. Still, the prince had to fight for his friend in the only way he knew how.

An old scribe, leaning on a staff, was haranguing the fifty young men assembled to compete for the two vacant posts in the kingdom.

'Gentlemen,' he rumbled, 'you've had years of school. You want government office. You crave the power attached to it. But has anyone told you what that office entails? You must wear clean linen and spotless sandals. Keep your eyes on your papyrus and your nose to the grindstone. You must steady your hand and curb your tongue. When your head aches from studying, study some more! Obey your superiors and strive to improve in all ways. If you wish to serve mankind, do not shrink from discipline. A monkey can follow commands, a lion can be learn to do tricks, but a lazy young scribe is hopeless. The only cure is the rod!' he said with a flourish. 'Proceed, gentlemen!'

Each candidate was given a sycamore writing kit, thinly coated with plaster. A cavity in the centre held the sharpened reeds serving as their pens. They moistened the two cakes of ink, one black, one red. Then every man invoked the great sage Imhotep, patron of scribes, spilling a few drops of ink in his memory.

For several hours, they had to copy inscriptions, answer grammar and vocabulary questions, solve mathematics and geometry problems, compose a sample letter, copy out the classics. Several gave up altogether, others lost their concentration. Then came the ultimate test, in the form of riddles.

The fourth and final one had Ramses stumped. 'How does the scribe transform death into life?' That was beyond the wisest scholar. His mind was blank. Missing this one, on top of inevitable lost points for minor errors, would eliminate him. He thought and thought, but saw no solution.

He might not become a royal scribe, but he would not stop trying to save Ahmeni. They could go deep in the desert with Setau and his snakes. The constant threat of death was preferable to a life without freedom.

Out in the courtyard, a baboon scurried down a palm tree and under the awnings, hopping on to Ramses's shoulder before the proctors had time to intervene. The prince sat quietly as the baboon seemed to whisper a few words to him, then vanish as suddenly as it had appeared.

For a few brief seconds, man and animal had merged into a single being. In his magical form as a baboon, Thoth, the god of learning, had infused the king's son with his thoughts. The human hand was moved by the animal spirit.

Ramses read the answer he had been given. 'The scribe uses his scraper to remove the plaster covered with writing. A new coat is then applied. Thus, he brings the dead plaster back to life, ready to be used again, like new.'

Ahmeni was so exhausted he could no longer lift a basket. His bones felt ready to break, his neck and shoulders stiffer than a plank. They could beat him if they liked, but he wouldn't move. It was such a waste. He dimly remembered the prospect of a wonderful future: reading, writing, copying hieroglyphs, following the teachings of the sages, preserving time-honored texts . . . One last time, he tried to hoist his load.

A strong hand lifted the burden from him.

'Ramses!'

'I'd like your opinion of this writing kit.'

The prince showed his friend a gilded palette carved like a column. Its capital was a lily, the cone-shaped top to be used for buffing inscriptions.

'Magnificent!'

'It's yours, if you can read me the text.'

'"May Thoth's baboon protect the royal scribe,"' he rattled off. 'That's for beginners!'

'Then I, Ramses, in my official capacity as royal scribe, hereby engage you, Ahmeni, as my private secretary,' he said. And he handed over the palette.

9

The reed hut at the far edge of a wheat field, deserted at night, was a perfect hideaway for Iset the Fair and Ramses, with Wideawake to stand guard.

Their young bodies were perfectly in tune. Playful, passionate, tireless, they found hour after hour of pleasure without exchanging a word.

Tonight, blissfully drowsy, Iset the Fair was humming, head on her lover's chest.

'I don't know why you're still with me,' Ramses said.

'Because you're a royal scribe now.'

'You could do better.'

'Better than my prince?' she laughed.

'You could have the *crown* prince.'

Iset made a face.

'Yes, I've considered it, but he doesn't appeal to me. Too fat, too dull, too underhanded. I couldn't bear to let him touch me. So I decided to love you.'

'Decided?'

'Some souls are made to give love, some to take it. I'll never belong to a man. Not even a king can own me. I've chosen you, Ramses, and you will choose me. We're two of a kind.'

Senses still reeling from his sleepless night with Iset the Fair,

Ramses was taking the back way to his scribe's residence when Ahmeni bustled out of an office and over the iris beds to intercept him.

'We need to talk.'

'I'm tired, Ahmeni. Can it wait?'

'No, it's too important.'

'Then at least get me something to drink.'

'Milk, freshly baked bread, dates and honey – the royal breakfast is served. But first you should know that the royal scribe, along with his personal assistant, is kindly requested to attend a reception at the palace tonight.'

'You mean . . . at my father's?'

'The one and only.'

'An invitation from Pharaoh! Or is this another one of your pranks, Ahmeni?'

'Relaying important news is one of your assistant's duties.'

'A royal reception . . .'

Ramses longed to meet his father again; as a royal scribe, he would not be allotted much time. What would he say? Should he protest, demand explanations, question the pharaoh's treatment, ask what was expected of the younger son, what plans Seti might have for him? Each word would have to be weighed.

'One more thing,' Ahmeni said, frowning.

'Yes?'

'A shipment of ink cakes came in yesterday, and I found two that were unacceptable, even though they had the seal of quality. I always feel I should check all our new supplies. Now I *know* I should.'

'Aren't you blowing this out of proportion?'

'It's inexcusable. I'm calling for an investigation in your name. A royal scribe sets the national standard.'

'As you see fit, Ahmeni. Now can I get some sleep?'

Sary was paying a courtesy call on his former pupil. Granted,

Ramses had no further need of a tutor. Admittedly, Sary had played no part in coaching the prince to first place in the highly competitive royal-scribe examination. Nevertheless, the prince's coup reflected favourably on his teacher. As the newly appointed director of the *Kap*, he was set for life.

'I must admit you amazed me, Ramses, but don't let it go to your head. You righted a wrong and rescued Ahmeni; isn't that enough?'

'I'm not sure I understand.'

'You asked me once to advise you behind the scenes, help you tell your friends from your enemies. The only true friend I see is Ahmeni. Others resent your success, but that won't hurt you, provided you get out of Memphis and settle in the south.'

'You sound like my brother.'

Sary was momentarily nonplussed. 'Don't read too much into things, Ramses. But stay away from the palace. This reception is not for you.'

'I am a royal scribe, am I not?'

'Believe me, your presence there will be neither welcome nor wise.'

'And if I choose to attend?'

'You'll be royal scribe – but without a posting. Don't cross Shaanar. If you do, you're your own worst enemy.'

Sixteen hundred sacks of wheat and as many of other grains had been brought to the royal palace. Thousands of fancy cakes and rolls would be baked; sweet beer and oasis-grown wine would flow. Thanks to the pharaoh's efficient stewards, by the time the first star appeared in the night sky, the guests at the reception would enjoy the best the palace had to offer.

Ramses was among the first to arrive at the monumental gates to the palace complex, flanked night and day by the pharaoh's private guard. The sentries knew Seti's younger son by sight, yet still checked his credentials before allowing him entry to the vast, almost forested, garden. An artificial lake reflected the ancient acacias. Here and there were tables laden with baskets of bread and sweets, stands with floral arrangements. Cup-bearers poured wine and beer into alabaster goblets.

The prince fixated on the central building, where he knew royal audiences always took place. The rooms were covered with shiny ceramics; visitors marvelled at the play of colours. Before he was sent to the royal academy, Ramses had played in the private suites and even ventured as far as the steps to the throne room. He still remembered his glimpse of Pharaoh's throne, its base carved with scenes showing Ma'at, the essence of truth and harmony. He also recalled a sound scolding from his nursemaid, the one who had suckled him well past the age of three.

Ramses had hoped that the royal scribes would be allowed inside the palace, but it was obviously not to be. Seti would simply have the guests gather in a vast courtyard, then would appear in a window and give a short speech reiterating the scope and importance of their duties and responsibilities.

How could he manage to speak to his father privately? The king had been known to mingle briefly with his subjects and greet a few of the most notable. He, Ramses, had achieved a perfect score on the scribes' examination; he alone had solved the final riddle. He would not be amiss in approaching Seti to ask why the king ignored him. If he was really meant to leave Memphis for some obscure post in the provinces, he wanted to hear it directly from Pharaoh.

All around him the royal scribes, their families and a host of courtiers who never missed important parties were drinking, eating, and making small talk. Ramses tried the heady oasis-grown wine, then the strong beer. Draining his goblet, he noticed a couple seated on a stone bench tucked under an archway.

A couple consisting of his brother Shaanar and Iset the Fair.

Ramses strode their way.

'You told me you'd made up your mind, my sweet. Is this how you show it?'

Iset was stunned, but Shaanar remained cool.

'You forget your manners, dear brother. Have I no right to converse with a lady?'

'If that's what you call her.'

'Don't be crude.'

Cheeks aflame, Iset the Fair fled the brothers, leaving them face to face.

'I can't put up with much more, Ramses. You are no longer needed in Memphis.'

'I am a royal scribe.'

'Brag all you want, but there will never be a post for you without my approval.'

'Your friend Sary warned me.'

'Sary is only trying to keep you out of trouble.'

'Just stay away from Iset.'

'How dare you try to intimidate me!'

'If I'm nothing, then I have nothing to lose.'

Shaanar backed down. 'Brother, you're right,' he said in his silkiest voice. 'No one should have to share a woman's affections. But let's leave the choice up to her now, shall we?'

'Agreed.'

'Then go and enjoy the party.'

'When will the king be addressing us?' Ramses asked.

'Oh, hadn't you heard? Pharaoh has left on a military inspection tour of the northern borders. He asked me to host this reception. And since you scored the highest on the latest exam, I've arranged a special reward for you: a hunt in the desert.'

Shaanar walked off.

Vexed, Ramses downed another goblet of wine. So he was

not to see his father after all. Shaanar had lured him here only to put him in his place. Drinking more than was sensible, Ramses kept to himself. Snatches of the other guests' chatter only served to annoy him. In a daze, he collided with an elegant-looking scribe.

'Ramses! Delighted to see you again.'

'Ahsha! Still here in Memphis?'

'I leave for the north tomorrow. The latest reports say the Trojan War is all but ended. The Greek barbarians wore down Priam's defences, and rumour has it that Achilles killed Hector. My first diplomatic mission will be to determine whether our intelligence is accurate. And you, old friend — a major post in the offing?'

'Not that I know of.'

'Everyone talks about the scribe competition. Some less than kindly, I may say.'

'I'll learn to live with that.'

'Wouldn't you like to go abroad? Oh, forgive me: I forgot that you're getting married. Soon, isn't it? Sorry I'll be away, but I do wish you all the best.'

Then an ambassador commandeered Ahsha, and the fledgling diplomat's mission was already under way.

Ramses was suddenly aware of his creeping intoxication: he was like a broken rudder, a house with a shaky foundation. Livid, he flung the goblet away, swearing never again to indulge in such unfit behaviour.

10

The hunting party left at dawn for the western desert. Ramses had left his dog in the care of Ahmeni, who was still intent on tracing the second-rate ink cakes.

From the safety of his sedan chair, Shaanar saw the hunters off. He would not venture into the desert, content with offering a parting invocation: 'May the gods protect these brave souls and bless their efforts with plentiful game.'

The procession of light chariots rode out. Ramses's was teamed with an army-veteran driver. It was a joy to be back in the desert where the ibex, bubal, oryx, leopard, lion, panther, stag, ostrich, gazelle, hyena and fox roamed free, with man as their only predator.

The master of the hunt had left nothing to chance. Well-trained dogs followed the chariots, some of which were laden with provisions and jugs of water. There were even tents in case the pursuit of some special quarry kept them out past dark. The hunters were equipped with lassos, new bows and a large supply of arrows.

'Do you like killing or catching?' the driver asked.

'Catching,' answered Ramses.

'All right then. You use the rope and I'll take the bow. Killing is a tool for survival. No hunter escapes it. I know who you are, son of Seti; but facing danger makes us equals.'

'Incorrect.'

'You think you're so superior?'

'No, you are, because of your experience. This is my first hunt.'

The former charioteer shrugged.

'Enough talk. Look sharp and let me know if you spot any prey.'

The veteran paid no attention when a panic-stricken fox and then a jerboa ran by. He left them for the other teams. Soon, the cluster of hunters scattered.

The prince sighted a herd of gazelles.

'Great!' his companion cried, already hot on their trail.

Three stragglers, old or sick, became separated from the herd and bolted towards a nearby gully, where a wadi flowed in the rainy season.

The chariot stopped.

'Time to walk now.'

'Why?'

'Too rocky here. Wheel damage.'

'But the gazelles will outrun us!'

'Don't think so. I know this place. They'll head for a cave, and then we'll get them.'

So they marched, for over three hours, intent on stalking, indifferent to the weight of their weapons and gear. When the heat grew too intense, they stopped to eat in the shade of a stone outcropping where succulents grew.

'Tired?'

'No.'

'Then you're a desert man. Either it knocks you flat or it gives you wings, and hot sand will do it for you every time.'

Pieces of rock broke loose and tumbled down to join the gravel in the river bed. It was hard to picture this dry red land with a life-giving river, trees and fields. The desert was the other world present in the heart of the human one. Ramses sensed how precarious his existence was. At the same time, he felt the power that nature stirred in the soul of the silent listener. God had created the desert to make man stop and hearken to the voice of the secret fire.

The charioteer checked the flint-tipped arrows. Two fletches with rounded edges weighted the opposite end of the shaft.

'Not the best, but we'll make do.'

'How far to the cave?'

'An hour, give or take. Want to turn back?'

'Let's get going.'

Not a snake, not a scorpion, no living thing seemed to dwell in this desolation. They had probably burrowed in the sand or beneath a rock, to come out only in the cool of evening.

'My left leg is bothering me,' said Ramses's companion. 'An old war wound. We may need to stop and rest.'

When night fell, the man was still in pain.

'Sleep,' he told Ramses. 'This leg will keep me awake. If I start to nod off, I'll wake you.'

First came a pleasant warmth. Then the sun left the gentle dawn behind and it was scorching. Emerging victorious from its nightly combat with the shadows and the life-devouring dragon, it grew too bright for mere mortals.

Ramses awoke.

His hunting companion had disappeared. The prince was alone – without food, water or weapon, and several hours' walk from his point of departure. He set off without delay, at a steady pace, husbanding his strength.

The man had deserted him, assuming he'd never survive the forced march back. Who had put him up to this? Who would want to pass premeditated murder off as a hunting accident? Everyone knew the prince was impulsive, the story would go. In pursuit of his prey, he had lost all caution, and now he was lost in the wilderness.

Shaanar! It had to be his sneaking, spiteful brother. Ramses refused to leave Memphis, so Shaanar sent him to cross the river of death. Boiling with rage, Ramses vowed not to make that journey. Instead, he unerringly retraced his path to the meeting place, advancing relentlessly as a conqueror.

A gazelle ran swiftly by, soon followed by an ibex with long, backward-curving horns, which studied him thoroughly before it bolted. The animals must be heading for a watering place the prince's companion had neglected to point out. He could choose to stay on track and die of thirst, or put his trust in the animals.

He opted for the animals.

By the time he had spotted ibexes, gazelles, oryxes and a thirty-foot tree in the distance, he was telling himself he should always follow his instincts. The tree had grey bark and a tangle of branches blooming with fragrant yellow-green flowers and bearing thin-skinned oval fruit up to three inches long, so sweet that hunters called it the 'desert date'. It also prickled with long, green-tipped thorns. In the shelter of its shade lay one of those mysterious springs that gushed from the desert with Set's blessing.

Leaning against the tree trunk, a man sat and ate bread.

Ramses moved closer and recognized him: the leader of the gang of grooms who had bullied Ahmeni.

'May the gods be with you, my prince. Are you lost, by any chance?'

With his dry lips, parched tongue and burning brow, Ramses had eyes only for the water skin on the ground by this hairy, stubble-faced creature's left leg.

'You're thirsty? What a shame. Nice, cool water, but too precious to waste on a dead man.'

Only ten paces between Ramses and his salvation.

'You had to show me which one of us was a prince. You got away, and now all the stable boys laugh at me.'

'I know you didn't plan this. Who's behind it?'

A twisted smile. 'For once I was glad to oblige. When your hunting partner offered me five cows and ten lengths of linen to finish you off, I didn't think twice. I knew you'd come here. Going back the same way you came with no water would have been suicide. You thought the gazelle and the ibex would save your life, but they only made you my trophy.'

The groom rose, flashing his knife.

Ramses sized up his opponent. He probably expected more fancy wrestling moves. Instead, he was facing an unarmed, exhausted teenager, desperately thirsty, in no shape to use technique against a much stronger and armed attacker.

Which left brute strength as the prince's only choice.

With an angry whoop, releasing all his energy, Ramses rushed at the groom. The man swung wide with his knife, then fell heavily backward into the prickly desert date tree, the thorns piercing his flesh like so many daggers.

The hunters could not complain. Their live catch included an ibex, two gazelles and an oryx now being guided by the horns. More or less resigned, the herd moved forward when their bellies were gently prodded. One man had a baby gazelle slung over his back; another held a terrified rabbit by the ears. There was a hyena lashed to boards that rested on two helpers' shoulders. A dog nipped and jumped from below in vain. Most of the specimens would be delivered to experts for observation and training. The hyena would be force-fed. Its fatty liver was considered a delicacy, and although the process was full of pitfalls, some breeders still kept trying. Other animals were tagged for temples. They would be offered to the gods, then consumed by humans.

The hunters had all regrouped at their point of departure, with the exception of Prince Ramses and his driver. The scribe in charge of the expedition made anxious enquiries. Waiting was out of the question. A chariot should be dispatched to search for them, but in which direction? If anything happened to the prince, it could mean the end of his career. Ramses might not have the brightest future in store for him, but his disappearance would not go unnoticed.

The scribe and two hunters stayed behind until mid-afternoon, while the rest of the party hurried back to the valley with the game, alerting the desert patrol on their way.

Fidgeting, the scribe composed a report on a plaster tablet, scraped it off, began again, gave up. There was no hiding behind official language. No matter how carefully he phrased it, two men had gone missing, and one was the king's younger son.

Then he thought he spied a silhouette moving slowly through the noonday sunlight. Optical illusions were commonplace in the desert, so he asked the two hunters to have a look. They agreed that it seemed to be a human walking in their direction.

Step by step, the outline grew clearer. Ramses had survived.

11

Shaanar relaxed as two highly skilled palace-trained cosmetologists gave him a manicure and pedicure. Seti's older son always took pains with his toilet. As a public figure and future sovereign of a rich and powerful country, he was required look his best at all times. He felt that refinement in personal appearance was the hallmark of a civilization that prized cleanliness and good grooming. He also enjoyed being pampered like a precious statue, massaged with perfumed oils, before his hairdresser took over.

Muffled shouts suddenly disturbed the peace in Shaanar's spacious quarters. He opened his eyes.

'What's going on? I do not allow—'

Ramses burst into the luxurious bathroom.

'The truth, Shaanar. I want it and I want it now.'

The heir apparent dismissed his manicurist and pedicurist. 'Calm down, dear brother. What truth might you have in mind?'

'Did you try to have me killed?'

'You must be dreaming! The very idea . . .'

'Two paid killers, working in tandem . . . one's dead now, the other one missing.'

'Please explain yourself. And may I point out that I am, after all, your brother?'

'If you're guilty, I'll find out.'

'Guilty? Choose your words carefully, Ramses.'

'You sent me on a hunt in the desert, and someone laid a trap for me.'

Shaanar took Ramses by the shoulders.

'I'm the first to admit we're very different, and there's no love lost between us. But does that mean we should work against each other, instead of facing reality and accepting what our destiny dictates? I want you out of Memphis, it's true. It's true I don't believe you'd fit in at court. All the same, I have never intended you any harm, and I despise violence. Please believe me: I am not your enemy.'

Ahmeni had always been particular about his scribe's equipment, cleaning the water pot and brushes twice if he cleaned them once, smoothing his palette to a perfect surface, changing scrapers and erasers as soon as they failed to meet his standards. As secretary to a royal scribe, he commanded a liberal supply budget, yet he continued to use the costly papyrus sparingly and composed rough drafts on scraps of limestone. In an empty turtle shell, he hand-ground his own mineral pigments to make the brightest red and the deepest black.

When Ramses returned from the hunt after all the others, Ahmeni was overjoyed. 'I knew you were safe and sound! If something was wrong with you, I'd sense it. And I haven't been wasting my time while you were gone. The case of the second-rate ink is moving forward.'

'What did you find out?'

'That we belong to a complex branch of the public service, with many different departments and plenty of susceptible officials. Your name and title opened doors for me. You may not be popular, but you're respected.'

The prince's curiosity was piqued. 'Details, please.'

'Ink cakes are an essential commodity in our country. Without ink cakes, no ink; without ink, no writing; without writing, no civilization.'

'And no scribes,' Ramses teased.

'As I assumed, ink production is highly regulated. Each cake of ink is inspected and stamped before it leaves the warehouse. In theory, an inferior product could never turn up in a top-quality shipment.'

'Meaning?'

'Something awfully fishy is going on.'

'Or else you've been working too hard and it's starting to show.'

Ahmeni pouted. 'You don't take me seriously!'

'I was forced to kill a man out in the desert. It was his life or mine.' Ramses related his tragic adventure in detail. Ahmeni hung his head.

'No wonder you think I'm silly, getting all worked up over ink cakes. The gods protected you! They'll always be with you, Ramses.'

'Let's hope they're paying attention.'

The reed hut was snug in the mild night air. Frogs croaked in the nearby canal. Ramses had decided to wait up all night for Iset the Fair. If she failed to appear, it would be over between them. Again and again he saw himself fight for his life, knocking the groom into the vicious thorns of the desert date tree. Conscious thought had played no part in his actions. A firestorm had swept through him, leaving him ten times stronger. Was it a fire from some mysterious world, the desert power of Set, his father's near namesake?

Until that moment, Ramses had believed he could control his own fate, defying gods and men, victorious in any combat. But he had forgotten the price to be paid in a fight, the stark fact of death. He had carried death like a sickness; he had transmitted it. He felt no regret, yet wondered whether the incident marked the end of his dreams or the frontier of an unknown country.

A stray dog barked. Someone was approaching the hut in stealth.

Perhaps he was being foolish. As long as the dead groom's partner in crime, the chariot driver, was still at large, Ramses's life was in danger. Perhaps the driver had tailed him here. Probably he was armed. It was the perfect spot for a surprise attack.

Ramses sensed the intruder's presence, without being able to see him or judge his precise location. He could have described each gesture, the length of each silent stride. As soon as the shadow approached the door to the hut, the prince sprang, pinning the intruder to the ground.

'What a welcome!'

'Iset! Why were you sneaking up on me?'

'Remember our agreement? Rule number one: be discreet.'

She tightened her grip on her lover, his desire already perceptible.

'Please keep attacking me.'

'Have you made up your mind for good?'

'The fact that I'm here should tell you something.'

'Are you going to keep seeing Shaanar?'

'Will you ever stop talking?'

She wore a loose tunic without a stitch underneath. Holding nothing back, she moulded her body to his. Iset was madly in love, to the point of forgetting she once planned to be queen of Egypt. It was more than physical attraction: Ramses had an inner power even he did not fully grasp. That power was what she found so utterly fascinating. She could no longer think straight. What would he do with her? Slowly destroy her? The throne would go to Shaanar, but already he seemed so pompous, so boring. Iset the Fair would never grow old and dull before her time. She was too fond of being young and in love.

The dawn found them still intertwined. Unexpectedly tender, Ramses stroked his mistress's hair.

'They say you killed a man in the desert.'

'Someone sent him to kill me.'

'For what reason?'

'Revenge.'

'Did he know you're the king's son?'

'He knew, but he'd been paid too well for that to matter. The driver I was teamed with set it up.'

Iset the Fair sat bolt upright. 'Have they brought him in?' she asked anxiously.

'Not yet. The police took my statement; there's a warrant out.'

'And what if—'

'Someone's plotting against me? Shaanar denies it. He honestly seemed shocked.'

'Watch out, though. He's a sly one.'

'Maybe you like them smart. Are you sure I'm the one you want?'

She kissed him with all the fierceness and rising heat of the sun.

Ahmeni's office was deserted. He had not even left a note. Ramses was convinced his secretary would never rest until he found the source of the second-rate ink. Obstinate, obsessive about his writing materials, he took the breach in quality as a personal affront and would stop at nothing until the case was solved and the perpetrators indicted. It was no use telling him not to overdo it. Though frail in body, Ahmeni had surprising reserves of energy to fuel his determination.

Ramses went to see the chief of police. Unfortunately, the investigation had proved fruitless. The sinister chariot driver had disappeared. The trail was cold. The prince's irritation showed, although the police official assured him no effort was being spared.

Disappointed, Ramses decided to be is own detective. He knew the Memphis army base contained a maintenance centre for chariots. As a royal scribe, he asked to see his counterpart who kept the log of chariots used in war and for hunting; the precious vehicles were carefully tracked. Ramses gave a detailed description of the missing charioteer, hoping the man had worked here.

The official referred him to the chief inspector of the royal stables by the name of Bakhen.

The man was examining a grey horse, too young for the yoke, and lecturing the sorry-faced driver. Bakhen looked about twenty, strongly built, with rough-hewn features and a short beard outlining his square jaw. He wore two copper bands around his bulging biceps. A gravelly voice added to the threat in his words.

When the misguided driver departed, Bakhen stroked the grey horse. It gazed at him gratefully. Ramses approached.

'Bakhen? I'm Prince Ramses.'

'Good for you.'

'I need some information.'

'Try the police.'

'They couldn't help me. Maybe you can.'

'Fat chance.'

'I'm looking for a driver.'

'I only work with horses and vehicles.'

'He's a wanted man.'

'What do I care?'

'You won't help identify a criminal?'

Bakhen glared at Ramses. 'Trying to hang an accessory charge on me? Prince or no, you'd better clear out of here.'

'I'm not going to beg.'

Bakhen burst out laughing.

'You don't give up easy, do you?'

'You know something and I'm going to get it out of you.'

'Some nerve, too.'

A horse whinnied. Bakhen ran to the stall where a splendid dark-brown stallion was bucking wildly against a tether.

'Easy, boy. Easy, now.' Bakhen's voice seemed to sooth the animal. The horse even let him come near. A beauty, Ramses thought.

'What's his name?'

'"The God Amon Decreed His Valiance." My favourite horse.'

The answer had come not from Bakhen but from a voice at the prince's back, a voice that sent shivers down his spine.

Ramses turned and made a deep bow to his father, the pharaoh Seti.

12

'We're leaving Ramses.'

The prince could hardly believe his ears, nor could he ask his father to repeat those three magic words. His happiness was so intense his head swam.

Seti went to his horse, perfectly calm now. He untied the tether, led the stallion to a light chariot, saw it hitched. At the main barracks door, the monarch's personal sentries stood alert.

The prince hopped in the chariot and stood to his father's left.

'Take the reins.'

Proud as a conqueror, Ramses drove to the launch where Pharaoh's fleet was making ready to sail southward.

Ramses had no chance to tell Ahmeni he was leaving. And what would Iset the Fair think when he didn't appear for their secret meetings? But his qualms paled against thrill of sailing on a royal ship, moving briskly with a strong tailwind.

As the expedition's official scribe, Ramses was to write a report and keep the ship's log down to the last detail. Captivated by the changing countryside, he found a great deal to record. It was nearly five hundred miles from Memphis to Gebel el-Silsila, their destination. The seventeen-day voyage was full of wonders for Ramses: the glistening river, the lush flood plain, the peaceful hilltop villages. Egypt was his for the taking, immutable, brimming with life, able to rise above its most humble forms.

Ramses did not see his father again on board. The days flowed as quickly as a single hour, and the ship's log grew thicker. In this sixth year of Seti's reign, a thousand soldiers, stone-cutters and sailors were to land at Gebel el-Silsila, the country's main site of sandstone quarrying. Here the Nile, forced between steep, narrow banks, was boiling with rapids, the cause of frequent wrecks and drownings.

From the prow of his ship, Seti oversaw the expedition. Unit leaders supervised the unloading of crates full of tools and food supplies. The workers sang and bantered, but the pace was unrelenting.

Before the end of the day, a royal messenger announced that His Majesty would reward each worker with five pounds of bread per day, one bunch of vegetables, one portion of cooked meat, sesame oil, honey, figs, grapes, dried fish and wine, plus two sacks of grain per month. Extra rations would help to ensure that the men would work their hardest.

The stone-cutters made short trenches, then extracted blocks of sandstone one by one from the quarry. There was no room for improvisation in their work. The unit leaders scouted and marked the veins of stone for the cutters. For the biggest blocks, the stone was notched and wedges of hard, dry wood were hammered in and moistened, causing the wood to expand and fracture the stone.

Some blocks were sent directly to on-site stonemasons; others were lowered down steep channels to the river landing and hauled on to barges to the appropriate temple construction project.

Ramses roamed the work site. Would he ever find words to describe this beehive of activity? How could he keep an accurate record of the expedition's production? Determined to be efficient, he examined each step in the operation, familiarized himself with the workers without interrupting their toil, learned the men's rough language, studied the tricks of their trade. When they put him to the test, he cut his first block of stone with a skill that surprised his detractors. The prince had long since abandoned his fine linen garments for a rough leather apron. He did not mind the heat or the sweat. He liked the quarry better than the court. The men were genuine, the stone kept them honest. Ramses left behind his life of ease.

He had decided. He would remain with the quarrymen, learn their trade, live their life. Far from the artifice of city life, he would find his strength harvesting blocks of sandstone for the gods.

This must be the message Seti was trying to send him: never mind your pampered childhood, your sheltered upbringing; discover your true nature in the stone and unforgiving southern sun. It had been a mistake to conclude that the encounter with the bull meant Seti intended to groom him for power. Now his father had shattered his illusions and shown him his true capacities.

Ramses had no desire to live in a gilded cage. Shaanar would make a much better figurehead. His mind at ease, Ramses slept on the ship's bridge, lost in the stars.

The previous day had been a productive one, but now the quarry was unnaturally quiet. Usually the men began to work in the cool of daybreak. Where were the unit leaders, why weren't they calling the roll?

Yielding to the quarry's magic, the prince explored the silent walkways between grey slaps of sandstone. By now they were imprinted in his mind. This landscape would remain with him for ever. He was deep in thought when he heard the ring of hammers.

Navigating the maze, Ramses watched for marks identifying the various units' territory. He was eager to turn in his scribe's kit, pick up a mallet, live with these hard-working men, share their ups and downs, forget that he ever belonged to the idle rich.

At the far end of the quarry, carved in the rock, was a chapel. To the left of the doorway stood a stela, an inscribed stone tablet. This one offered a prayer to the rising sun. Before it stood Pharaoh Seti, arms raised, palms open, celebrating the rebirth of the light just beginning to bathe the quarry.

Ramses knelt and listened.

When the prayer was finished, Seti turned to his son.

'What were you seeking in this place?'

'My path in life.'

'Four perfect feats distinguished the creator,' Pharaoh declared. 'He gave birth to the four winds, so that each living thing may breathe. He made water and the yearly flood for the benefit of rich and poor alike. He made each man the same as his neighbour. Finally, he stamped the human heart with the memory of the West and the great beyond, so that sacrifices would be made to the unseen. But men have trespassed against the creator. Some attempt to debase the world he has made. Are you one of those?'

'I . . . I killed a man.'

'Is the meaning of life to destroy life?'

'It was self-defence. A force came to guide me.'

'Then own up to what you did and stop feeling sorry for yourself.'

'I want to find the real culprit.'

'Don't waste your time on foolishness. Are you prepared to make a holy sacrifice?'

The prince nodded.

Seti ducked inside the chapel and reappeared with a yellow dog in his arms.

'Wideawake!' Ramses beamed.

'This is your dog, then,'

'Yes, but—'

'Take a rock and crush his head. Offer him up to the spirit of this quarry. You will be cleansed of your offence.'

Pharaoh released the dog. It ran straight for Ramses, smothering him with kisses.

'Father . . .'

'Now.'

Wideawake begged to be petted.

'I refuse.'

'You dare to defy me?'

'I wish to join this company of quarrymen and never return to the palace.'

'You'd give up your title over a dog?'

'He trusts me. I owe him my protection.'

'Follow me.'

Seti, Ramses and Wideawake climbed up a narrow hillside trail to a craggy overlook.

'If you had killed your dog, you would have been the vilest of destroyers. Your choice has brought you to the next stage in your journey.'

Ramses was overjoyed.

'I'll prove myself here!'

'No, you won't.'

'I don't mind hard work.'

'Quarries like this one provide eternal life for our civilization. A king must visit frequently and check that the work is done correctly. The gods must dwell for ever in beauty. To work with the quarrymen is to study the art of government. Stone and wood make no allowances. Pharaoh is the creation of Egypt; Pharaoh never stops creating Egypt. Building temples, the pride of the people, is the greatest act of love.'

Each of Seti's words was a blaze of light expanding Ramses's mind. Ramses was a thirsty traveller, his father a cool, fresh spring.

'Then I do belong here.'

'No, my son. Gebel el-Silsila is only a sandstone quarry. You have yet to experience granite, alabaster, limestone. There is no rest for you, no trade where you can settle. It is time to return to the north.'

13

In his spacious office, Ahmeni was sorting his notes. A number of low-level bureaucrats had opened up to him, more or less willingly, with satisfying results. A sleuth at heart, Ahmeni sensed he was homing in on the truth. There was no doubt someone was running a profitable deception. When he found out exactly who, his pursuit would be merciless.

As he finished his summary, Iset the Fair barged in to Ramses's residence, forcing the door to his secretary's office.

Ahmeni stood up, feeling awkward around this self-assured young beauty.

'Where is Ramses?' she bluntly enquired.

'I don't know.'

'I don't believe you.'

'Suit yourself, but that's the truth.'

'I hear Ramses tells you everything.'

'We're close, but he left without warning.'

'It doesn't seem possible!'

'I wish I could make you feel better, but I can't tell a lie.'

'You don't seem very concerned for him.'

'Not in the least.'

'Because you know where he is and you just aren't telling me!'

'I'm telling you I don't know.'

'You depend on him for your living.'

'Ramses will be back soon, mark my word. If anything had happened to him, I'd sense it. We're joined for life. That's why I don't feel worried.'

'Of all the—'

'He's coming back.'

Vague and contradictory rumours circulated at court. Some claimed Seti had exiled Ramses in the south. Others said the princes had been sent to inspect the dykes in preparation for the annual flood stage. Iset the Fair was beside herself. She had never been treated this way. The first night he had failed to appear at their hideaway, Iset thought he was hiding, playing a joke on her. She had called his name over and over. A sudden chorus of toads and lizards, stray dogs and cats had responded. Panic-stricken, she'd fled into the night.

Her insolent young prince had made her feel so stupid – and so concerned for him. If Ahmeni was telling the truth, it meant Ramses had been kidnapped.

One person, only one, knew what had really happened.

Shaanar was finishing lunch. The roasted quail was heavenly.

'Why, Iset! What a pleasure to see you. Some dessert, perhaps? Not to brag, but my chef's fig purée is really the best in town.'

'Where is Ramses hiding?'

'My dear lady, how would I know?'

'I thought you made it your business to know all the latest developments.'

Shaanar smiled admiringly. 'Touché!'

'Please tell me.'

'Sit down and have some figs with me. You won't regret it.'

The young woman chose a comfortable chair with a green seat cushion.

'Fate has put us in a unique position. No use denying it. Don't you agree?'

'I'm not sure I understand,' Iset replied.

'You and I get along so well. You ought to think twice before you commit to my brother. My dear, consider your future.'

'What would you know of my future?'

'With me it could be wonderful.'

Iset the Fair took a good look at Shaanar. He tried to appear elegant, attractive, self-assured, already playing the king. Yet he had none of Ramses's magnetism or physical presence.

'Would you really like to know where my brother is?'

'Very much.'

'I'm afraid it may be upsetting.'

'I'll take a chance.'

'If you were mine, I would never neglect you like this.'

'I'm fine on my own.'

Slumping, he opened up to her. 'Ramses signed on as a scribe with the Gebel el-Silsila sandstone mining project. A job for a minor bureaucrat, requiring him to spend months in the south rubbing elbows with quarrymen. My father has once again demonstrated what a good judge of character he is: he put my brother in his place. Now would you like to discuss your prospects with me?'

'Shanaar, I feel weak, I—'

'I warned you.' He rose and took her right hand.

His touch disgusted her. Yes, Ramses was apparently in disfavour. Yes, Shaanar would be king, and the woman who shared his life would bask in glory. Scores of well-bred young women were dying to marry him.

She struggled free of his grip, shouting, 'Leave me alone!'

'Don't settle for less than you deserve, Iset.'

'I love Ramses.'

'Who cares about love? It's no concern of mine, and you'd soon find it doesn't matter. All I ask of you is to be beautiful, bear me a son, serve as my consort. Turning me down would be madness.'

'Then I've gone mad.'

Shaanar reached out to her. 'Don't leave, Iset. Or else . . .' Shaanar's round face loomed menacingly. 'I'd hate for us enemies. Let me appeal to your intelligence.'

'Goodbye, Shaanar. Follow your star. I'll follow mine.'

Memphis was a noisy, bustling city and a busy shipping hub. Commercial traffic was closely regulated, with an army of scribes to record the cargoes. Among the storehouses along the docks was one exclusively for office supplies, including dozens of cakes of pigment.

Ahmeni, as private secretary to the pharaoh's younger son, was allowed free entry. He first inspected the finest-quality ink, but without results.

His slight stature was an advantage in navigating narrow streets crowded with shoppers and donkeys laden with fruit, vegetables or sacks of grain. He ranged as far as the temple of Ptah, recently enlarged by Seti. In front of the vast colonnade stood colossal pink granite statues of god-kings. The young scribe loved the old capital. Founded by Menes, unifier of the Two Kingdoms, north and south, it reminded him of a chalice prized by the goddess of gold. The lotus-covered lakes, the flowers on every corner delighted the senses. A wonderful place to relax in some leafy retreat, admiring the Nile. But he was not here for pleasure. Skirting the munitions depots, Ahmeni made his way to the door of a small factory supplying ink for the city's finest schools.

He was given an icy reception, but Ramses's name got him into the workroom. One of the pigment grinders, nearing retirement age, was most cooperative. It bothered him that some newer manufacturers had lowered standards, yet retained the status of royal purveyors. Ahmeni eventually got him to part with an address on the north side of town, beyond the limits of the ancient white-walled citadel.

The young scribe avoided the teeming quays and crossed Ankh-taoui, 'Life of Two Lands'.* Past an army barracks, he ventured into a densely populated outlying area of the city. Low multi-family dwellings stood next to imposing mansions; craftsmen's shops abounded. After several false starts, he got directions from women out sweeping their stoops and visiting neighbours. Ignoring his fatigue, Ahmeni doggedly pursued the latest lead in the case of the poor-quality ink cakes.

A hairy, club-wielding man of forty stood guard at the door to the factory.

'Hello, there. May I come in?'

'Employees only.'

'You might want to make an exception. I'm private secretary to a royal scribe.'

'On your way, young man.'

'The scribe in question is Ramses, the son of Seti.'

'The shop is closed.'

'Then it's the perfect time for me to look around.'

'Against company policy.'

'If I look around now, I won't have to come back with a warrant.'

'Get lost.'

Ahmeni wished he weren't such a weakling. Ramses would have had no trouble tossing this lout into the nearest canal. Still, there had to be a way . . .

He saluted the guard, pretended to leave, then climbed a ladder to the roof of a granary near the back of the building – and waited. Once night fell, he lowered himself through the skylight. He examined the company's stock in the light of an

* Memphis was at the intersection of upper and lower Egypt.

oil lamp he found on a shelf. There were two rows of ink cakes, each one stamped with the official seal of inspection. The first row was a disappointment: all top quality. The second, however, contained cakes that were too small, too light, uneven in colour. Ahmeni chose one at random and wrote a quick sample, enough to convince him he had found the scene of the crime.

In his triumph, the young scribe did not register the footsteps. The guard whacked him over the head, slung the limp body over his shoulders and threw it in the nearest communal dump, where waste was burned each day just before dawn.

That would show the little snoop. He'd never talk now.

14

The refuse disposal man's small daughter rubbed the sleep from her eyes as her father led her slowly through the hushed backstreets of the far north side. He had to finish his rounds before dawn, setting fire to the rubbish in communal dumps maintained between blocks of houses. A daily schedule of waste disposal was one of the government's strictest health measures. The work was repetitive, but the pay was good and he felt he was making a useful contribution to society.

On this block lived two families who were easily the biggest slobs on his route. Several warnings had not had the least effect; there would have to be a citation. Grumbling about the failings of mankind, he picked up the rag doll his little girl had dropped and soothed the child. When he was done, they would eat a hearty breakfast and then have a nap in the shade of a tamarisk. Their favourite spot was the park by the goddess Neith's temple.

Luckily, the dump was less full than usual. The rubbish man set his torch to several spots so the fire would start quickly.

Daddy . . . I want that big doll.'

'What, sweetheart?'

'That big dolly over there.'

The little girl pointed through the smoke to where a human arm stuck out of the refuse.

'I want it, Daddy.'

Alarmed, the man jumped into the enclosure, hoping his feet wouldn't burn.

An arm . . . the arm of a thin young man! He carefull lifted the unconscious form. The back of the head was crusted with blood.

On the return voyage, Ramses had not seen his father. His log would be quite complete and his entire report would be entered in the royal annals of the important events in year six of the reign of Seti. Putting aside his writing kit and scribe's clothing, he also spent time with the crew and shared in their work, learning to tie knots, raise sails, even man the rudder. Above all, he studied the wind, a manifestation of the mysterious god Amon, puffing out sails and guiding ships to safe haven: the invisible made clear, yet still invisible.

The ship's captain played along, since the king's son forgot his position and refused the privileges of rank. He set him to the thousand and one tasks that make up a sailor's life. Ramses didn't balk, but swabbed the deck and rowed with the best of them. Sailing north required a thorough knowledge of river currents and a stout-hearted crew. Feeling the boat glide over the water, working with the water to achieve the best possible speed, was an intense pleasure.

The expedition's return was cause for celebration. Spectators crammed the banks of Memphis's main harbour, tellingly named 'Safe Journey'. As soon as their feet touched the pier, the sailors were greeted with garlands of flowers and cups of cool beer. There was ceremonial dancing in their honour, praises sung to their courage and the goodness of the river that guided them.

Graceful hands slipped a garland of blue flowers around Ramses's neck. 'Will this be sufficient reward for a prince?' asked Iset the Fair mischievously.

Ramses made no attempt to escape. 'You must be furious,' he told her. He took her in his arms; she pretended to resist.

'I'm just supposed to forget that you left without any notice?'

'I had no choice.'

'Surely you could have found some way to let me know.'

'Pharaoh said jump; I jumped.'

'You mean—'

'My father took me with him to Gebel el-Silsila. Believe me, it was no exile.'

Iset the Fair snuggled closer. 'Sailing for days and days . . . how you must have talked!'

'It was no pleasure cruise. I worked as a scribe, a stone-cutter and a sailor.'

'Why did he want you to go?'

'Only he knows the reason.'

'I saw your brother. He told me you were finished, heading for a second-rate government post in the south.'

'My brother thinks everything is second-rate, except for himself.'

'But you've come back now, and I'm yours.'

'You have the looks and brains to be a queen.'

'Shanaar still wants me to marry him.'

'What's stopping you? You're not very likely to get a better offer.'

'I have a better lover. I can't live without you now.'

'The future . . .'

'I care only about the present. My parents are in the country, the house is empty. Doesn't that sound more inviting than a reed hut?'

He shared Iset's longing, but was it love? Ramses found no answer. For now the physical passion was enough, the intoxicating sensation of their bodies merging, swirling sub-limely into one. Iset's caresses aroused him again and again. He never had enough of her. It was so hard to leave her,

naked and languid, her arms pulling him back when he tried
to slip away.

For the first time, Iset the Fair had mentioned marriage.
Ramses bridled: much as he enjoyed her, he was not prepared
for anything more permanent. They might be young, but they
were of marriageable age. There could be no objection to their
union. Still, Ramses did not feel it was time. Confident that
she would win him over, Iset did not protest. The more she
got to know her prince, the more she believed in him. She
listened to instinct rather than reason. Anyone with so much
love to give was an irreplaceable treasure.

Ramses made his way to the centre of town, near the palace
complex. Ahmeni must be expecting him any moment, eager
to report on his case.

An armed police guard stood at the entrance to Ramses's
residence.

'What's going on?'

'Are you Prince Ramses?'

'Yes, I am.'

'Your secretary has had an accident. Police matter, I'm
afraid.'

Ramses ran straight to his friend's bedside.

Ahmeni lay still, his head bandaged, a nurse attending him.
'Quiet,' she ordered Ramses. 'He's sleeping.' She ushered the
prince out of the room.

'What happened to him?'

'He was left for dead in a rubbish dump on the north side
of town.'

'Will he live?'

'The doctors think so.'

'Has he said anything?'

'A few words, nothing that made any sense. The painkillers
make him very drowsy.'

*   *   *

Ramses went to see the assistant chief of police, busy inspecting the southern precincts. The official deeply regretted that he was unable to furnish any information. An investigation at the scene of the crime had turned up no witnesses. Intensive questioning had not resulted in a single lead. Just like Ramses's missing charioteer, the attacker had disappeared, perhaps even fled the country.

He got home just in time to see Ahmeni regain consciousness. His bandaged face lit up at the sight of his friend.

'You're back! I knew you'd come back!' His voice was shaky, but clear.

'How do you feel?'

'I found it, Ramses, I found it!'

'Too bad you almost lost your life in the process.'

'I've got a good hard head, though, see?'

'Who hit you?'

'The guard in the place where I found the counterfeit ink cakes.'

'So you really did solve your mystery.' Ahmeni's face glowed with pride. 'Tell me how to get there,' said Ramses.

'It's dangerous. Take the police with you.'

'Don't worry, and rest now. The sooner you're back on your feet, the sooner we'll work on the case together.'

Following Ahmeni's directions, Ramses easily found the suspect factory. Three hours past sunrise, and not a soul inside. Intrigued, the prince had a look around the neighbourhood, but nothing seemed out of the ordinary. The small ink factory appeared to have been abandoned.

To make sure, Ramses stayed around until evening. There was plenty of activity in the neighbourhood, but no one left or entered the scene of the crime.

He questioned a water-bearer serving the nearby shops.

'Do you know that building?'

'They make ink there.'

'Why is it closed?'

'No one's been here for a week. It's strange.'

'Has the owner been by?'

'I couldn't tell you.'

'Who ran the business, then?'

'We never saw a boss there, only workers.'

'What about customers?'

'Never paid attention.' The water-bearer moved on.

Ramses decided to borrow Ahmeni's method. He climbed up to the granary room and crossed to the ink factory.

Within seconds, he saw that the workroom was deserted.

Along with the other royal scribes, Ramses had been summoned to the temple of Ptah, the god who created the world through the word. Each scribe appeared before the high priest and gave a succinct accounting of his recent activities. The master reminded them that they should have respect for words as their raw material and model their speech on the teachings of the sages.

When the ceremony was over, Sary congratulated his former student.

'I'm proud to have been your guardian. In spite of what your detractors say, you seem to be following the path of knowledge. Never stop learning, and you will become a man of consequence.'

'Is that more important than finding my inner truth?'

Sary was affronted. 'I thought you were finally settling down, but I hear rumours.'

'What rumours?'

'Strange stories . . . that you're tracking down a missing chariot driver, that your private secretary was injured in an assault.'

'They're more than stories.'

'It's best to leave these matters in official hands. The

police have more resources at their disposal. They'll get results, believe me. You're too busy. The most important thing is for you to live up to your title.'

A private lunch with his mother was a rare privilege and one Ramses duly appreciated. Playing an active role in the government, she found her days filled with affairs of state and perfomring the daily liturgy, not to mention her countless court obligations. The Great Royal Wife had very little time for herself or her family.

In the soothing shade of a pavilion, low tables had been set with alabaster plates. Tuya, fresh from a meeting to choose an elite women's choir for the temple of Amon, wore a long, pleated linen gown and thick golden collar. Ramses had boundless affection for his mother, mixed with a growing admiration. She was a woman beyond compare, born to be queen despite her modest birth. Tuya alone could inspire Seti's love and help rule his kingdom.

On the menu were lettuce, cucumbers, a prime cut of beef, goat cheese, a round honey cake, spelt wafers, oasis wine cut with water. The queen enjoyed this break in her day and never permitted outsiders or favour-seekers to join her. Her private garden, nestled around a tranquil pool, was as much a part of her nourishment as the meals that her staff composed so carefully.

'How did things go on your trip to Gebel el-Silsila?'

'I lived the life of a stone-cutter, then a sailor. I learned to respect those men.'

'But neither life was the one for you.'

'My father did not wish it.'

'He wants to see you grow.'

'Do you know of his plans for me?'

'You're not eating.'

'I don't understand why I have to be kept in the dark.'

'Do you fear Pharaoh or trust him?'

'My heart knows no fear.'

'Then throw your whole being into the struggle ahead. Never look back, have no regrets or remorse. Avoid envy and jealousy. Count each second you spend with your father as a heavenly gift. Nothing else should matter.

The prince ate his beef, perfectly grilled and seasoned with garlic and herbs. A great ibis punctuated the flawless blue of the sky.

'I need to ask a favour. The police won't help me.'

'That's a serious accusation, son.'

'I think it's well founded.'

'Do you have proof?'

'None at all, and that's why I've come to you.'

'I'm not above the law.'

'If you demand a real investigation, it will happen. Right now, no one seems interested in finding out who tried to have me killed. No one will name the businessman who put the seal of inspection on second-rate ink and passed it off as top quality, even to royal scribes. My friend Ahmeni almost died when he discovered the factory. When I got there, it was closed and the neighbours are scared to talk. That means someone important is involved, so important that everyone's petrified.'

'And you think you know who it is?' Ramses was silent. 'I'll see what I can do.'

15

Pharaoh's ship was sailing north. Some distance out of Memphis, they had tacked towards one of the lesser branches of the Nile. Now they were deep in the Delta.

Ramses was dazzled.

The opposite of the desert, this was the territory of the god Horus.* Where Seti ruled, the river valley cut a narrow swath of green through the vast desert. Here, water was all-powerful. The heart of the Delta was a huge swamp, thick with papyrus plants, teeming with birds and fish. There were no towns, not even villages, only a few fishermen's shacks on islands that were really no more than the tops of submerged hillocks. The light shimmered, unlike the Valley's harsh, direct sun. The reeds danced in the wind that blew down from the sea.

Black flamingos, along with ducks, herons and pelicans, shared this vast domain of meanders and backwaters. Here a ring-tailed wildcat plundered a kingfisher's nest, there a snake slithered under some bushes, producing a cloud of multi-coloured butterflies. Man was not yet master of this place.

The ship gradually slowed, carefully steered by a captain

* The gods divided the universe between the warring brothers Horus and Seti.

familiar with these treacherous waters. On board were twenty seasoned sailors; at the prow stood their supreme ruler. His son was secretly observing him, fascinated by his presence. Seti *was* Egypt, Egypt incarnate, with a thousand years of pharaonic rule reinforcing his awareness of divine grandeur and the pettiness of men. In the eyes of his people, Pharaoh remained a mysterious personage. His true home, they believed, was the starry heavens; his earthly presence served as a link with the other world; his gaze opened the door to that world for his people. Without him, the country would be overrun by barbarians; with him, the future was a promise of eternity.

Ramses was keeping a log of the expedition, just as he had on the first trip with his father. This time, he had no idea what the purpose of the voyage was. Neither his father nor the crew would discuss it. The prince noted an underlying tension in the men, as if danger lurked. At any moment, a monster might rear up and devour the vessel.

As before, Seti had given him no time to say goodbye to Iset the Fair and Ahmeni. Ramses imagined the former's fury, the latter's concern. Still, he would follow his father anywhere he chose to lead, resisting the pull of love or friendship.

A channel opened, easing their progress, and the ship went ashore at a grassy islet with an odd wooden tower on it. The king went down a rope ladder; Ramses followed. Pharaoh and prince climbed the wooden tower with battlements of wattle.

Seti's attention was so focused that Ramses dared not ask any questions.

'Look, Ramses!'

So high in the heavens that it seemed to touch the sun, a flock of migrating birds flew south in a V.

'They come from beyond the known world,' Seti revealed, 'from the infinite spaces where the gods give life to all things. At home in the ocean of energy, those birds have a human head and feed on sunlight, but when they draw close to

85

earth, they turn into swallows or other migratory birds. Study them always, for they represent our ancestors, their spirits persuading the sun not to set the world on fire. These birds inspire a pharaoh's thoughts and show him a path mere mortals cannot see.'

As soon as night fell and the first stars appeared, Seti taught his son about the heavens. He told him the names of constellations, explained the endless movement of the planets, the sun and the moon, the meaning of the dekans. Pharaoh's power, he declared, should extend to the far ends of the cosmos, so that no land was beyond his grasp.

Ramses listened with his heart as well as his ears. He took his fill of the nourishment offered him, not wasting a crumb. Dawn came much too soon.

The royal barge was stuck in the dense undergrowth. Seti, Ramses and four sailors armed with spears, bows and throwing sticks set off in a light papyrus boat. Pharaoh told them which way to row.

Ramses felt transported to another world, altogether different from the Valley. No trace, here, of human activity. Tufts of papyrus grew so tall they sometimes blocked the sun. If his shipmates hadn't daubed him with a greasy repellent, he would have been eaten alive by the insects swarming around them in a deafening buzz.

The skiff made its way through a watery glade, then glided into a sort of lake with two small islands cresting in the centre.

'The holy cities of Pe and Dep,' revealed Pharaoh.

'Cities?' Ramses asked, astonished.

'Where the souls of the just come to rest; their city is all of nature. When life sprang up from the primeval ocean, it took the shape of a hillock emerging from water. Here are the two sacred mounds which you may conceive of as the chosen residence of the gods.'

Following his father, Ramses alighted at the 'holy cities' and paused in prayer at a humble reed hut that served as a shrine. Embedded in the ground in front of it was a staff with a spiral-carved head.

'This is the symbol of function in life,' the king explained. 'Everyone must find his function and fill it, before attending to personal concerns. A pharaoh's function is to be the gods' first servant; if he thought of serving himself, he would be no better than a tyrant.'

The unsettling, shifting surroundings kept them all constantly watchful and on edge. Only Seti seemed serene, as if in perfect command of this unreadable landscape. Without the tranquil certainty in his father's expression, Ramses might have thought they would drift for ever through the groves of giant papyrus.

Suddenly the horizon cleared and the boat sped through greenish water towards a bank where fishermen worked. Naked, hirsute, they lived in rudimentary huts, worked lines, purse nets and hoop nets, slit the fish with long knives, gutted them and dried them in the sun. Two of them were carrying a Nile perch, so huge that the pole it was strung on sagged in the middle.

Unaccustomed to visitors, the fishermen looked alarmed and hostile. Huddling together, they brandished their knives.

Ramses advanced to meet their aggressive stares.

'Bow to your Pharaoh,' he commanded.

Arms rose, hands open, knives fell to the spongy ground. Pharaoh's subjects prostrated themselves before their sovereign. Recovering, they asked him and his men to share their meal.

The fishermen joked with the sailors, and the sailors produced two jars of beer. When sleep overcame the men, Seti addressed his son in the torch light that kept away insects and wild animals.

'Here are the poorest of men, yet they fulfil their function and await your support. Pharaoh assists the weak, protects the widow, feeds the orphan, responds to anyone who is in need. He is the faithful shepherd guarding his flock night and day, the shield protecting his people. He is the one God has chosen to fill the supreme function, so that it may be said: 'In his day no one went hungry.' There is no task more noble than becoming Egypt's *ka*, my son, the whole country's nourishment.'*

Seti left Ramses to spend several weeks with the fishermen and papyrus gatherers. He learned to identify many different edible fish, build light boats, find his way through the maze of canals and swamps, hone his hunting skills. He listened to these natural athletes tell of struggling for hours to land an enormous fish.

Their life was rough, but they had no desire to leave it. The Valley seemed tame and bland in comparison. A few days in civilization was enough for them: they sampled the women's charms, ate their fill of meat and vegetables, and headed home to the Delta.

The prince absorbed their power, adopted their way of looking and listening, hardened in their company, never complaining when he ached with fatigue, and once again forgot his privileged position. The fishermen marvelled at his strength and cleverness; his daily catch soon equalled three of theirs. But before long jealousy replaced admiration, and the men shied away from the king's son.

It was the end of his dream: to become someone else, relinquish the mysterious force that drove him, live no differently from a young stone-cutter, sailor or fisherman. Seti had brought him to this frontier, this wild place where

* *Ka*: a spiritual element within a human being that was said to survive the body.

land and sea merge, to put him in touch with his true being, stripped of childish illusions.

His father had left him here. But the night before his departure, had he not seemed to be marking out a course for Ramses, steering him towards kingship? His words had been for no ears but his son's.

No – it had been a dream, a moment of grace, nothing more. Seti spoke to the wind, the water, the vastness of the Delta; his son was only a stand-in. Bringing him to the ends of the earth, his father had shattered his vain hopes and fantasies. Ramses's existence would not be that of a monarch.

His father's personality was imposing and inaccessible, yet he felt close to Seti. He longed to sit at his father's feet, to show him all he was capable of, to surpass himself. The fire that burned in Ramses was no ordinary one; Seti had discerned it, he was sure, and the art of kingship was the secret he had been slowly unveiling.

No one would come for Ramses: it was his decision when to leave.

He stole away before dawn, as the fishermen lay sleeping around the campfire. He stroked hard, steering his light papyrus craft due south. He followed the stars, then his instinct, until he rejoined a main branch of the river. He paddled doggedly on, aided by a tailwind, focused on his goal, taking only short breaks to snacking on dried fish. Ramses tried to work with current rather than fight it. Cormorants flew overhead, the sunlight streamed down.

There, where the Delta ended, stood the white walls of Memphis.

16

The heat was stifling. Man and beast slackened their pace, waiting for the Nile's annual flooding, which brought a long period of rest except for those choosing to work on Pharaoh's construction projects. The harvest was in; the parched earth seemed about to die of thirst. But the Nile had turned chestnut brown, heralding the rise in water level that was the key to Egypt's prosperity.

In the cities, shade was at a premium. Market vendors hung makeshift awnings. The most dreaded time of year was upon the country: the five days left over from the harmonious cycle of twelve thirty-day months. This period was ruled by the terrifying lion-headed goddess Sekhmet. She wanted to wipe out the human race for rebelling against the sun, except that the creator once again came to the rescue, convincing Sekhmet he was drinking human blood when it was really rye beer. On five extra days in each year, Sekhmet was free to unleash her plagues and pestilence on the land, still determined to exterminate man, with all his evil, cowardice and cunning. Day and night, the temple walls echoed with litanies to appease the goddess. Pharaoh conducted a secret liturgy that would set the year to right again, turn death to life, provided the king was just.

During these five dreadful days, economic activity ground to a virtual halt. Plans and trips were postponed, ships stayed in port, fields lay deserted. A few made last-minute repairs to their dykes, fearing that the avenging goddess's anger would take the form of heavy winds. Without Pharaoh's intercession, would anything be left of Egypt when she was done?

The chief of palace security had intended to shut himself in his office until New Year's Day, when everyone would breathe a sigh of relief, then celebrate. Unfortunately, he had just been summoned by Queen Tuya, and could not stop wondering why. Ordinarily he had no direct contact with the Great Royal Wife, receiving his orders from her chamberlain. What would cause her to sidestep the usual procedure?

Like most court officials, he was terrified of the great lady. She believed the court should set an example and demanded the highest standards. No one displeased her twice.

To this point, the chief of palace security had enjoyed an uneventful career, climbing through the ranks without stepping on anyone's toes. He never made waves and quickly became entrenched in each new job. Since his appointment to the palace, all had gone smoothly.

Until today.

Had one of his underlings been spreading lies about him, eyeing his job? Was someone close to the royal family out to ruin him? What charges could have been levelled against him? The questions plagued him. Before long he had severe headache.

Trembling, one eyelid twitching uncontrollably, the chief of security was admitted to the queen's reception room. Although he was taller, she seemed to tower over him.

He bowed low.

'Majesty, may the gods favour you and keep you—'

'Yes, yes,' she interrupted. 'Please sit down.'

The Great Royal Wife motioned towards a comfortable chair. The palace official dared not look up. A wisp of a woman, but so full of authority!

'You've learned, I suppose, that a palace groom was hired to kill my son Ramses.'

'Yes, Majesty.'

'And you also know that the driver who was hunting with Ramses probably did the hiring.'

'Yes, Majesty.'

'You are no doubt aware of the investigation's current status.'

'There's every chance it will be long and complicated.'

'Every chance'? Strange choice of words. Perhaps you'd rather not see the truth come out?'

The security chief hopped to his feet, as if stung by a hornet.

'Of course I would . . . I wouldn't—'

'Sit down and listen carefully. I have the feeling someone wants the investigation dropped, written off as a simple case of self-defence. Ramses survived, his assailant is dead, the man who hired him vanished into thin air. Why stir up trouble? My son has pressed for results, but the police have failed to turn up a single lead. Something is very wrong here. Are we no better than a barbarian tribe, utterly lacking the concept of justice.'

'Your Majesty! You know how dedicated the police are, how—'

'All I know is that they've been unresponsive. I hope it's temporary. If someone is blocking investigation, I need to know who it is. And you are going to find out for me.'

'You want me—'

'You have more leeway than the police. Find the charioteer who set a trap for Ramses and bring him in.'

'Majesty, I—'

'Will you or won't you?'

Slumping, the chief of palace security felt one of Sekhmet's arrows pierce him. How would he be able to satisfy the queen without taking risks, ruffling feathers? If the villain behind the scenes turned out to be someone important, he could end up facing much more than Tuya's wrath. But if he failed the queen, he was finished.

'Of course I will do as you wish, but it may be difficult.'

'You have already said so. If it were a routine matter, I wouldn't summon you personally. I also need your help with one more investigation, fortunately much less sensitive.'

Tuya told him about the ink deception and the mysterious factory where the counterfeit cakes had been made and stored. Thanks to detailed information from Ramses, she could pinpoint the location. She wanted the name of the owner.

'Is there a connection to your son's case, Majesty?'

'Unlikely, but who knows? I'm depending on you for answers.'

'Most certainly, Majesty.'

'Excellent. Now get to work.' The queen withdrew.

The chief's head throbbed. He wondered dejectedly if magic might not be his only recourse.

Shaanar was in his glory.

Gathered around him in one of the palace state rooms were scores of merchants from all over the world. Cypriots, Phoenicians, Aegeans, Syrians, Lebanese, Africans, yellow-skinned Orientals, pale-faced men from the mists of the north had responded to his invitation. Seti's Egypt had such international influence that being called to his court was considered an honour. Only the Hittites, who increasingly resisted Seti's overtures, were not represented.

Shaanar firmly believed that international trade was the best hope for humanity. In the ports of Phoenicia, in Bylbos or Ugarit, ships from Crete, Africa, the distant Orient berthed side by side. Why should Egypt remain isolated in the name of preserving her identity and traditions? Shaanar admired his father, but wished the pharaoh were more forward-looking. If it was up to him, he would drain the greater part of the Delta and create a series of merchant ports on the Mediterranean. Like his ancestors, Seti was obsessed with keeping the Two Lands intact. Instead of building defences and increasing the size of the army, wouldn't it be better to trade with the Hittites, dispensing considerable aid to the most warlike factions, if necessary?

When he ascended to the throne, Shaanar planned to abolish armed confrontation. He hated the army, the generals and soldiers, the limited vision of die-hard military men, the will to dominate by force. War was not a lasting means of exercising power; sooner or later conquered nations turned the tables on their conquerors. On the other hand, trapping them in a web of economic forces that only a ruling elite could understand and control was virtually certain to eliminate any attempt at resistance.

Shaanar was grateful that fate had made him the older son and heir apparent. His restless, brash brother posed no threat to his grandiose plans. A worldwide trade network he would run singlehandedly, alliances based on economic interest, a united empire where local character and customs would disappear . . . The thought was exhilarating.

What did Egypt matter? It could serve as his base, but would soon be too small for him. The south, mired in tradition, had no future at all. Once Shaanar's plan succeeded, he would settle in some friendly capital and make it his base of operations.

Foreign merchants were not customarily received at the palace; Shaanar's invitation was a mark of his interest. He was preparing for his role as Seti's successor, in the not-too-distant future, he hoped. persuading Seti to modify his views was no easy task. Still, any ruler respecting the law of Ma'at must bow to the demands of the moment. Shaanar was confident that his reasoning was strong.

The reception was an unqualified success. The foreign merchants promised to send Shaanar their craftsmen's finest vases for his collection, famous throughout the Near East, as far as Crete. He would give almost anything for a perfect piece of pottery with delicate curves and seductive colours. Pride of ownership only heightened his aesthetic pleasure. Alone with his treasures, Shaanar felt a deep satisfaction that no one could take away.

One of his informers approached him as he ended a cordial conversation with an Asian dealer.

'Trouble,' the informer whispered.

'What kind?'

'Your mother isn't satisfied with the official investigation.'

Shaanar frowned.

'One of those ideas she gets?'

'No, more serious.'

'She wants her own investigation?'

'The chief of palace security is already on it.'

'He's useless.'

'If his back's to the wall, he could cause problems.'

'Let him sniff around, then.'

'What if he actually gets somewhere?'

'Quite unlikely.'

'We could warn him off.'

'Who knows how he might react? There's no reasoning with imbeciles. Besides, the trail is cold.'

'What are your orders?'

'Watch him and report to me.'

The informer disappeared into the crowd and Shaanar returned to his guests. Despite the irritating news, he remained the perfect host.

17

Day and night, the river patrol controlled traffic in the northern harbour of Memphis. Arrivals and departures were strictly regulated to prevent accidents. Each vessel was identified and made to wait if no berths were available.

The officer in charge of the main canal kept watch almost absent-mindedly. At lunchtime, the traffic slowed. From his white, sun-baked tower, the patrolman surveyed the scene, not without satisfaction: the Nile, the canals, the green to the north that marked the start of the Delta. In less than an hour, when the sun began to descend from its zenith, he would go home to the southern suburbs and enjoy a much-needed siesta, then play with his children.

His stomach grumbled. He munched on wafer bread stuffed with fresh greens. His work was more tiring than it appeared: it required great powers of concentration.

All at once, a strange apparition.

At first he thought it was a mirage, the summer sunlight at work on dark-blue water. Then, forgetting his snack, he fastened his gaze on the incredible little craft threading between two barges laden with wine jars and sacks of grain.

A papyrus rowing boat, all right — with a champion oarsman going at a furious clip.

These light skiffs were not ordinarily seen outside the watery maze of the Delta. More important, this one was not

96

on his list of the day's authorized arrivals! The patrolman flashed a mirror signal to the emergency squad.

Three fast boats manned with expert rowers manoeuvred to intercept the skiff. Soon two guardsmen escorted Prince Ramses ashore.

Iset the Fair vented her fury.

'Why won't Ramses see me?'

'I have no idea,' replied Ahmeni, the back of his head still bandaged.

'Is he ill?'

'I hope not.'

'Has he mentioned me?'

'No.'

'You could be a bit more informative, Ahmeni.'

'It's not in my job description.'

'I'll be back tomorrow.'

'As you like.'

'Can't you try to be helpful? I'd be glad to reward you for letting me in to see him.'

'My salary is more than adequate.'

The young woman shrugged and left.

Ahmeni was puzzled. Since his return from the Delta, Ramses had shut himself up in his room and refused to talk. He picked at the meals his friend brought in to him, reread the sage Ptah-hotep's maxims, or stayed out on the terrace gazing at the city and the pyramids of Giza and Saqqara in the distance.

While unable to engage the prince's interest, Ahmeni still informed him about his latest discoveries in the counterfeit ink case. The scraps of documents found at the deserted factory left no doubt that it belonged to a highly placed person, employing quite a few workers, but beyond that Ahmeni had run into an impenetrable wall of silence.

Wideawake had covered his master with sloppy kisses and

stayed by his side every minute, afraid of losing Ramses again. Playfully alert or curled up at the prince's feet, he kept a constant watch. The yellow, floppy-eared dog with the curlicue tail was Ramses's only confidant.

On New Year's Eve, Iset lost patience with her lover. Flouting his ban, she joined him on the terrace where he sat deep in thought, the dog at his side. Wideawake bared his teeth and growled, ears at attention.

'Call him off!' Ramses's icy stare kept her from coming closer. 'What's going on? Won't you please speak to me?'

Ramses turned coldly away. 'You have no right to treat me this way. I was out of my mind with worry. I love you, and now you won't even look at me!'

'Leave me alone.'

Iset fell to her knees. 'Is that all you have to say?' Wideawake stopped threatening. 'What do you want of me, Ramses?'

'Look at the Nile, Iset.'

'May I stand by you?' He said nothing, she inched closer; the dog made no move.

'The star called Sothis is about to appear,' he told her. 'Tomorrow, it will rise in the east with the sun to announce the inundation.'

'The same as every year.'

'Don't you understand that this year will be like no other?'

His serious tone so impressed Iset the Fair that she could not pretend.

'No, I don't.'

'Look at the Nile.'

She clung tenderly to his arm.

'Don't be so enigmatic. I'm not your enemy. What happened in the Delta?'

'My father made me see myself for what I am.'

'What do you mean?'

'I have no right to run away; it's no use hiding.'

'I believe in you Ramses, whatever your fate may be.'

He stroked her hair softly. She looked at him, speechless: whatever he had gone through on this journey had transformed him. The adolescent was now a man, a man of mesmerizing beauty. She could not take her eyes off him. She was hopelessly in love.

The experts who measured the river waters had picked the exact day the Nile would crest, flooding into Memphis.

The festival was proclaimed; the cry went from street to street, telling how Isis had finally found her dead husband Osiris and brought him back to life. Shortly after dawn, the dyke to the town's main canal was opened and the waters coursed mightily through. So that the waters might increase but not destroy, thousands of votive statues of the god Hapi were thrown into the Nile. The manifestation of the Nile's life-giving inundation, Hapi was depicted as a full-breasted man, with tufts of papyrus in his headdress, carrying a tray full of food. Each family would keep a vial of flood water to guarantee their prosperity through the coming year.

At the palace, everyone grew restless. In less than an hour they would form a procession that Pharaoh would lead to the Nile, where he was to make his ritual offering. And all were wondering exactly where they would be placed in the official hierarchy.

Shaanar paced, asking the chamberlain the same question for the tenth time.

'Has my father assigned my place?'

'Not yet.'

'This is madness. Ask the priest in charge.'

'The king himself will determine the order of the procession.'

'Everyone knows what the order will be!'

'Please forgive me. I have no further information.'

Shaanar smoothed the pleats of his long linen robe and fiddled with his three strands of carnelian beads. He would have preferred something fancier, but dared not outshine his father. The rumours seemed to be true: that Seti meant to make certain changes in protocol, with the queen's consent. But why hadn't he been consulted? If his parents excluded him, he must be falling out of favour. Who could be at the bottom of this except his power-hungry brother?

It had been a mistake to underestimate the boy. The lying snake had stabbed him in the back. Tuya listened to Ramses's lies and influenced her husband.

Yes, that was Ramses's plan: to move to the head of the procession, appearing directly behind his father and mother at an important public ceremony. To show that he had become the favourite son.

Shaanar demanded an audience with his mother.

Two priestesses had just finished dressing the Great Royal Wife. Her crown was adorned with two tall feathers, a symbol of how she incarnated the breath of life nurturing all of Egypt. The queen's earthly made the dry season end, the fertile flooding begin anew.

Shaanar bowed to his mother.

'No one will tell me what I'm doing in the ceremony today,' he said.

'Are you complaining?'

'I think I should be at my father's side when he makes the offering.'

'That's entirely up to him.'

'He must have informed you of his decision.'

'Don't you trust your father's judgement? You're usually the first to praise his decisions.'

Shaanar fell silent, regretting that he had appealed to his

mother. While always even-handed, she made him uncomfortable. She simply seemed able to see right through him.

'Rest assured,' he continued, 'that I bow to Pharaoh's wisdom.'

'Then what cause have you to worry? Seti will act in the best interests of Egypt. That's the essential thing, don't you agree?'

To keep his hands and mind occupied, Ramses was copying out one of Ptah-hotep's maxims on a sheet of papyrus: 'If you are a leader giving orders to many, seek each occasion to be efficient, in order for your manner of governing to be free from error.' The prince pondered this idea in his mind as if the long-dead author were addressing him directly.

In less than an hour, a priest would come and assign him a role in the ritual procession. If his instinct was correct, he would take Shaanar's usual place. There was no reason to suppose Seti wanted to shake up the established order, but why else had the procession's protocol been shrouded in mystery? Pharaoh must be planning a surprise for the surging crowd on the riverbanks. He would put Ramses where Shaanar's usually stood.

No law required the king to name his eldest son as his successor. Not even high birth was necessary. A number of pharaohs and their consorts had come from a modest background, without court connections. Tuya herself had been a penniless girl from the provinces.

Ramses relived his three encounters with his father. None of them had been accidental. Seti had jolted him into an awareness of his true nature, brutally stripping him of all his illusions. Just as a lion was born to be king of the jungle, Ramses felt he was destined to rule.

Contrary to his original belief, he was not free to choose. Fate had determined his path in life, and Seti was making sure that he did not stray from it.

*   *   *

Spectators crowded the parade route from palace to river. The New Year's festivities provided one of their few opportunities to see the Pharaoh, his queen their children, and an array of high government officials.

From the window of his palace suite, Shaanar studied the onlookers who would momentarily witness his shameful dispossession. Seti had not even given him a chance to defend himself and explain why Ramses would never make a proper king. The monarch's judgement was clouded. He would stick to his arbitrary and unjust decision.

It would not be a popular one at court. Shaanar would be able to organize an opposition that Seti could not ignore. The most influential officials were on his side. Let Ramses make a few false moves, and Shaanar would soon have the upper hand again. And if Ramses failed to make his own blunders, he could count on some help from his brother.

The high priest begged the king's older son to follow him. The procession would soon be under way.

Ramses followed the priest.

The procession stretched from the palace gates to beyond the temple district. The prince was led to the head of the line. After the grand marshal, the royal couple came first. The white-robed temple priests, their shaved heads gleaming, watched Seti's son advance and noted his magnetic presence. Some people still saw him as an immature, sport-loving youth, destined forever to play second fiddle.

Ramses walked on.

He passed powerful lords and elaborately dressed ladies, inspecting the younger prince on the occasion of his first official appearance. It was no dream. This important New Year's Day, his father would place him in line for the throne.

The priest suddenly halted.

He escorted Ramses to a spot behind the high priest of

Ptah, far behind the royal couple, far behind Shaanar who stood proudly to the right of his father, still Seti's designated successor.

18

For two days, Ramses refused to eat or speak to anyone.

Ahmeni, sensing how deeply disappointed his friend was, stayed in the background like a quiet, helpful shadow. Yes, Ramses had made his first official appearance, and from now on would have a role in various state occasions. Unfortunately, he would hardly be more than a face in the crowd. In everyone's eyes, Shaanar was still heir to the throne.

Wideawake sympathized with his master and stopped demanding his usual walks and play sessions. But having to care for the floppy-eared yellow dog finally brought Ramses out of his self-imposed exile. He called for his pet to be fed, and when Ahmeni brought in a meal for the prince as well, he gave in and ate it.

'I'm a conceited fool, Ahmeni. My father taught me a valuable lesson.'

'Stop torturing yourself.'

'I thought I was smarter than that.'

'Is power so important to you?'

'Not power, but the chance to be what I am. I was so sure I was born to be Pharaoh. All along, my father was showing me why it can never happen. I was blind.'

'Can you accept your destiny?'

'Do I still have one?'

Ahmeni feared for his friend's sanity. Ramses's despair

was so profound that he might decide to risk his life in breakneck adventures. Only time would ease the disappointment, but patience was not among the prince's virtues.

'Sary is having a party tonight,' Ahmeni said softly. 'Would you go with me?'

'If you want me to.'

Ahmeni tried to contain his delight. Everyday pleasures, he thought, would help Ramses find the road to recovery.

Their childhood teacher and his wife had invited the best younger set to a fishing party, stocking their garden pond for the occasion. Each guest was given a stool and an acacia fishing pole. The biggest catch would be awarded a splendid papyrus relating the adventures of Sinoueh the Sailor, a classic tale enjoyed by generations of cultivated Egyptians.

The young scribe seemed intrigued by this novel entertainment, so Ramses handed his pole over to his friend. Ahmeni didn't seem to understand that neither his devotion nor Iset's love could quench the fire that ravaged the prince's soul. Time would only serve to fan the insatiable flame. It must be fed. No matter what his fate dictated, he would not accept second best. Only two people fascinated him: his father and mother, the king and queen. It was their vision he wished to share, and none other.

Sary laid an affectionate hand on his former pupil's shoulder.

'You don't feel like fishing?'

'It's a great idea. The party of the season.'

'With you here, it had to be.'

'Don't make fun of me, Sary.'

'I wasn't joking. The court respects you now. More than one person has mentioned how impressive you looked in the New Year's procession.'

The affable professor seemed to be sincere. He led Ramses to a tent where cool beer was being served.

'There's no better job than being a royal scribe,' he said enthusiastically. 'You gain the king's confidence, you have access to the treasury, the storerooms, you receive a share of excess temple offerings, you're outfitted with fine clothing, horses, a boat, you have a beautiful residence, you collect revenues from your properties, devoted servants tend to your every need. Your hands stay soft and white, your back unbent, there's no heavy lifting, no hoes, picks, or shovels, no forced labour, and your orders are carried out to the letter. Your palette, reed pens and papyrus are the keys to prosperity. They'll make you a rich and respected man. Fame and glory, you ask? They go with the job! The voices of scribes are heard through the centuries, while their contemporaries fade into oblivion.'

'"Be a scribe,"' Ramses recited from memory, '"for a book is more durable than a stela or pyramid; it will preserve your name better than any monument. As heirs, scribes have their books of wisdom; their writings are priests that offer prayers for the departed. Their son is the tablet upon which they write, the stone engraved with hieroglyphs their wife. The strongest buildings crumble and disappear, yet the works of the scribes last through the ages."'

'Splendid!' exclaimed Sary. 'You haven't lost one bit of all I taught you.'

'I think you mean the teachings of our elders.'

'Of course, of course . . . but I *was* the one who led you to them.'

'And I thank you for it.'

'I'm prouder of you by the day, my boy. Be the best royal scribe you can, and the rest will take care of itself.'

Sary had to go and play host. Chitchat, drinking, fishing, whispered lies and secrets – Ramses found the atmosphere stifling. He had nothing in common with these people who never looked beyond their limited, privileged horizon.

His older sister took him gently by the arm.

'Happy?' asked Dolora.

'Doesn't it show?'

'What do you think of my outfit?'

He stepped back to look at her. Her dress was too gaudy, her wig too elaborate, but at least she seemed a bit perkier than usual.

'You look like the perfect hostess.'

'A compliment from you? How very unusual!'

'That should make it special.'

'You looked awfully good in the New Year's procession, I hear.'

'I stood there and didn't say a word.'

'Exactly. The court was expecting a different kind of behaviour.'

'What kind?'

A wicked gleam came into Dolora's eyes. 'A protest – even an attack. When you don't get your way, you usually react much more strongly. Is our lion turning into a lamb?'

Ramses clenched his fists, fighting the urge to slap her.

'Do you know what I want, Dolora?'

'What our brother has, and it can never be yours.'

'You're wrong. I'm not envious. I'm only looking for my own true path.'

'Ramses, there's not much going on at this time of year, and Memphis can be so hot. We're leaving soon for our place in the Delta. Come with us. We never see you. You can teach us to row, we can swim and catch some really big fish.'

'My work—'

'Come, Ramses. Now that you're recognized as a member of the royal family, why not spend some time with us? You need to unwind.'

There were cries as the biggest fish of the day was landed. Dolora rushed to congratulate the winner, while Sary presented the first prize.

Ramses waved to Ahmeni.

'My line broke,' confessed the secretary.

'Let's go.'

'Already?'

'The contest's over, isn't it?'

Shaanar, expensively dressed as ever, approached them.

'Sorry I'm so late. You could have given me some fishing tips.'

'Ahmeni stood in for me.'

'Not feeling well?'

'Whatever.'

'Ramses, I'm glad to see how well you're controlling yourself. Even so, I thought you'd want to thank me.'

'For what?'

'The only reason you were included in New Year's procession was because I insisted. Seti was afraid you might not behave correctly, with good reason, I might add. Fortunately, you did very well. Keep it up and we'll stay on the best of terms.'

Shaanar and his retinue moved along. Sary and Dolora bowed to him; his unannounced arrival was a social coup.

Sitting in the dark on his terrace, Ramses scratched his dog behind the ears. Wideawake closed his eyes; this was heaven. The prince contemplated the circumpolar stars, the ones that were said to shine eternally. According to the sages, they represented the hearts of Pharaohs who had passed though the judgement hall of the dead and been restored to life everlasting.

A naked Iset put her arms around his neck. 'All you care about is that dog. You make love to me and then leave me alone in bed!'

'I don't fall asleep like you do.'

'Kiss me and I'll tell you a little secret.'

'I can't stand bribery.'

'I got your sister to invite me along to the Delta. That way you won't be stuck alone with your relatives, and some people will thank us. You know they're placing bets that we're secretly married.'

She wound herself around him, affectionate and catlike, until the prince could no longer ignore her caresses. He picked her up, carried her across the terrace to the bed, laid her down and covered her body with his.

Ahmeni was happy: Ramses was back to eating with his usual gusto.

'We're all ready to go,' the secretary announced proudly. 'I made sure everything's packed correctly. We can use a holiday.'

'You deserve one. Planning to catch up on your sleep?'

'When I start on a project, I can't rest until it's finished.'

'You won't have to work at my sister's.'

'I'm afraid I will. I'm still a bit behind after my accident.'

'Ahmeni! Will you ever learn to relax?'

'Like master, like servant,' he joked.

Ramses took him by the shoulders. 'You're not my servant. You're my friend. Please follow my advice and take a few days off.'

'I'll try, but . . .'

'What is it?'

'The counterfeit ink, the abandoned warehouse . . . I have to get to the bottom of it.'

'Are you sure it's in your best interest to keep trying?'

'We'd be doing the country a favour.'

'Oh, you wouldn't want to neglect your civic duty.'

'Ramses, I know you agree with me.'

'I asked my mother to help us.'

'That's great!'

'Nothing new has turned up, though.'

'It will. We're going to get them.'

'Ahmeni, I couldn't care less about this ink business. But I do want to get my hands on the man who tried to kill you and find out where he got his orders.'

The fierce determination on Ramses's face made his secretary tremble.

'I won't let you down, Ahmeni.'

Sary had chartered an elegant boat that could hold thirty passengers comfortably. How delicious to float down the broad, flooded Nile to a comfortable hilltop villa surrounded by palm trees! The heat would be more bearable in the country and the lazy, enchanting days would flow peacefully along.

The captain was in a hurry to leave. The harbour patrol had just cleared them for departure. If he missed his turn, there was likely to be a two-or three-hour wait.

'Ramses is late,' his older sister whined.

'Iset the Fair is here, though,' Sary reminded her.

'Did they send his baggage?'

'It was all loaded before the sun came up.'

Dolora angrily stamped her feet. 'Here comes his secretary!'

Ahmeni ran up in fits and starts.

'Ramses has disappeared,' he panted.

19

A floppy-eared yellow dog at his side, the traveller had a reed sleeping mat slung over his shoulders; in his left hand he carried a leather sack for his clothing and sandals, in his right a walking stick. When they stopped to rest, he spread the mat beneath a tree and slept, with his faithful watchdog to protect him.

Prince Ramses had completed the first stage of his journey by boat, the second on foot. Taking narrow roads across river bluffs, he had stopped with villagers he met along the way. He was refreshed to find a peaceful, unchanging world that moved to an ancient cycle of seasons and festivals.

Ramses had not told Ahmeni or Iset the Fair his plans. He wanted to set off alone, like any Egyptian going to visit relatives or look for off-season work on one of the royal construction projects.

In certain towns he took the ferry, sitting with people too poor to own even the most rudimentary boat. Dozens of light craft, all different sizes, went by in both directions. Some were full of children who stood and jostled each other until they all fell in the river. Then they launched into a furious race.

The winter months, the time for recreation and travel . . . Ramses felt the people of Egypt breathing, joyful and serene in the knowledge that Pharaoh protected them. He heard Seti mentioned with respect and admiration, felt proud to be his son, vowed to live up to the privilege, even if he remained a simple royal scribe, tallying the wheat harvest or registering decrees.

On the northern edge of Faiyum, the lush province ruled by Sobek, the crocodile god, lay the royal harem of Merur, a vast complex tended by the finest gardeners in the kingdom. Many considered it the most beautiful domain in Egypt. Elderly ladies left the court and retired here, surrounded by lovely young women who were brought here to train as weavers, to study poetry, music, dance. They learned to make gemstones and enamel jewellery. The harem buzzed with constant activity.

Before approaching the gates, Ramses changed his simple kilt, put on his sandals, dusted off his dog. When they were presentable, he approached a surely-faced guard.

'I'm here to see a friend.'

'Your letter of introduction, young man?'

'I don't need one.'

The guard bristled. 'What makes you think so?'

'I'm Prince Ramses, the son of Seti.'

'A likely story! A king's son would travel with a retinue.'

'I have my dog.'

'Move along, boy. Enough of your jokes now.'

'Out of my way. It's an order.'

His firm tone and commanding gaze took the guard by surprise. Should he throw this imposter out or check on his story?

'What's your friend's name?'

'Moses.'

'Wait here.'

Wideawake sat in the shade of a persea tree. The air was fragrant. Hundreds of birds flocked in the harem's groves. Could life be any sweeter?

'Ramses?'

Pushing the guard aside, Moses ran towards Ramses. The friends embraced, then walked through the gate, followed by Wideawake, who sniffed longingly at the guardhouse kitchen.

Moses and Ramses went down a flagstone alley that wound through the sycamores, ending at a broad pond with white lotuses in full bloom. They sat down on a bench made from three blocks of limestone.

'What a wonderful surprise, Ramses. Have you been sent to work here?'

'No, I wanted to see you.'

'You came alone, without an escort?'

'Would that shock you?'

'No, it's quite in character. What have you been up to since we left school?'

'I became a royal scribe and I was led to believe my father wanted me to be his successor.'

'Would Shaanar ever settle for that?'

'It was only a dream, of course, but I was absolutely certain. When my father chose a public occasion to put me in my place, I realized how badly mistaken I'd been. Even so . . .'

'Go on.'

'A force is still alive in me, the force that made me overstep my boundaries. I can't settle for less than excellence. What should we do with our lives, Moses?'

'That's the only important question, I agree.'

'What's your answer?'

'I have no more idea than you do. Here I help run operations, supervise the weavers and potters. I have my own private quarters with five rooms and a garden. The food is wonderful. Thanks to the harem library, I've become a Hebrew full of the wisdom of the Egyptians! What more could I ask?'

'A girlfriend?'

Moses smiled. 'Plenty of women here. Have you found someone?'

'Maybe.'

'Who?'

'Do you know Iset the Fair?'

'Fit for a king!' He whistled. 'I envy you. But why the "maybe"?'

'She's gorgeous and she's smart. I love being with her, but I can't really say I love her. I thought love would be different, more intense, more—'

'Stop worrying! Live for today. Isn't that the song the harpists sing at our banquets?'

'Moses, have you found love here?'

'I've certainly found lovers. But it's not enough. I feel a fire inside me, the same as you do, a force I can't name. Should we stoke the fire or try to forget it's there?'

'We have no choice, Moses. If try to ignore it, we'll flicker like shadows and die.'

'Do you think that the world is light?'

'Light is in this world.'

Moses looked up at the sky.

'In the secret heart of the sun.'

Ramses made his friend look away. 'Don't look straight at it or you'll go blind.'

'I plan to find out what's hidden there.'

A frightened cry interrupted their conversation. They saw two girls fleeing down a nearby lane, as fast as their slender legs would carry them.

'Now it's your turn for a surprise,' said Moses. 'Let's find out what scared those poor girls out of their wits. They're two of my weavers.'

The prankster was still in plain sight. With one knee bent, he retrieved a snake, admired its dark-green skin, and popped it into a sack.

'Setau!'

114

The snake charmer seemed not the least surprised. He answered Ramses's astonished questions, explaining that he was here to deliver snake venom to the harem laboratory, his best customer. And it was always a pleasure to spend a few days with Moses. Now they could have a grand reunion, make up for lost time, then go their separate ways again.

'I've taught Moses a thing or two. Close your eyes, Ramses.'

When the prince was told to open them again, Moses, steady as a rock, held a thin dark-brown wand in his right hand.

'Not much of a trick,' the prince said.

'Take a closer look,' urged Setau.

The wand came alive and began to wriggle. Moses let go of a good-sized snake, which Setau quickly recovered.

'A nice piece of magic, and completely natural. A cool head, a steady hand, and you can fool anyone, even a king's son.'

'Teach me to use your magic wand.'

'Why not?'

The three friends found a quiet fruit grove where Setau could hold class. Handling live snakes required dexterity and precision.

A troupe of slim girls went over a dance routine. Wearing straight knee-length kilts with straps that criss-crossed over the shoulders, hair pulled back in bead-trimmed ponytails, they coordinated their acrobatic moves.

Ramses had been admitted as a friend of Moses, a favourite with the harem dancers, though today they did little to lighten his mood. Compared with his friends, Setau was blithe. He had already found his true calling, studying snakes and dealing with the constant threat of sudden death. Moses wished he could also find his life's work, but instead he was caught in a tangle of administrative tasks. His performance was nevertheless so outstanding that he was in line for his own directorship once there was an opening.

'One day,' he promised Ramses, 'I'm going to leave it all behind.'

'What do you mean?'

'I'm not quite sure, but I do know I can't stand it here much longer.'

'We'll leave together.'

A perfumed dancer brushed against the two friends, failing to raise their spirits. When the dance routine was over, however, they let themselves be talked into staying for refreshments. By the blue-tinted pond, the dancers and their teachers showered Prince Ramses with questions about the court, his work as a royal scribe, his future plans. His answers were unforthcoming, almost curt. The disappointed girls started playing a game, quoting poetry their friends had to identify, a good way to show off their literary knowledge.

Ramses noticed that one of the group remained silent. Younger than her companions, with shiny jet-black hair and blue-green eyes, the girl was stunning.

'What's her name?' he asked Moses.

'Nefertari.'

'Why so shy?'

'She's new at the harem and comes from a humble family. Her gifts as a weaver are what brought her here. Now she's the best at everything she tries, and the society girls resent her.'

The dancers decided to try their luck with the prince again. Was it true that he planned to marry Iset the Fair? Even so, a prince was supposed to have a bigger heart than other men, with room . . . Ramses turned his back on their teasing and took a seat beside Nefertari.

'My sitting here probably bothers you.' Disarmed by his frankness, she gazed at him anxiously. 'Excuse the intrusion, but you seemed so alone.'

'I was only thinking.'

'Is there something on your mind?'

'We have to write an essay on one of Ptah-hotep's maxims.'

'My favourite author. Which one will you choose?'

'I'm not sure yet.'

'What are you studying here, Nefertari?'

'Floral design. I love arranging flowers for the gods and I hope to spend most of my time in the temple.'

'An austere existence for a young girl.'

'I like meditation. It gives me strength. The sacred writings say that silence makes the soul grow like a flowering tree.'

The dance instructor was rounding up her students; they had to change before grammar class. Nefertari stood to go.

'Wait. May I ask you a favour?'

'The teachers are strict, they don't like us to be late.'

'Tell me which maxim you've chosen.'

Her smile would have melted the most hardened warrior.

'"A perfect word is rarer than green stone, yet the servant girl grinding wheat at the millstone may possess it."'

Airy and luminous, she vanished.

20

Ramses stayed another week at the Merur harem without finding a chance to see Nefertari again. Moses's efficiency was rewarded with extra assignments, leaving him little time to spend with his friend. However, the talks they did have were a source of strength for them both, and they vowed to keep a keen edge on their heightened consciousness.

The news that Seti's younger son was visiting quickly spread through the harem. Elderly noblewomen asked to speak with him; some, it was clear, had tired all their earlier listeners. Any number of instructors and administrators had requests for him. The head of the harem showed him every consideration, hoping Ramses would put in a good word with his father. It became a major undertaking to find a quiet corner where he could sit and read. Feeling like a prisoner in paradise, he gathered his bag, his reed mat and walking stick, and left without a word to anyone. Moses would understand.

Wideawake had been eating too much, as usual. A few days of walking would get him back in shape.

The chief of palace security was exhausted. In his entire career he had never worked so hard, running all over town, arranging meetings with bureaucrats, checking and rechecking facts, then calling some of his contacts in for

118

further questioning and threatening them with the direst consequences.

Had there really been pressure to close the investigation, or had the wheels of bureaucracy simply ground to a halt? It was hard to tell. He had definitely received some veiled threats himself, but there was no way to trace them to their source. At any rate, he had more to fear from the queen than from the most ruthless politician or businessman.

When he was sure that despite every effort he had come up against a brick wall, he appeared before Queen Tuya.

'Your Majesty, rest assured of my complete dedication.'

'I'm more interested in results.'

'You asked me to find the truth, whatever it might be.'

'I did.'

'I don't think you'll be disappointed, because—'

'Let me be the judge. The facts, please.'

The security chief hesitated. 'Allow me to point out that my responsibility . . .' A look from the queen cut short his attempt to give himself credit. 'The truth can be difficult to hear, Your Majesty.'

'I'm listening.'

He swallowed hard.

'Well, I have two catastrophes to report.'

Ahmeni carefully copied out the decrees that were a standard part of the royal scribe's duties. Although piqued at Ramses's failure to confide in him, he knew the prince would be back. He continued to do his job as if nothing were out of the ordinary.

When Wideawake came bounding into his lap and covered his cheek with soft, moist kisses, Ahmeni forgot his hurt feelings and greeted Ramses enthusiastically.

'I was sure I'd find your office empty,' the prince confessed.

'Who would take care of business, then?'

'I don't think I would have put up with being deserted like that.'

'No, and you wouldn't have to. The gods gave us different roles in life, and I accept mine.'

'Ahmeni, forgive me.'

'I swore I'd be your faithful servant and I'll keep my word. I don't want demons from hell to slit my throat! So you see, I'm only thinking of myself. How was your trip?'

Ramses told him about the harem, Moses, Setau, but skipped his brief encounter with Nefertari — a moment of grace he stored in his mind like a jewel.

'You came back just in time,' Ahmeni informed him. 'The queen wants to see you as soon as possible and Ahsha has asked us to dinner.'

Ahsha showed them through the official residence the Foreign Service had just assigned him, in the centre of town, not far from the State Department. Young as he was, he already had the polish of a seasoned diplomat. Impeccably groomed, he wore the latest Memphis fashion, simple in cut but bold in colour. His natural elegance was underscored with a new-found self-assurance. Ahsha was obviously on his way.

'You seem to be doing well,' Ramses remarked.

'I was in the right place at the right time. My report on the Trojan War turned out to be very accurate.'

'Just what did you conclude?'

'That the Trojans are heading for defeat. I disagree with the theory that Agamemnon will show mercy; we can expect mass destruction and slaughter. However, Egypt will not take sides in the conflict. It would serve no purpose for us to get involved.'

'True. Seti's goal is to keep the country at peace.'

'That's exactly why he's so worried.'

Ramses and Ahmeni blurted out in unison, 'Do you mean war?'

120

'The Hittites are making trouble again.'

In Year One of his reign, Seti had found himself with a Bedouin uprising on his hands. Incited by the Hittites, they had invaded Palestine and proclaimed an independent kingdom. Bloody faction fighting ensued. Once it settled down, Pharaoh led a campaign to pacify Canaan, annex southern Syria and check on the Phoenician ports. During Year Three, Egypt had come close to direct confrontation with the Hittites, but the opposing forces had both held their positions and then retreated to their bases.

'What do you know for sure?' Ramses asked Ahsha.

'It's classified information. You may be a royal scribe, but you don't work for the State Department.'

With his right index finger, Ahsha smoothed his impeccably trimmed little moustache. Ramses thought he might even be serious, until he saw the teasing in his friend's bright eyes.

'The Hittites are causing us trouble in Syria,' Ahsha informed them. 'Certain Phoenician princes, for a tidy consideration, are willing to take their side. The king's military advisers recommend a rapid strike, and the last I heard, Seti agreed with them.'

'Will you be sent on the expedition?'

'No.'

'What's the matter? Not enough friends in high places?'

'Not exactly.' Ahsha's fine face tensed slightly, as if Ramses had finally gone too far. 'I've been given another mission.'

'What kind?'

'I can't say, and this time I mean it.'

'A secret mission!' exclaimed Ahmeni. 'Fascinating, but won't it be dangerous?'

'I serve my country.'

'You really can't tell us?'

'I'm leaving for the south. Don't ask me anything more.'

*   *   *

121

Wideawake knew when he was being spoiled: a lavish meal, served in the queen's private garden. He licked Tuya gently to show his gratitude. Ramses chewed impatiently on a twig.

'He's a good dog. You're lucky to have him, son. Care for him well.'

'You wanted to see me. Here I am.'

'How was your stay in Merur?'

'You always know everything!'

'I'm supposed to be Pharaoh's eyes and ears.'

'Do you have news for me?'

'The chief of security did much better than I thought. We've made progress, but the news isn't good. The chariot driver is dead. His body was found in a deserted barn south of the city.'

'How did he end up there?'

'There are no reliable witnesses. And as far as the ink deception goes, we're no closer to identifying the owner. The scroll where his deed was registered is missing from the archives.'

'Someone paid to have it removed, you're suggesting.'

'Yes. Someone rich and powerful enough to buy silence.'

'Government corruption makes me sick. We can't turn our backs on this!'

'Do you think that I intend to?'

'Mother!'

'I'm happy with your reaction,' she said warmly. 'Never accept injustice.'

'Where do we go from here?'

'The chief of security has reached an impasse. It's in my hands now.'

'Tell me what I can do to help you. Anything.'

'You'll go that far for the truth?' The queen's smile was ironic and indulgent.

'I can't even find the truth that's inside me.' Ramses was afraid to say more and risk looking ridiculous to his mother.

'A real man does more than hope. He acts.'

'Even when fate works against him?'

'Then he has to change his fate. If he can't, he should lower his sights and not pin the blame on others.'

'Suppose Shaanar is our mastermind.'

The queen's face clouded with sadness. 'That's a horrible thought.'

'But I can't get it out of my mind, and neither can you.'

'You're my sons, and I love you both. You may not have much in common, you may both be too ambitious, but even so, who can imagine your brother would stoop so low?'

Ramses was shaken. His urge to rule had blinded him to the point of suspecting the most sinister plots.

'My friend Ahsha hears rumours of war.'

'He's well informed.'

'Does my father plan to fight the Hittites?'

'He may be forced to.'

'I want to go with him and defend my country.'

21

In Shaanar's wing of the palace, the atmosphere was leaden. His staff and attachés walked on eggshells, following every rule to the letter. No laughter or conversation broke the tension.

The news had come down late that morning: two elite regiments were being mobilized for a quick response. In plain terms, war against the Hittites! Shaanar was appalled. This would compromise the trade relations he was just beginning to establish and the healthy rewards he envisioned.

A senseless confrontation would result in a climate of uncertainty that was bad for business. Like too many of his predecessors, Seti was heading into a quagmire. The same outdated obsession with defending the empire, flexing Egypt's muscle – such a waste of resources! Shaanar had not yet succeeded in undermining the king's war council. He had planned to expose them for what they were: a bunch of shortsighted old hawks with delusions of grandeur. If this expedition failed, Shaanar would get rid of them for good.

With Pharaoh, his prime minister and his chief of staff at the front, who would be left to run the country? Queen Tuya, of course. Lately she consulted less frequently with her older son, it was true, and they sometimes had words; still, the affection between them was real. The time had come to clear the air. Tuya would understand his views;

furthermore, she could influence Seti to delay declaring war. Shaanar requested that this be worked into her busy schedule as soon as possible.

Tuya granted him an afternoon audience in her reception rooms.

'Such an official setting, Mother dear!'

'Something tells me that this is no private matter.'

'You're right, as usual. Where did you get your sixth sense?'

'Flattery doesn't work on mothers.'

'All right. I've come to ask how you feel about war.'

'I don't like it. Who does?'

'My father's decision seems a bit precipitate.'

'Do you believe he would ever act on impulse?'

'Of course not, but the circumstances . . . the Hittites . . .'

'Shaanar, do you like new clothes?'

'Of course,' he murmured, on unsure ground. 'You know I—'

'Come with me.'

Tuya led her son to a side room. On a low table lay a wig with long panels of wavy hair, a shirt with full sleeves, an ankle-length skirt, pleated and fringed, and a broad sash to tie it all together.

'Nice, isn't it?'

'Beautiful tailoring.'

'This is your uniform. Your father has chosen you as standard-bearer, his right hand in the Syrian campaign.'

Shaanar blanched.

The king's standard-bearer carried a staff carved with a ram's head, one of the symbols of Amon, the god of victory. Pharaoh's elder son would therefore be in the front ranks, next to his father, and ride into battle with him.

Ramses fumed.

What was keeping Ahmeni? He was supposed to be back

with the decree listing the names of Seti's war party. The prince was eager to see where he figured in it. Rank was not what he wanted, only the chance to fight.

'You're finally back! Where's the list?' Ahmeni hung his head. 'What's the matter?'

'Read it yourself.'

By royal decree, Shaanar was named standard-bearer, to ride at the right hand of Pharaoh. Ramses's name was nowhere to be found.

Every barracks in Memphis was on war alert. The next morning, the infantry and charioteers would start for Syria, with the king himself in command.

Ramses hung around headquarters all day long. When his father left the council room, at nightfall, the prince dared approached him.

'May I beg a favour, Highness?'

'Speak.'

'I want to go with you.'

'My decree is final.'

'I don't care about being an officer. I only want a chance to destroy the enemy.'

'Then my decision was correct.'

'I don't understand.'

'It's pointless to wish for something unrealistic. To win a war, you have know how to fight. That's not the case with you, Ramses.'

Once he recovered from his frustration and disappointment, Shaanar was not displeased with his new assignment, a fine addition to his string of honours. Furthermore, a future pharaoh was required to prove himself in battle, a tradition since the days of the First Dynasty. A king must be able to defend his territory and resist invasion. However deplorable Shaanar considered this, the people viewed it as essential.

126

Shaanar therefore bowed to necessity. The situation seemed almost amusing when he spotted Ramses staring longingly as the vanguard marched by.

The army going off to war, like any exceptional event, was cause for celebration. A holiday was declared and any potential worry for the troops was drowned in beer. It was virtually certain that Seti would return victorious.

Despite his new-found status, Shaanar was uneasy. In battle, even the best-prepared soldier could be caught off guard. Imagining himself wounded or disabled made him feel sick. At the front, his first concern would be self-preservation. Danger could be left for the professionals.

Once again, luck was with him. During this campaign he would have the chance to talk with his father and plan for the future. That prospect made it worth the effort, no matter how trying it might prove to leave behind the comforts of palace life.

Ramses's disappointment was an excellent sendoff.

The provincial recruits annoyed Bakhen. When war was imminent, volunteers signed up in droves, dreaming of feats of danger and foreign lands. But this bunch of backward peasants would never make it past the outskirts of Memphis. They would soon head back to their fields. As chief inspector of the royal stables, Bakhen was also in charge of training new soldiers.

He was exceptionally strong, with a short beard outlining his square jaw. All the volunteers obeyed when he ordered them to lift a sack full of stones, hoist it over their right shoulders, and run around the barracks until he told them to stop.

The process of elimination was harsh and swift. Few of them knew how to pace themselves. Panting, the dropouts put down their sacks. Bakhen waited until fifty or so were left before he stopped them.

He couldn't believe his eyes. One recruit looked familiar, a head or more taller than the other runners, and far less winded.

'Prince Ramses! You don't belong here.'

'I want to complete basic training and get my certificate.'

'But . . . you don't need one! All you'd have to do is—'

'I don't think that's fair, and neither do you. A sheet of papyrus doesn't make a soldier.'

Caught unawares, Bakhen twisted the leather band accentuating the size of his biceps.

'This is tricky . . .'

'You're not afraid, are you?'

'Me, afraid? Get back there with the others.'

For three interminable days, Bakhen pushed the men to the outer limits of their endurance. Twenty made the grade. Ramses was one of them.

On the fourth day, they were introduced to weapons: bludgeons, swords and shields. After a brief explanation of their use, Bakhen let the young men start sparring.

When one of them got his arm hurt, Ramses laid his sword on the ground. The others followed suit.

'What do you think you're doing?' roared Bakhen. 'Get back to work, or clear out of here!'

The recruits did as told. Anyone slow or clumsy was dismissed. Out of the original contingent, only twelve would continue to train as professional soldiers.

Ramses was still in the running, his enthusiasm unflagging through the next ten days of drills.

'I need an officer,' Bakhen announced on the eleventh morning.

All but one of the trainees showed equal ability in handling an acacia bow that could shoot an arrow fifty yards in open fire.

Pleasantly surprised, Bakhen produced a much taller bow,

its front reinforced with horn, then placed a copper ingot a hundred and fifty yards from the archers.

'Take this bow and pierce the target.'

Most of them barely managed to bend the bow. Two shot the arrow, but fell far short of the target.

Ramses was last in line; like his fellow recruits, he was allowed three tries. Bakhen eyed him ironically.

'A prince should never become a laughing stock. Better archers than you have already failed the test.'

Intent, Ramses focused on the target until nothing else existed.

Bending the bow took a major effort. His muscles aching, Ramses pulled the ox-tendon bowstring.

His first shot landed to the left of the target. Bakhen snorted.

Ramses exhaled. Without drawing a new breath, he sent the second arrow sailing right over the copper ingot.

'Last chance,' Bakhen reminded him.

The prince closed his eyes for more than a minute and visualized the target, convincing himself it was not so far away, that he was becoming the arrow, that all the arrow wanted was to enter the heart of the ingot.

The third shot was a deliverance. The arrow whizzed through the air like an angry hornet and went straight through the target.

His comrades cheered. Ramses handed the longbow back to Bakhen.

'I've added one more test,' the instructor announced. 'Hand-to-hand combat, with me.'

'Is that standard procedure?'

'It's my procedure.'

'Give me my officer's certificate.'

'First fight me and show you're a match for a real soldier.'

Ramses was taller than Bakhen, but lighter and much less

experienced. He would have to rely on lightning reflexes. The instructor attacked without warning. The prince dodged him, but Bakhen's fist grazed his shoulder. Five times running, the instructor hit thin air. Incensed, he finally grabbed his opponent's left leg and knocked him down. Ramses broke loose with a kick to Bakhen's face and a quick chop to the back of his neck.

Ramses thought the fight was over, but Bakhen was not about to give up so easily. He staggered to his feet and rammed his head into the prince's chest.

Iset the Fair daubed her lover's torso with a salve so effective the pain was becoming bearable.

'I have the healer's touch, wouldn't you say?'

'I'd say I was stupid.'

'The brute could have killed you.'

'He was doing his job. I thought I had him. At the front, I'd be dead.'

Iset rubbed him more gently, reaching lower. 'I'm so glad you didn't go! I think war is evil.'

'A necessary evil, sometimes.'

'You have no idea how much I love you.'

Supple as a lotus stem, she wrapped her body around her lover's.

'Forget about fighting and war. Wouldn't you rather have me?'

Ramses made no attempt to resist the pleasure she offered. But something else gave him greater happiness, something he hadn't mentioned to Iset: the officer's certificate on his desk.

22

The army's return was marked with celebrations. The palace had anxiously followed dispatches from the front. The Lebanese rebels held out only a few days, after which they swore eternal allegiance to Egypt and pledged to be Pharaoh's faithful subjects. In return for his lenience, Seti had demanded a large quantity of top-grade cedar, to raise new masts in front of temples and build several barques of the gods for ceremonial use. The princes of Lebanon unanimously proclaimed that Pharaoh was the incarnation of Ra, the divine light, who gave them life.

Because he had moved so swiftly, Seti was able to enter Syria without encountering resistance. The Hittite king, Muwattali, had not had time to muster troops and decided to observe things from a distance. Unprepared for a siege, the walled city of Kadesh, symbol of Hittite power, had opened its gates to the Egyptian forces. Seti, to his generals' surprise, had settled for placing a stela in the heart of Kadesh instead of razing the fortress. The military was quick to second-guess this unconventional tactic and speculate about its long-range consequences.

As soon as the Egyptian army was out of sight, Muwattali dispatched a large contingent and regained control of Kadesh.

Then came negotiations. To avoid a bloody confrontation, the two sovereigns agreed through their ambassadors that the Hittites would stop inciting unrest in Lebanon and the Phoenician ports, and Egypt would refrain from attacking Kadesh or its surrounding territory.

Peace was concluded. Precarious, to be sure, but still peace.

As heir apparent and now commander, Shaanar presided at a banquet for more than a thousand people, offering the finest food, vintage wine from Year Two of Seti's reign, and the stirring spectacle of naked young girls who danced to the music of flute and harp.

The king made only a brief appearance, letting his elder son bask in the glory of a successful mission. As *Kap* alumni on the rise, Moses and Ahmeni had been invited. So had Setau, decked out in a sparkling robe lent by Ramses.

Ahmeni, single-minded as ever, mixed with Memphis city fathers, steering the conversation towards recent factory closings. Despite his persistence, he learned nothing new.

Setau was hustled away by Shaanar's head steward. A snake was loose in the milk locker. Setau found a likely chink in the wall, stuffed heads of garlic inside and plugged it with a dead fish. The poor creature would never come out again. The steward's relief was short-lived, since Setau had taken an instant dislike to him. When he accidentally freed a red-and-white reptile with fangs set deep in the upper jaw, Shaanar's assistant took off like a rabbit. Moron, thought Setau. Anyone can see this species is perfectly harmless.

Moses, attractive and manly, was surrounded by young women, as usual. Most of them wished they could talk to Ramses, but Iset was guarding him jealously. The group of classmates were making a fine reputation for themselves: Moses seemed destined for an important administrative position and Ramses's courage would win him a command in the army, since there was no place for him at court.

The two friends slipped out between dances and met in the garden, beneath a persea tree.

'Did you hear Shaanar's speech?' asked Moses.

'No. Iset wasn't interested.'

'Your older brother openly proclaims himself the true victor in this campaign. Thanks to him, Egyptian losses were kept to a minimum, and diplomacy, not warfare, won the day. Moreover, he insinuates that Seti is growing older, worn out by his responsibilities, and should soon be ready to appoint a regent. Shaanar already has already outlined his programme: pro-trade, anti-war, economic cooperation with Egypt's worst enemies.'

'He's disgusting.'

'Not an appealing character, I grant you, but his plans do merit consideration.'

'Reach out a hand to the Hittites, Moses, and they'll cut off your arm.'

'War is no solution.'

'Shaanar will leave Egypt a second-rate, bankrupt power. The land of the Pharaohs is in a class by itself. When we let our guard down, the Asian invaders came. It took all we had to uproot them and send them packing. If we lower our defences, we'll be exterminated.'

Ramses's vehemence surprised his friend.

'Spoken like a leader, I admit, but is that the right direction?'

'The only one that will keep our territory intact and protect the home of the gods.'

'The gods . . . do the gods exist?'

'What do you mean?'

Before he had time to reply, a flock of girls surrounded him and Ramses, asking all sorts of questions about their future plans. Iset promptly came to her lover's rescue.

'Your brother cornered me,' she confessed.

'What did he want?'

'He still thinks I should marry him. Ask anyone at court, he says, anyone close to the government – it won't be long before Seti names him as regent. I can be Great Royal Wife, he tells me.'

A strange sensation washed over Ramses. He was suddenly transported to Merur, contemplating a serious young girl as she copied out Ptah-hotep's maxims by lamplight. Iset the Fair was alarmed by the look on his face.

'Are you all right?'

'You know very well that I've never been sick in my life.'

'You seemed so far away.'

'I was thinking. So did you accept his proposal?'

'I've given my answer.'

'Congratulations. You'll be my queen, I'll be your humble servant.'

She pummelled his chest; he grasped her wrists.

'I love you, Ramses. I want to spend my life with you. How can I make you understand that?'

'Before I can become a husband and father, I need a clearer vision of my future. Give me time, Iset.'

In the fragrant night, silence was slowly gathering. The musicians and dancers had left, along with the older courtiers. Here and there, in the vast palace gardens, information was being exchanged and sorry plots hatched – classic Memphis one-upmanship.

From the kitchens, a cry shattered the quiet.

Ramses was first on the scene. He found Shaanar's head steward armed with a poker, beating a cringing old servant. The prince put the attacker in a strangle hold. When he dropped his weapon, the old man fled, huddling behind the other dishwashers.

Moses ran in. 'Stop, Ramses. You'll kill him!'

The prince loosened his hold. The steward, red-faced, choked and gasped for breath. 'That old man is only a

Hittite prisoner,' he said hoarsely. 'He has to be taught to follow orders!'

'Is that how your treat your workers?'

'Only Hittites.'

Shaanar, so richly attired he outdid his most elegant guests, dispersed the crowd now gathering in the kitchen. 'Move along now. I'll take care of this.'

Ramses grabbed the steward by the hair and shoved him to the floor.

'I accuse this coward of torture.'

'Come, come, dear brother. Don't get carried away! My steward can be a bit strict, but after all—'

'I'll bring charges and testify in court.'

'And I thought you hated Hittites!'

'This old man is no threat to us. He's a palace servant and deserves fair treatment, according the law of Ma'at.'

'No speeches, please! Let it drop, and I'll owe you a favour.'

'I'll testify, too,' declared Moses. 'We don't need your bargains.'

'Let's not let things get out of hand,' soothed Shaanar.

'Take the steward,' Ramses told Moses, 'and hand him over to our friend Setau. Tomorrow I'll request a special hearing.'

'That's illegal confinement!'

'Do you plan to appear in court with your steward?'

Shaanar caved in: too many reliable witnesses – better not get involved in a losing battle. The steward would merely be sentenced to exile in a desert oasis.

'I won't stand in the way of justice,' he concluded blithely.

'Justice for all,' Ramses countered.

'That's what I meant,' hissed Shaanar.

'If this is how you plan to govern the country, I'll lead the opposition.'

'You're blowing this out of proportion.'

'I'm stating facts. Complete disregard for others must be part of your grand design.'

'That's going too far, Ramses. You owe me respect.'

'I owe respect the Lord of the Two Lands. Still Seti, the last I heard.'

'Go ahead. Mock me, while you have the chance. Tomorrow you'll have to obey me.'

'Tomorrow is a long way off.'

'That leaves you time to hang yourself with your own rope.'

'Are you planning to treat me like a Hittite prisoner?'

Exasperated, Shaanar stomped off.

'Your brother is a dangerous man,' observed Moses. 'Do you really need to challenge him like that?'

'I'm not afraid of him. Now explain what you meant by that comment about the gods.'

'I have no idea. All I know is that strange thoughts run through my mind and tear me apart. Until I can figure out what my voices mean, I'll have no peace.'

23

Ahmeni refused to give up. His status as private secretary to Ramses, the royal scribe, opened doors for him, and once inside he knew how to make friends. Contacts in several government departments were soon helping him find information. He was able to check the list of ink manufacturers and the names of their owners. As Queen Tuya had discovered earlier, the documents concerning the suspect factory had mysteriously disappeared.

At an impasse, Ahmeni hit on a different, less direct method: identifying merchants who dealt with the royal scribes and referring to the lists of property in their names, hoping that this would lead back to the north-side factory. Days of tedious research ended in utter frustration.

Only one approach remained: a systematic search of the waste dumps, beginning with the one where he had nearly died. Before committing important documents to papyrus, a conscientious scribe wrote a draft on a scrap of limestone. Eventually it would be discarded in a pit with the with thousands of others used in official business.

There was no guarantee that such a draft existed for the deed to the abandoned factory. Nevertheless, Ahmeni began devoting two hours a day to the search, refusing to consider the odds of succeeding.

*   *   *

Iset the Fair disapproved of Moses. The brooding Hebrew was a bad influence; each time he visited, Ramses grew moody. Her solution was to lead the prince on a dizzying round of social events, while avoiding any further mention of marriage. Before he knew what was happening, the prince was bouncing from one mansion, garden party, society ball to the next, like any idle young nobleman, leaving his private secretary in charge of business.

Egypt was a dream come true, a garden of delights, a bountiful mother. There was a wealth of happiness to be found in the shade of a palm tree, the honeyed flesh of a date, the sighing wind, the beauty of the lotus and scent of the lily. Add to all that the passion of a woman in love, and you approached perfection.

Iset thought she had finally won Ramses's heart and mind. His spirits were high, his verve was matchless. In and out of bed, they rode on a wave of pleasure. Wideawake concentrated on educating his palate with the help of some of the city's finest chefs.

It seemed as though Seti's two sons were set on their respective paths: Shaanar would be a statesman, Ramses a social lion. Iset the Fair was quite content with this arrangement.

One morning, she woke to find Ramses missing. Without even doing her face, she ran anxiously out to the garden and called her lover. When there was no answer, she grew frantic. Finally she found him, sitting near the well, meditating by a bed of irises.

'What's wrong?' she asked. 'You gave me such a fright. I can tell something's on your mind,' she said, kneeling beside him.

'I'm not cut out for the life you want me to live.'

'That can't be. Look how happy we are!'

'It's not the kind of happiness I need.'

'Don't ask too much of life: it will turn against you.'

'When it does, I'll be ready.'

'Is pride a virtue?'

'If it means you demand the best from yourself, then yes. I need to have a talk with my father.'

Since the truce with the Hittites, Pharaoh was no longer under fire. There was general agreement that Seti had been wise to avoid a wider war with an uncertain outcome, even if the odds seemed to favour the Egyptian army.

Shaanar's propaganda campaign had failed to convince anyone other than himself that he had played a decisive role in the conflict. According to the ranking officers, the king's son had excelled at watching from the sidelines.

Pharaoh listened and worked.

He listened to his advisers, a few of whom were honest, carefully weighing information, separating the wheat from the chaff, and never deciding in haste.

He worked in his vast office in the main palace, by the light from three tall, barred windows. The walls were white and bare, the furnishings simple and austere: a broad table, a straight-backed armchair for the monarch and woven rush seats for his visitors, a cabinet for his papyrus documents.

Here, in solitude and silence, the Lord of the Two Lands set the course of the world's most powerful nation, trying to steer it according to the law of Ma'at, the incarnation of universal order.

The silence was suddenly broken by shouts from the inner courtyard where the king and his councilors stationed their chariots.

From one of his office windows, the king could see that a horse had just been spooked and had broken the rope to its hitching post. Now it was galloping around the yard and kicking wildly at anyone in its path. It knocked down a guard, then an elderly scribe who had been too slow in taking cover.

As the animal caught its breath, Ramses ran out from behind a pillar, jumped on its back, and pulled hard on the reins. The bucking horse reared again and again in a vain attempt to throw the rider. Beaten, the animal snorted, strained, then quieted.

Ramses jumped off. A soldier from the royal guardsmen came up to him.

'Your father wishes to see you.'

For the first time, the prince was admitted into the Pharaoh's office. Its spareness surprised him. Instead of the regal luxury he expected, the room was almost bare and utterly plain. The king was seated, studying a papyrus scroll.

Unsure how to act, Ramses stopped short a few feet from his father, who failed to offer him a seat.

'That was dangerous business,' Seti said.

'Yes and no. I've ridden that horse, and it's not a mean one. It must have been standing too long in the sun.'

'Still, it was much too risky. My guardsmen would have handled it.'

'I was trying to help.'

'Help yourself get noticed?'

'Well . . .'

'Be honest.'

'Calming a wild horse is no easy task.'

'Am I to conclude that you staged the incident for your own benefit?'

Ramses flushed indignantly. 'Father! How could you—'

'A pharaoh studies strategy.'

'Would that seem like a good one to you?'

'At your age, a trick like that would not bode well for the future. But the way you reacted when I accused you convinces me you're sincere.'

'I will confess I was trying to find a way to talk to you.'

'About what?'

'When you left for Syria, you wouldn't take me along

140

because I couldn't fight like a soldier. While you were gone, I took care of that. I won the rank of officer.'

'A hard-fought battle, I hear.'

Ramses barely concealed his surprise.

'You knew already?'

'So you're an officer now.'

'I can ride, fight with a sword, lance, shield, or as an archer.'

'Are you fond of war, Ramses?'

'It's necessary, isn't it?'

'War causes great suffering; is that something you wish to propagate?'

'Is there another means of ensuring our country's freedom and prosperity? We never go on the offensive, but when we're attacked, we retaliate. Which is as it should be.'

'If you were me, would you have destroyed Kadesh?'

The young man thought for a moment.

'I'd need to consider the facts first. I know nothing about your campaign, except that the peace was preserved and the people of Egypt feel more secure. Giving you an unfounded opinion would be sheer stupidity.'

'Aren't there other subjects you'd like to bring up?'

The prince had wrestled with the questions for days and nights on end, struggling to repress his urge to act. Should he share his suspicions about Shaanar with the pharaoh, tell him that the heir apparent was spreading false claims to his father's victory? Ramses was sure he could find the words to convey his righteous outrage, to convince his father that Shaanar was a snake in the grass.

Now that he was here, denouncing his brother seemed pointless and libellous. How could he play the informer? How could he ever have thought he was one step ahead of Seti? Still, he could not bring himself to lie.

'It's true that I wanted to tell you something.'

'Then why not tell me?'

'I'm in no position to sling mud.'

'Why not let me be the judge?'

'You already know what I was planning to say. If that's not true, my dreams amount to nothing.'

'You seem to go from one extreme to the other.'

'There's a fire that burns in me, a demand for something I can't define, a need that love or friendship alone can never satisfy.'

'Coming from someone your age, that sounds final.'

'Will time make it any easier?'

'Count on no one but yourself, and life may give you more than you expect.'

'Can you tell me what this fire is, Father?'

'Refine the question. Then the answer will come to you.' Seti looked down at the scroll he was studying. The conversation was over.

Ramses bowed. As he turned to go, his father's low voice stopped him cold.

'Your timing is good. I was planning to send for you. Tomorrow, as soon as I celebrate the rites of dawn, we leave for the turquoise mines in the Sinai peninsula.'

24

In this eighth year of Seti's reign, Ramses marked his sixteenth birthday on the eastern desert road to the famous mines at Serabit el-Khadim. Although closely patrolled, the route remained dangerous enough that no one ventured here lightly to brave thirst, evil spirits and pillaging Bedouins. Undeterred by the threat of arrest and imprisonment, they freely attacked caravans forced to cross the Sinai peninsula.

While this expedition was far from warlike in nature, a contingent of soldiers was guarding the pharaoh and the miners. The king's participation made it exceptional. His departure was announced just before the evening rites, and he left the next morning. Queen Tuya was to govern in his absence.

Ramses had been given his first important assignment: lead officer of the infantry detachment, reporting to Bakhen, who had been appointed commander. When the troops assembled, the two greeted each other icily, unwilling to risk a confrontation with the king looking on. Besides, it would be a long journey; they would have to learn to work together. Bakhen lost no time in relegating Ramses to the rear guard, where, he claimed 'a neophyte can do the least harm to his troops'.

More than six hundred men formed the guard contingent. They would also escort the precious stone safely home from the remote and arid land where the goddess Hathor appeared in the form of turquoise.

The desert road itself presented few difficulties: it was well-marked and well-maintained, studded with small forts and watering spots. It ran through hostile territory, up red and yellow mountains so high that they awed the men who were seeing them for the first time. Some were convinced that evil genies lurked in the peaks, ready to pounce on their souls. But Seti's presence and Ramses's self-assurance brought them back to their senses.

Ramses had hoped for a test of his worth that would convince his father, so the uneventful journey was a disappointment. He had no trouble asserting his authority over the thirty foot soldiers assigned to him. They had all heard about his talent for archery and how he had controlled a stampeding horse; they all hoped serving under him would bring a promotion.

At Ramses's insistence, Ahmeni had agreed to stay behind. In the first place, it would be too hard on his frail constitution. Furthermore, he had just made a discovery in a waste dump close to the suspect factory: a fragment of limestone with a bizarre inscription. It was too soon yet to say whether it represented a solid lead, but the young scribe intended to follow up on it. Ramses begged him to be careful. Ahmeni would have Wideawake to guard him, and could call on Setau if needed. Their friend was still prospering, selling venom to temple laboratories and ridding posh villas of the odd cobra.

The prince found himself watching his back. Much as he loved the Egyptian desert where he had almost lost his life, the Sinai made him uneasy: too many looming boulders, too many disturbing shadows, too much chaos. Despite Bakhen's denials, Ramses was apprehensive about a Bedouin attack. Nothing direct, with such a large force of Egyptians, but they still might attempt to pick off stragglers; even worse, they could sneak into camp at night. The prince made his men take special precautions, doubling his orders. He had a run-in with Bakhen, resulting in the decision to put Bakhen in charge of security, yet taking Ramses's misgivings into account.

One evening, the king's son left the rear guard to work his way up the column, bivouac by bivouac. His men had been short of rations and wanted some wine. He was told to see the expedition's director of operations and escorted to the tent that served as his office. Ramses lifted the tent flap, bent low, and stared in silent amazement at the man who sat there cross-legged, studying a map by lamplight.

'Moses! What brings you here?'

'Pharaoh's orders. I'm in charge of logistics and making a better map of the region.'

'I'm in command of the rear guard.'

'I hadn't heard. Bakhen doesn't have much use for you, it seems.'

'We're getting along better now.'

'Let's go outside. It's too cramped in here.'

The two young men had a similar build, athletic and powerful, which made them seem older than their years. Their boyhood was gone for good.

'I was glad when the call came,' Moses confessed. 'The harem had nothing left to offer me. I was ready to pack it in.'

'I thought Merur was a dream job.'

'Not for me. Sweet young things began to grate on my nerves, the arts-and-crafts crowd was too competitive, and I'm not cut out to be an administrator.'

'Is this desert any better?'

'A thousand times! I love it here: the stone faces, the sense that something out there is watching you. I feel at home.'

'Do you still feel that fire we talked about?'

'It's not as strong now. My cure isn't far away. It's somewhere in these dry rocks and secret ravines.'

'I'm not so sure.'

'You don't hear the desert call to you?'

'Not this one. I only sense danger.'

'The soldier in you,' Moses said huffily.

'Speaking of that, my men are short on wine. Your operation must be breaking down.'

Moses burst out laughing. 'Yes, I'm responsible for that. I thought it would be better for the rear guard to stay alert.'

'A little wine would help with their morale.'

'Our first contest of wills,' Moses noted. 'Who'll come out on top?'

'Neither of us. We have to act for the good of the group.'

'My friend, you take this command you've been given so seriously. Could it be a way to escape from yourself?'

'You ought to know me better than that.'

Moses looked Ramses straight in the eye. 'You'll get a small supply of wine if you promise to try to appreciate the Sinai.'

'It's not like Egypt.'

'I'm not Egyptian, Ramses.'

'Of course you are.'

'You're wrong.'

'You were born and raised in Egypt. Your future's there.'

'You're an Egyptian. I'm a Hebrew, with different ancestors. Perhaps they lived here . . . I can feel their footsteps, guess their hopes and disappointments.'

'This desert is getting to you.'

'You can't understand.'

'Don't you trust me any more?'

'You know I do.'

'I love Egypt more than my life, Moses. Nothing is more precious to me than my country. If you think you've found yours, then I do have some idea how you feel.'

The young Hebrew sat down on a rock. 'A country . . . no, this desert is not a country. I love Egypt as much as you do, I appreciate the opportunities I've been given. But all along I've felt another place calling me home.'

'This is the first other place you've seen. Is it the right one?'

'It may not be, I grant you.'

'We'll cross other deserts together, and you'll come back to Egypt. The light that shines there is unique.'

'How can you be so sure of yourself?'

'Because in the rear guard I have no time to worry about the future.'

In the dark desert night, their chiming laughter filtered up to the stars.

The donkeys set the pace, the men followed. Each carried his weight, none lacked food or water. At several points the king ordered the expedition to halt while Moses took readings for his map. He and his team of surveyors followed dried river beds, scaled cliffs, chose new landmarks to be charted later.

Ramses still felt a vague apprehension. He and three experienced foot soldiers kept a constant watch to keep his friend safe from a Bedouin ambush. Moses knew how to take care of himself, but he still might fall into a trap. Fortunately, nothing of the sort occurred, and Moses accomplished the feat of collecting enough data for a detailed new map. Future travellers would thank him.

After dinner, the two friends sat by the fire and talked into the night. Grown used to the calls of hyenas and wildcats, they were comfortable with their rough existence, far from the mansions of Memphis and the harem of Merur. They waited for the dawn, convinced each new day would hold some clue to the inner mysteries they strove to unveil. Often they would fall silent and listen to the darkness. It seemed to whisper that their youth could overcome any obstacle.

*   *   *

The long cortège drew to a halt.

In the middle of the morning, it was unheard of; Ramses gave his men the order to put down their gear and prepare for combat.

'Wait,' said a soldier with a long scar across his chest. 'With all due respect, sir, I think a prayer of thanks is more in order.'

'Explain yourself, soldier.'

'We're there, sir.'

Ramses took a few steps to one side. A rocky, forbidding plateau was outlined in the desert sunlight.

Serabit el-Khadim, domain of the goddess Hathor, the sovereign lady of turquoise.

25

Shaanar was seething.

For the tenth time, the queen had refused to give him a more active role in the interim government, claiming that his father had left no specific directive concerning him. His position as heir apparent gave him no authority to deal with matters beyond his comprehension.

The king's older son had to bow to his mother's wishes and stifle his disappointment. He saw now that his network of friends and informers was still too weak to counter Tuya effectively. Instead of moping, Shaanar moved to consolidate his position.

He hosted a quiet dinner for several influential and tradition-minded courtiers, where he played the part of a forthright young man, eager for their advice. Swallowing his pride, he was the model son, whose only ambition was to follow in his father's footsteps. It went over very well. Virtually certain of becoming the next king, Shaanar garnered even more political support.

However, he seemed to be losing his grasp of foreign relations, while his primary goal remained establishing commercial ties with other nations, both friendly and hostile. He needed to gauge the exact state of diplomatic relations, but how was that possible without a competent and cooperative inside source? His network of trade contacts was not enough:

businessmen focused on profit, not their governments' true intentions.

The ideal solution would be finding a diplomat who worked closely with Seti – ideal, but almost a pipe dream. Nevertheless, Shaanar needed first-hand information to develop his own strategy and be ready, when the time came, to make sweeping changes in Egyptian policy.

The word 'treason' came to mind, making him smile. What would he ever betray except the past, except tradition?

From the flat, rocky top of Serabit el-Khadim, the view was a chaotic jumble of mountains and valleys. The turquoise plateau was the only peaceful spot in this harsh, disturbing landscape.

Ramses looked down in amazement. In places, the precious stone showed thought the rocky surface. Elsewhere it was less accessible. Generation after generation of miners had dug tunnels and passageways. Between expeditions, they stowed their tools underground. There was no permanent operation, since turquoise extracted during the hotter months tended to crack and fade.

Old hands supervised the newcomers and the operation was soon in full swing. The shortest possible stay in the Sinai was the most desirable. The men repaired the stone huts where they would camp; any shelter from the cold night air was welcome. Before they went into the mines, Pharaoh led devotions in the little temple to Hathor, asking the sky goddess to aid and protect them. The Egyptians had not come to harm the mountain, but to harvest precious stones for the temples. The stones they cut and polished would shine with the star queen's eternal and life-giving beauty.

Soon the sound of chisels, mallets and shears rang out, along with the shouts of the miners. They worked in small groups, which Seti visited in turn. As for Ramses, he toured the stelae erected by earlier expeditions. It was his way of paying homage to the mysterious powers of earth and sky, as well as the men who had worked here before him and their legendary finds.

Moses worked hard as director of operations, making sure each member of the expedition was housed and fed, each shrine supplied with incense. Because they honoured the gods, the men were blessed with treasures such as the huge hunk of turquoise a lucky young miner discovered.

Given the site's configuration, there was no threat of a surprise attack. No one could scale the steep slope leading to the plateau without being spied by the lookouts. Ramses, therefore, had one of the easier assignments in camp. For the first few days, he worked his unit with iron discipline, then realized it was ludicrous. While maintaining basic security, he soon relaxed the men's routine and let them indulge in the long siestas they loved.

The prince grew restless with little to do. He offered his help to Moses, but his friend refused, needing to be in control. He had no luck with the miners, either, who said the tunnels were no place for a prince. Finally Bakhen blew up and ordered Ramses to mind his own business and stop interfering with everyone else's work.

So Ramses concentrated on his men. He learned all about their careers, their families, listened to their complaints, argued with them on certain points, conceded others. They wanted better retirement pay and more recognition from the government, considering that they often served under difficult conditions and far from home. Few of them had ever seen combat, but all had worked in the quarries, on state construction projects or expeditions like this one. The life was hard, but they were rather proud of their profession, and anyone lucky enough to accompany the Pharaoh could dine out on his recollections for years to come!

Ramses observed. He learned the day-to-day operation of a work site, understood the necessity for a hierarchy based on ability, not social position. He learned to tell the hard workers from the slackers, the diligent from the easily distracted, the talkers from the silent types. And his gaze kept returning to the stelae placed by their ancestors, the sacred aspirations of their desert shrines pointing towards the heavens.

'Inspiring, aren't they?'

His father had surprised him.

Dressed in a simple kilt, the same as those his Old Kingdom counterparts wore, he remained every inch the Pharaoh, radiating a strength that fascinated Ramses more each time they met. Seti needed no special adornment: his mere presence was enough to assert his authority. No other man possessed this magic: all relied on artifice or attitude. Seti appeared, and chaos turned to order.

'They put me in touch with the past,' Ramses confided.

'Stone has a voice. Unlike ours, it is always true. A destroyer's monuments will be destroyed, a liar's actions have no lasting effect. Pharaoh's sole strength is the law of Ma'at.'

Ramses's head spun. Was his father accusing him? Had he been destructive or untrue? His impulse was to scramble over the edge of the plateau, climb down and disappear in the desert. But what crime had he committed? He waited for his father to continue, but the king simply gazed into the distance.

Shaanar . . . yes, his father must be referring to Shaanar, without naming names! He knew what his heir was up to and was advising Ramses of his real position. His fate was changing again! The prince felt certain that Seti was about to tell him something important, and his disappointment was in proportion to his expectations.

'What is the goal of this expedition?' asked the king.

Ramses hesitated. Was there more than it seemed to his question?

'To bring back turquoise for the gods in their temples.'

152

'Does our country's prosperity depend on precious stones?'

'No, but what would we do without their beauty?'

'Wealth that is based on profit is hollow and cannot last. Each person, each thing, has its special worth, which you must find and value. Cherish what is irreplaceable.'

Ramses felt a light suffusing his heart and bracing him. Seti's words were engraved in his mind for ever.

'The humble and the great alike depend on Pharaoh for their just share. Never favour one over the other. Convince them that the community takes precedence over the individual. What is good for the hive is good for the honeybee, and the bee must serve the hive that gives it life.'

The bee, one of the symbols used in writing Pharaoh's name! Seti was instructing him once again, slowly revealing the secrets of kingship.

Ramses was staggered.

'Producing wealth is essential, distributing it even more so. When one caste controls the riches, trouble and discord will follow. Smaller shares, more equally portioned out, sow the seeds of joy. A pharaoh's reign must be like a banquet: when it ends, no one leaves hungry. Observe, my son, and continue to observe. For if you are not a seer, you will never seize the meaning of my words.'

Ramses spent a sleepless night, his eyes fixed on a blue vein running down one side of the plateau. He asked Hathor to lift the dark clouds in the midst of which he seemed to be struggling, inconsequential as a wisp of straw.

His father had a specific plan, but what was it? Ramses had stopped thinking he might become king one day, but then why would Seti, who never wasted words, favour him with his teachings? In the same situation, Moses might have a clearer understanding, but the prince had to forge his own path, and do so alone.

Shortly before dawn, he noticed a shadowy form leaving

the main tunnel. In the fading moonlight, it looked like a demon scurrying between doors to the underworld. But the demon in question had a human shape and clutched something to its chest.

'Who goes there?'

The man froze for an instant, turned to look at the prince, then ran towards the rockiest part of the plateau, where the only building was a tool shed. Ramses took off in pursuit.

'Stop!'

The man ran faster. So did Ramses. He caught up to the apparition as they reached the plateau's steeper edge.

The prince dived, tackling the man's legs. The fugitive fell, still clutching his right hand to his chest. With his left, he grabbed a stone and tried to smash his attacker's brains. Ramses elbowed him in the throat, knocking the wind out of him. The man staggered to his feet, lost his balance and pitched backward.

A scream, a second cry of pain, then the sound of a body tumbling from rock to rock and finally landing with a thud.

When Ramses worked his way down, the thief was dead, still holding a sack full of turquoise. Ramses had seen the man before. It was the chariot driver who had arranged to have him killed.

26

None of the miners knew much about the culprit. It was his first expedition and he had kept to himself. He had been an asset in the mines, spending hours in the deepest tunnels and winning the respect of his colleagues.

The penalty for stealing turquoise was so stiff that the last time it had happened was ancient history. The thief had got what he deserved, the men thought: it was the law of the desert. Due to the serious nature of his offence, the criminal was not given a proper funeral. His mouth and eyes would not be open in the next world; he would not be able to negotiate the rows of doors to the netherworld; he would fall prey to the goddess of destruction.

'Who hired this man?' Ramses asked Moses.

The Hebrew consulted his lists. 'It seems that I did.'

'You?'

'The director of the harem offered me several workers to bring along here; I signed them on.'

Ramses breathed easier. 'The dead thief was the chariot driver who left me in the desert.'

Moses turned pale. 'You didn't think—'

'Not for an instant, but someone must have played you for a fool.'

'The harem director? He's innocent as a lamb.'

'And probably as gullible. I need to get back to Egypt, Moses, and find out what's behind this.'

'I thought you were giving up the quest for power.'

'I still have to know the truth.'

'It may not be pretty.'

'Are you keeping something from me?'

'No, I swear it. But who would dare to take on Pharaoh's younger son?'

'More people than you or I might imagine.'

'If it's a plot, the instigator will stay out of reach.'

'You're giving up on me, Moses?'

'The whole affair is madness. If you're not Seti's successor, who would want to harm you?'

Ramses said nothing about his latest conversations with his father. They were a secret well of thought he would return to again and again before he understood their meaning.

'Will you help me, Moses, if I need you?'

'Do you even need to ask?'

In spite of the incident with the turquoise thief, Seti did not alter the expedition's timetable. Only when the correct quantity of stone had been mined would the king give the signal for their return to Egypt.

The chief of palace security ran all the way to the queen's chambers. Tuya's messenger had told him to come at once.

'At your service, Majesty.'

'Tell me about your investigation.'

'But . . . it's finished!'

'Really?'

'I found out everything I could.'

'About the charioteer, for instance?'

'Poor soul . . .'

'Can you explain how a dead man could leave on a mining expedition and be caught stealing turquoise?'

The security chief shrivelled. 'That's . . . it's impossible!'

156

'Are you saying I'm insane?'

'Your Majesty!'

'I see three possibilities. You were in on the plot, you were incompetent, or both.'

'Majesty . . .'

'You didn't even try.'

The palace official threw himself at the queen's feet.

'They lied to me, they fooled me, I promise I'll—'

'I don't like snivellers. Now tell me who paid you off.'

The security chief's disjointed explanation gave ample evidence of how unfit he was for his job, a fact hitherto concealed by his skill at public relations. Afraid of compromising his position, he had never dared push too hard. He had tried to do right. He begged the queen's mercy.

'You can serve as my older son's doorman. At least try to screen his visitors.'

The ex-security chief made an impressive show of his gratitude, unaware that the Great Royal Wife had already left the audience chamber.

Ramses and Moses swept into Merur like a whirlwind, pulling their chariot up short in front of the administration building. They had taken turns driving, each trying to outdo the other in skill and endurance. With several stops for fresh horses, they had made the journey from Memphis in record time.

The clatter of their arrival roused the harem director from his afternoon nap.

'Have you lost your minds!' he shouted. 'This is no army post!'

'The Great Royal Wife sent me here on a mission,' revealed Ramses.

The director laid his twitching hands on a bulging belly.

'Ah. But is that any reason to cause a disturbance?'

'It's an emergency.'

'Here, in my establishment?'

'Under this very roof. I'm here for you.'

Moses nodded. The director recoiled a step or two.

'You must be mistaken.'

'One of the men you sent with me on the Pharaoh's mining expedition turned out to be a wanted criminal,' the Hebrew explained.

'My dear fellow, you're raving!'

'Who recommended the man to you?'

'I have no idea what man you're talking about.'

'Let's consult your records,' demanded Ramses.

'Do you have a warrant?'

'Will the queen's state seal serve the purpose?'

The director resisted no further. His search almost over, Ramses was elated. Moses, though more restrained, was also excited by the prospect of learning the truth.

The records relating to the turquoise thief were a disappointment. He had posed not as a veteran charioteer, but a miner with several expeditions behind him, who had come to teach stone-cutting at Merur, specifically turquoise. So that was why the head of the harem thought of him as soon as Moses was named to run the mining operation.

The harem official had obviously been duped. With the groom and the driver both dead, there were no more leads, and the instigator of the plot seemed even farther out of reach.

Ramses had taken more than two hours of archery practice, hitting target after target. He used his anger to hone his concentration, to channel his energy rather than waste it. When his muscles began to ache, he went for a long and solitary run through the harem's gardens and orchards. He knew that in this acute state of confusion, only intense physical activity could calm his mind.

The prince never felt tired. His old wet nurse always said she had never seen a sturdier infant. Never sick a day in his life, neither the cold of winter nor the heat of summer seemed to affect him. He slept soundly and had a tremendous appetite. By the age of ten, he had the athletic physique that daily exercise had continued to strengthen and tone.

Jogging between two rows of tamarisk trees, he heard a song no bird could ever sing. He stopped to listen.

It was a woman's voice, a lovely one. He moved silently closer and saw her.

In the shade of a willow tree, Nefertari was practising a tune on the lute, an instrument imported from Asia. Her voice, sweet as summer fruit, drifted on the breeze ruffling the willow fronds. To the young woman's left was a writing board covered with numbers and geometric figures.

Her beauty was almost unreal. For an instant, Ramses wondered if he might be dreaming.

'I see you. Why do you hide from music?'

He stepped from behind the bush concealing him.

'What were you doing there?'

He found no explanation; his embarrassment made her smile.

'You're dripping wet. Have you been running?'

'I came here hoping to identify a man who tried to have me killed.'

Nefertari's smile vanished. Her seriousness was equally enchanting.

'But you couldn't?'

'I'm afraid not.'

'You won't give up.'

'How do you know that?'

'Because you never give up.'

Ramses bent to examine her drawings. 'Are you studying mathematics?'

'Calculating volumes.'

'To design new temples?'

'I enjoy learning; I don't worry about tomorrow.'

'Is it all work here, or do you spend time with friends?'

'I'd rather be alone.'

'Don't demand too much of yourself.' The blue-green eyes clouded over. 'I didn't mean to offend you; please forgive me.'

An indulgent smiled flitted over her lightly made-up lips. 'Will you be staying a while at the harem?'

'I go back to Memphis tomorrow.'

'Firmly resolved to learn the truth, I'm sure.'

'Can you blame me?'

'The truth can be dangerous.'

'But I want it, Nefertari, and always will, no matter what the cost.' He saw a hint of encouragement in her eyes. 'If you come to Memphis, I hope you'll dine with me some evening.'

'I have several more months of study here at the harem. Then I'll return to my home province.'

'And the man you left behind?'

'You ask too many questions.'

Ramses felt stupid. Around this calm, self-possessed young woman, he was on unsure footing.

'Be happy, Nefertari,' he said in parting.

27

The old diplomat was proud to think that he had served his country long and well. His advice had helped three pharaohs make a minimum of foreign policy; he appreciated Seti's circumspection. It was good to have a leader more concerned with keeping peace than with short-lived military triumphs.

A happy retirement awaited him in Thebes, not far from the temple of Karnak. He would rediscover the family he had so neglected with all his travelling. The last few months of his career had brought him a special pleasure: mentoring the exceptionally gifted Ahsha. He learned quickly and grasped what was essential. When Ahsha returned from the south, after a spectacular success with a delicate information-gathering mission, he had sought out the senior man, seeking guidance. In the end, Ahsha became almost a son to him. Their sessions grew less theoretical; he shared his insider's knowledge and practical secrets gleaned from years of experience. Sometimes Ahsha arrived at his conclusion even before he did, with an understanding of the international situation that was both pragmatic and visionary.

His secretary announced a visit from Shaanar, who humbly requested a few moments of his time. The pharaoh's elder son and heir apparent could not be turned away. Despite his growing fatigue, the high-ranking diplomat received the moon-faced prince, full of his own importance and superiority. The small brown eyes, however, revealed the quick mind behind them. Considering this young man a lightweight would be a disastrous error.

'Your visit is an honour,' said the diplomat.

'I come because of my great admiration for you,' Shaanar said warmly. 'It's no secret that your advice has shaped my father's Asian policy.'

'That's an overstatement. Pharaoh makes his own decisions.'

'Based on your reports from the field.'

'Diplomacy is a difficult art. I do my best.'

'With excellent results.'

'When the gods are willing. Would you care for a cup of beer?'

'With pleasure.'

The two men sat in an archway where a cool wind blew in from the north. A grey cat jumped on the old man's lap, curled up and went to sleep. A servant poured the light, refreshing beer, then withdrew.

'You must be surprised that I called on you.'

'A bit, yes.'

'I hope our conversation will remain confidential.'

'Oh, strictly.'

Shaanar paused. The old diplomat was rather amused by this visit. He was used to dealing with favour-seekers, yet Shaanar's respectful attention was flattering.

'From what I hear, you're planning to retire soon.'

'I've said openly that I'll step down in a year or two, if the king agrees.'

'I'm sorry to hear it.'

'Well, I'm starting to feel my age.'

'Too bad that nothing can replace your experience.'

'We have men who can learn from it. I think you know Ahsha? The best young diplomat I've ever seen.'

'Is your approval of Seti's decisions unqualified?'

'Perhaps you could rephrase the question.'

'All right. Is our hostile attitude towards the Hittites still justified?'

'You don't know the Hittites.'

'They want to trade with us, don't they?'

'They want to take over Egypt and will never, never stop trying. There is no alternative to the king's policy of active defence.'

'What if I had another policy?'

'Discuss that with your father, not with me.'

'You're exactly the person I want to discuss it with.'

'I beg your pardon?'

'Provide me with private updates on developments in Asia, and I'll make it worth your while.'

'I'm afraid that's impossible. Any facts presented at our council meetings are classified information.'

'Then those are the facts I need.'

'Did you hear me? Impossible.'

'One day I'll run those meetings. Remember that.'

The diplomat flushed. 'Is that a threat?'

'You haven't retired quite yet. I'd value your experience. My policies will change the world, I promise you. Agree to be my ally behind the scenes, and you won't regret it.'

The old diplomat rarely lost control of himself, but now he was furious. 'I don't care who you are, what you're asking is out of the question!' he shouted. 'How can you consider betraying the pharaoh of Egypt – betraying your own father?'

'Please calm down.'

'I won't calm down! This is outrageous behaviour from a future ruler. Your father will hear about it.'

'That wouldn't be wise.'

'Get out of here!' he yelled, turning almost purple.

'Are you forgetting who I am?'

'I wish I could!'

'Not a word to anyone,' Shaanar demanded.

'Don't count on it.'

'In that case, I'll have to keep you from talking.'

'Whatever do you—'

Gasping, the old diplomat clutched his chest and collapsed. Shaanar quickly summoned his servants. They laid him out on a couch and ran for a doctor, who pronounced him dead of a massive heart attack.

Shaanar had been lucky: a risky step, but a satisfying outcome.

Iset the Fair was sulking.

She refused to set foot outside her parents' home or admit Ramses to see her. Fatigue, she claimed, had ruined her complexion. This time she would make Ramses pay for his sudden disappearance and long absence. From behind an upstairs drapery, she eavesdropped on Ramses and her maid.

'Please give your mistress my wishes for a speedy recovery,' said Ramses, 'and tell her I won't be back.'

'No!' cried Iset. She threw back the curtain, flew down the stairs and into Ramses's arms.

'I'd say you're looking fine,' he told her.

'Don't go away again or I really will get sick.'

'Do you want me to go against orders from the king?'

'Those dull old expeditions . . . My life is so hard without you.'

'You can't go anywhere, I suppose.'

'Of course I go out, but all the men are after me. So tiresome. With you around, they wouldn't bother me.'

'Would a little souvenir make you feel better?' Ramses produced a small box. Iset's eyes grew wide in astonishment.

'Open it.'

'Is that an order?'

'It's up to you.'

Iset the Fair lifted the lid and caught her breath in admiration. 'For me?'

'By permission of the head of the expedition.'

She kissed him fervently. 'Put it around my neck for me.'

Ramses did as he was told. The turquoise necklace made Iset's green eyes sparkle with pleasure. She was truly the fairest of them all.

Ahmeni stubbornly pursued his search of the city dumps, undeterred by the prospect of failure. The night before, he thought he might have found some new pieces of the puzzle, connecting the address of the workshop to the name of the owner, but in the end there was not enough to go on. The words were faded, with letters missing.

His time-consuming investigation did not interfere with his work as Ramses's private secretary. He performed his tasks flawlessly. The prince was receiving more and more mail every day. Each piece had to be answered promptly and in carefully chosen language. Concerned with maintaining the prince's impeccable reputation as a royal scribe, he had put the finishing touches on the official report of the Serabit el-Khadim expedition.

'You're making a name for yourself,' Ramses remarked.

'I'm not interested in gossip.'

'People say you deserve a better job.'

'I took a vow to serve you.'

'Think about your career, Ahmeni.'

'I'm exactly where I want to be.'

The prince sometimes felt unworthy of Ahmeni's loyalty and friendship, which he counted among his blessings. His friend always forced him to seek a higher standard.

'Any breaks in your investigation?'

'No, but I'm not giving up. What about yours?'

'My mother did all she could, but the trail's gone cold again.'

'There's a name that nobody will say out loud.'

'And maybe they shouldn't. Slander is a serious offence.'

'You're talking sense. I like that. You know, every day you seem more like Seti.'

'I'm his son.'

'So is Shaanar — but it's hard to believe that you come from the same family.'

Ramses paced nervously. Moses, all set to go back to his job at Merur, had just been summoned to the palace. There was no complaint about his role in the mining expedition; in fact, both miners and soldiers had said how well he had run the operation and hoped his work would serve as an example. Still, infighting and back-stabbing were always a possibility; perhaps Moses's popularity reflected badly on someone higher up.

Ahmeni wrote on, unflappable.

'Aren't you worried?'

'Not for Moses. He's cut from the same cloth as you. The harder you test him, the stronger he gets.'

Ramses was hardly reassured. Moses was so assertive that he easily inspired jealousy rather than admiration.

'Instead of fretting,' Ahmeni advised, 'why don't you read the latest royal decrees?'

The prince began to go through them, but had difficulty concentrating. He kept jumping up to walk around the terrace.

Shortly before noon, he saw Moses emerge from a nearby government building. Unable to wait a moment longer, Ramses bolted down the stairs to meet him.

His friend looked perplexed.

'Out with it!' said Ramses.

'I've been offered a post in the royal construction corps.'

'No more Merur?'

'No, I'd be building palaces and temples, going from site to site as an overseer, working with the project supervisor.'

'Are you going to take it?'

'Doesn't it sound better than watching the grass grow at the harem?'

'Then it's a promotion! Ahsha is in town and so is Setau. We're going out tonight.'

28

The four old classmates celebrated. Dancing girls, dinner, wine, dessert – a nearly perfect evening. Setau told a few snake stories and revealed his foolproof formula for meeting women: he would slip a snake in their private chamber, then come to the rescue. Somewhat unethical, he admitted, but it certainly saved time.

Each of them talked about where he was heading. Moses had his new assignment; the other four would stay with their chosen careers. There would be so much to talk about the next time they met!

Setau was the first to leave, with a doe-eyed Nubian dancer. Moses had to get a few hours' sleep before his journey to Karnak, where Seti was building on a grand scale. Ahmeni, unaccustomed to drinking, dozed in a nest of cushions. The night was fragrant.

'It's strange,' Ahsha said to Ramses, 'the city seems so peaceful.'

'Why would it be any other way?'

'Travel as I do and you'll see. We're not as safe as we think. To both the north and the south we have aggressive neighbours who'd jump at the chance to take over our nice, rich country.'

'The Hittites to the north, of course; but what about the south?'

'Don't forget the Nubians.'

'But they've been under our domination always.'

'That's what I thought, until I was sent there on a fact-finding mission. People opened up to me, and the picture that emerged was quite different from the official version of our relations.'

'You're being enigmatic.'

Aristocratic Ahsha did not seem cut out for long journeys through inhospitable countries. However, his breeding served him. Always even-tempered, he kept a cool head in the most trying situations. His inner resources and quick thinking surprised those who chanced to underestimate him. Ramses suddenly realized that from now on he would give serious consideration to any opinion Ahsha offered. His elegant façade was misleading. Beneath it was a tough-minded, confident individual.

'Does the term 'state secrets' mean anything to you?'

'Your speciality,' said Ramses ironically.

'This one concerns you directly. As your friend, I think you deserve to hear it a few hours ahead of Shaanar. Tomorrow morning, he'll be called to a special meeting of the pharaoh's advisory council.'

'Are you breaking your word just to help me?'

'I'm not betraying my country, because I'm sure you have a role in what's about to happen.'

'Explain.'

'I've already hinted that I think there's trouble in Nubia. Not the experts' opinion, but we shall see. I don't mean isolated protests, but a genuine uprising leading to significant casualties – unless the Egyptian army moves quickly to crush it.'

Ramses was dumbfounded.

'An incredible theory. It will never sell.'

'I wrote a report, stating my arguments point by point, with facts to back them up. I'm no soothsayer, just an accurate observer.'

'The Viceroy of Nubia and his generals will say you're mad!'

'Certainly. But Pharaoh and his council will read my report.'

'Why should they agree with your conclusions?'

'Because they reflect the truth, and the truth is what guides our sovereign, I'm sure you'll agree.'

'I do, but—'

'Then believe me and prepare yourself.'

'For what?'

'When Pharaoh decides to put down the revolt, he'll want to take one of his sons with him. It's your turn this time – the chance you've dreamed of to prove yourself as a soldier.'

'And if you're wrong . . .'

'Not a chance. Be at the palace tomorrow morning. Early.'

The council meeting caused a stir in the usually quiet wing of the palace Pharaoh chose for it. His 'Nine Only Friends', some generals, a few high officials, arrived; usually, the king simply met with his vizier and selected matters for his own further study. Now, without any hint of trouble in the air, a special meeting of the broader council had been called.

Ramses approached the vizier's assistant and requested an audience with Pharaoh. He was asked to wait. Since Seti never wasted words, the prince thought the proceedings would be brief; such was not the case. The meeting ran through lunchtime and well into the afternoon, which was most unusual. It could only mean that opposing viewpoints were being debated, and the king would hear all sides before determining his course.

As the day progressed towards sunset, the Only Friends left the council room, looking grave. Behind them came the generals. A quarter-hour later, the vizier's assistant fetched Ramses.

He was led in to see not Seti, but Shaanar.

'I wish to see Pharaoh.'

'He's busy. What can I do for you?'

'I'll come back later.'

'I'm authorized to act on Pharaoh's behalf. If you refuse to speak to me, I'll report you. Our father won't be happy. You keep forgetting the respect you owe me.'

The threat failed to deter Ramses. He was in this game for good.

'We're brothers, Shaanar. Have you forgotten?'

'But our positions . . .'

'That's no reason we can't be closer.'

Confused, Shaanar lowered his voice. 'Of course not – but you're so impulsive, so headstrong . . .'

'You go your way and I'll go mine. I have no more delusions of grandeur.'

'What . . . which way is it that you're going?'

'The army.'

Shaanar rubbed his chin. 'That will be perfect for you. Now why did you want to see Pharaoh?'

'I want to fight with him in Nubia.'

'Where did you hear about a war in Nubia?' Shaanar asked, startled.

Ramses was cool. 'I'm a royal scribe and an infantry officer. What I lack is combat experience. Give me a chance, Shaanar.'

Shaanar rose, paced the room, returned to his seat.

'Don't count on it.'

'Why not?'

'Too dangerous.'

'Do you fear for my safety?'

'A prince of the blood must not take unfounded risks.'

'Then why does Pharaoh march at the head of the army?'

'Enough, Ramses. It's no place for you.'

'It is!'

'My decision is final.'

'I'll appeal it to Father.'

'Don't cause trouble, Ramses. The country has problems enough without a breach in protocol.'

'Don't you get tired of standing in my way, Shaanar?'

The heir apparent's moon face hardened.

'What are you implying?'

'Will you sign my commission?'

'That's up to the king.'

'You can recommend it.'

'I need to think.'

'Think quickly.'

Ahsha studied the office. A good-sized room, two well-placed windows to keep the air circulating, walls and ceiling decorated with floral borders and a pattern of red and blue. Several chairs, a low table, well-woven mats, storage chests, a papyrus cupboard. Yes, his new State Department office was quite satisfactory, at least at this stage. Most men his age would be content with far less.

Ahsha dictated letters to his secretary, welcomed colleagues curious to meet this boy wonder. His final visitor was Shaanar, always on the lookout for new contacts in the department.

'A corner office,' the prince remarked.

'I consider myself fortunate.'

'The king was most impressed with your report on Nubia.'

'May my every effort please His Royal Highness.'

Shaanar shut the door to the office and spoke confidentially. 'I'm also most impressed with your work. Ramses fell for it! He can't wait to march off to war! Naturally, to tantalize him I refused at first, then gave in little by little.'

'Does he have his commission?'

'Pharaoh will agree to take him along, and Nubia will be his first engagement. Ramses doesn't realize the Nubians are ferocious fighters and it may turn out to be a bloodletting. His trip to the turquoise mines has him convinced he's a warrior. On his own, he never would have insisted on going to Nubia. We have him right where we want him now, don't we?'

'I hope so.'

'And what about you, Ahsha? I take care of my friends, and you're doing brilliantly. A little patience, two or three more first-rate reports and reviews, and you're headed for the top.'

'My only ambition is to serve my country.'

'Mine, too, of course. But the higher up you are in the State Department, the more effective you can be. Do you have any interest in Asia?'

'The prime focus of our diplomatic efforts?'

'Egypt needs professionals of your quality. Learn all you can, then be my eyes and ears. You won't regret it.'

Ahsha bowed to his prince.

Although the Egyptian people disliked armed conflict, they were not upset by Seti's departure for Nubia. How could the black tribes resist a powerful and well-organized army? The expedition was closer to a police operation than a real war. The unrest would be firmly quelled, the rebels dispersed, and Nubia would come back into the fold.

Thanks to Ahsha's alarmist report, Shaanar knew that the Egyptians would meet with considerable resistance. Ramses would try to prove his valour with youthful abandon. Historically, Nubian arrows and war axes had cut short the career of many unwary young soldiers, convinced of their superiority. With any luck, the same failing would be Ramses's downfall.

Life could not be better. Shaanar had his pawns lined up in winning position. Pharaoh had more work than he could do without damaging his health. In the near future he would be obliged to name his older son as co-regent and give him more decision-making power. Self-control, patience, working behind the scenes: those were the keys to success.

Ahmeni ran to the harbour, slowly, haltingly, and found it hard to elbow his way through the crowd that had gathered to see off the expedition. The waste dump he had just finished exploring had yielded an important, perhaps even crucial, clue.

His rank as Ramses's secretary got him behind security line. Panting, he reached the pier.

'The prince's boat?'

'There,' an officer answered, pointing far down the Nile.

29

Leaving Memphis on the twenty-fourth day of the second month of the winter season, in Year Eight of Seti's reign, the Egyptian army moved swiftly southward. At Aswan, they disembarked and re-embarked below the boulders of the First Cataract. At this time of year, the Nile was high enough to get them through the more dangerous channels, but Pharaoh preferred using boats equipped for the final stage of the river voyage to Nubia.

Ramses was enchanted. Commissioned as the expedition's scribe, he was under his father's direct command and travelled on the same ship. Its bow and stern curved upward, well out of the water. Two rudders, one to port, one to starboard, made for quick handling. From the single stout mast, one huge sail puffed out in the north wind as the sailors worked the ropes.

In the centre of the vessel was a large cabin divided into berths and working quarters. Smaller cabins for the captain and two steersmen were found near the two ends of the boat. The royal vessel, like the rest of the fleet, was a lively, happy place. The sailors and soldiers felt it was almost a pleasure cruise, and their officers played along. They were all acquainted with the king's directives: no attacks on civilians, no forced enlistment, no arbitrary arrests. A military convoy should inspire fear and enforce respect for the established order, but must never become synonymous with terror and pillage. Any member of the expedition failing to obey the honour code would be severely punished.

Nubia fascinated Ramses. He spent the river voyage glued to the bow. Parched hills, isles of granite, a thin band of green at the desert's edge, a deep-blue sky: a stunning land of fire and absolutes. Cows lazed on the riverbanks, hippopotamuses in the water. There were crested cranes, pink flamingos, swallows diving over palm trees where baboons scampered. Ramses felt at home in this wild place. It was like him: burning, unquenchable.

For more than two hundred miles between Aswan and the Second Cataract, the convoy progressed calmly, stopping in peaceful villages and distributing goods. This was Wawat, 'the Burning One', an area long ago subdued and settled. So powerful was this country's appeal that Ramses felt as if he moved in a waking dream.

He snapped to attention when an incredible sight appeared in the distance. The fortress of Buhen had brick walls thirty feet tall and twelve thick. At each corner of the crenellated battlements was a watchtower from which Egyptian lookouts scanned the Second Cataract and the surrounding region. No Nubian raid could penetrate the line of defensive forts along this border; Buhen was the largest, with three thousand permanent troops and a constant shuttle of couriers.

Seti and Ramses entered the fortress through the main gate, facing the desert. It was barricaded with two double doors, connected by a wooden bridge; an enemy would have been repelled by a shower of arrows, javelins and slingshot. Notched embrasures were placed in the wall to allow for deadly crossfire.

Part of their contingent was already visiting the town that had sprung up at the foot of the fortress, featuring a barracks, trim houses, warehouses, workshops, a market and a waste-disposal system. The troops would enjoy a few hours of leave before heading into Kush, the next province south. Today was a lark.

The king and his son were welcomed in Buhen's great hall, which also served as the provincial courtroom. Today, however, the commandant offered his distinguished visitors refreshments, including dates and cool beer.

'I expected the Viceroy of Nubia,' said Seti.

'He'll be arriving soon, Majesty.'

'I thought this was his residence.'

'Yes, but he went to assess the situation in Irem, south of the Third Cataract.'

'The situation? An uprising, you mean?'

The commanding officer's eyes shifted away from Seti.

'That's putting it too strongly.'

'Would the viceroy travel so far just to arrest a few robbers?'

'No, Your Majesty, we monitor the region closely and—'

'Then why have your reports been underestimating the problem, these past few months?'

'I tried to remain objective. There's a little unrest in Irem, true, but—'

'Two caravan attacks, a well under rebel control, an investigating officer murdered – you call that a little unrest?'

'We've seen worse, Your Majesty.'

'To be sure, but the ringleaders were caught and punished. This time, you and the viceroy have made no arrests, and the perpetrators think they've outsmarted you. They're putting together a serious revolt.'

'My role is purely defensive,' protested the commandant. 'No Nubian revolt could get past our fortifications.'

Seti's anger rose. 'Do you suppose we can hand the provinces of Kush and Irem over to rebel forces?'

'Not for a moment, Your Majesty.'

'The truth, then.'

The officer's spinelessness disgusted Ramses. Cowards

like that were unworthy to serve their country. If he were his father, he would have stripped the man of his rank and sent him to the front lines.

'I thought it served no purpose to alarm our troops. The number of incidents has been so small.'

'Our losses?'

'Nonexistent, I hope. The viceroy left with an experienced patrol. The very sight of them will bring the Nubians to their knees.'

'I'll wait here three days, no longer. Then I'll act.'

'I'm sure it won't be necessary, Majesty. At least we will have had the opportunity to entertain you! Tonight there's a small reception—'

'I won't be there. See that my soldiers are well taken care of.'

The Second Cataract was unforgiving. The Nile churned between tall cliffs. Narrow channels struggled through huge slabs of basalt and granite, splashing and foaming. At each twist, the rapids gathered more energy. In the distance, ochre sand streaked the red banks, studded with blue boulders. Here and there palms added a hint of green.

Ramses, watching, tumbled along with the river, battled the rocks with it, finally won. Between him and the river there was total communion.

The little town of Buhen was light-hearted, far removed from a war that no one believed existed. The thirteen Egyptian fortresses would have repelled invaders by the thousand. Besides, a large share of Irem was farmland, which always meant stability. Following the example of pharaohs past, Seti was simply flexing his military muscle to impress the population and reinforce the peace.

Touring the encampment, Ramses found that none of the soldiers seemed to have fighting on their minds. He observed them napping, feasting, making love to gorgeous Nubian women, playing dice, talking about home – but not sharpening their swords, even though the Viceroy of Nubia had failed to return from his pacifying mission in Irem.

Ramses made note of the human propensity to fail to prepare for the worst, or even conceive of it. Reality was so unsavoury that mirages seemed a safer way out of their shackles. Individual man was both evasive and criminally negligent. The prince vowed he would never shrink from facts, even if they did contradict his hopes. Like the Nile, he would rush up against boulders and come out on the other side.

At the western edge of the encampment, towards the desert, he saw a crouching figure digging in the sand, as if burying treasure. Intrigued, Ramses approached the man, sword in hand.

'What are you doing?'

'Shh! Not a sound!' ordered a barely audible voice.

'Answer me.'

The man straightened up. 'Now you've done it! It got away.'

'Setau! You joined the army?'

'Of course not! I'm convinced a black cobra was nesting in that hole . . .' Dressed in his strange garment full of pockets, ill-shaven, his swarthy complexion and black hair shining in the moonlight, Setau would hardly be mistaken for a soldier.

'The best magicians like their venom from Nubian snakes. It works the best, they say. An expedition like this is a godsend!'

'You're not afraid of snakes, but what about war?'

'I don't smell blood yet. These lame-brained soldiers spend their time stuffing their faces and getting drunk. Probably the least dangerous thing they do.'

'It won't stay this calm.'

'You can read the future?'

'Do you think Pharaoh would haul this many men to Nubia just for show?'

'What do I care, as long as I catch some snakes? They're huge down here, wonderful specimens! Instead of sticking your neck out on the battlefield, you ought to come and hunt with me. We'd do well together.'

'I'm under my father's orders.'

'I'm a free agent.' Setau stretched out on the ground and fell fast asleep. He was the only man in Egypt unperturbed by the thought of snakes crawling over him in the night.

Ramses contemplated the cataract and shared the Nile's endless strain. The night was just breaking up when he sensed a presence behind him.

'Did you forget to sleep, son?'

'I was guarding Setau. Several snakes came up to him, stopped and then went away. Even in his sleep, he exerts his power. Isn't it the same for a ruler?'

'The viceroy is back,' Seti revealed.

Ramses looked at his father. 'Did he pacify Irem?'

'He ended up with five dead, ten wounded, and beat a hasty retreat. That was about the sum of it. Your friend Ahsha's predictions were more accurate than I would have hoped. Remarkably observant, and his analysis was solid.'

'Sometimes he makes me uncomfortable, but he's brilliant.'

'Unfortunately, he knew better than my advisers.'

'Does this mean war?'

'It does, Ramses. There's nothing I like less, but Pharaoh can allow no rebellion to go unchecked. Otherwise, it would be the end of the reign of Ma'at, a descent into chaos, bringing unhappiness to everyone, mighty or humble. Egypt protects itself against invasion from the north by controlling Canaan and Syria. In the south, there's Nubia. A king who weakens, like Akhenaton, puts his country in danger.

180

'We're going to fight?'

'We'll hope that the Nubians will listen to reason. Your brother was quite insistent that I sign your commission. He seems to think you have the makings of a soldier. But we face a formidable opponent. Once the Nubians are stirred up, they will fight to the death, ignoring their wounds.'

'Do you think I'm not ready for combat?'

'There's no need to take unnecessary risks.'

'I want to live up to the trust you've placed in me.'

'Don't you also want to live?'

'Keeping my word comes first.'

'Then fight, if we're forced to; fight like a lion, a lion and a falcon, a flash of lightning. Or else you will be beaten.'

30

Reluctantly, the army left Buhen and pushed beyond the Second Cataract, the safety net of thirteen forts, and on into Kush. The region was pacified, supposedly, but the Nubians were renowned as fighters. It was no great distance to the viceroy's second residence at the garrison of Shaat, on the island of Sai. A short way downstream, Ramses found another island, Amara, and fell in love with its wild beauty. If there were ever an opportunity, he would ask his father to build a chapel there, a shrine to Nubia's splendour.

At Shaat, the men's carefree attitude vanished. Less strategic than Buhen, the citadel was full of refugees; Irem's rich farm plain had fallen into rebel hands. Emboldened by their victory and the viceroy's lack of retaliation, two tribes had passed the Third Cataract and were heading north. The old dream came to life again: regaining control of Kush, driving out the Egyptians, destroying the line of forts.

Shaat would be the first one in their path.

Seti ordered the alert to be sounded. Archers in the battlements, catapults in the turrets; in the trenches and at the foot of the high brick walls, the infantry.

Then Pharaoh and his son, accompanied by a downcast viceroy, were briefed by the garrison commander.

'The news is grim,' he confessed. 'In the last week, the uprising has grown to alarming proportions. Usually the natives are preoccupied with tribal warfare. We never worried about them joining forces against us. Now they have. I sent messengers to Buhen, but . . .' He glanced at the crestfallen viceroy and said no more.

'Go on,' ordered Seti.

'We could have nipped it in the bud if we'd moved quickly. Now I wonder if it wouldn't be better to evacuate the fort.'

Ramses was stunned to realize how cowardly and ill-prepared most of the border commanders appeared to be.

'Are the Nubians really so ferocious?'

'Wild animals,' the commandant answered. 'Death and suffering mean nothing to them. They enjoy fighting and killing. And their war cry! Absolutely blood-curdling. I wouldn't blame anyone for running from a Nubian attack.'

'Running? You mean desertion?'

'When you see them fight, you'll understand. Keeping them vastly outnumbered is the only way to subdue them. And right now, we're not sure whether they number in the hundreds or thousands.'

'Leave for Buhen with the refugees and take the viceroy with you,' Seti commanded.

'Should I send reinforcements?'

'We'll see; my messengers will keep you informed of the situation. Block the river routes and put all the forts on high alert.'

The viceroy retreated, still fearing repercussions. The commandant prepared the evacuation. Two hours later, a long column of refugees set off northward. Remaining at the Shaat garrison were Pharaoh, Ramses and a thousand suddenly sombre troops, murmuring that ten thousand bloodthirsty savages were going to overrun the fort and hack every last Egyptian to pieces.

Seti gave Ramses the task of telling them the truth. The young prince explained facts and discounted rumours. Then he did more: he appealed to their courage, reminded them each of their pledge to protect their country, even if it meant laying down their lives. His words were simple and direct. His enthusiasm was catching. Learning that the king's son would be fighting with them, as one of them, renewed their hope. Ramses's spirit, along with Seti's gifts as a strategist, would save them from certain doom.

The king had decided to advance instead of waiting to be attacked. Engaging the enemy seemed preferable, despite the possibility of retreat in the face of superior numbers. At least it would be settled.

He spent a long evening poring over maps of the Kush region with Ramses, teaching him how various geographic features were represented. The prince basked in his father's attention, learning quickly and vowing to remember each detail. No matter what happened, tomorrow would be a glorious day.

Seti retired to the king's chamber. Ramses stretched out on a makeshift bed. His dreams of victory were disturbed by muffled exclamations and laughter from the next room. He got up to investigate.

Lying on his stomach, Setau grunted his appreciation as a giggling Nubian masseuse kneaded his muscular back. Her fine features could have graced a Theban noblewoman. Her magnificent body was a deep, glowing ebony.

'She's fifteen and her name is Lotus,' the snake charmer told him. 'She has magic hands. Would you like to try a massage?'

'No, thanks. She might not be able to resist me.'

'She even likes snakes! Handles all the most dangerous species. We've already harvested a load of venom. I can't believe my luck! I knew this expedition was a good idea.'

'Tomorrow the two of you will be guarding the fortress.'

'You're attacking?'

'Advancing.'

'All right. Lotus and I will be the gatekeepers. And try to catch ten cobras.'

In the chill of early morning, the foot soldiers had to don their winter tunics, to be removed once the Nubian sun began to shine. Ramses, driving a light chariot, was at the head of the contingent, just behind the scouts. Seti was in the middle of the ranks, guarded by his own special detachment.

At the sound of trumpeting in the distance, Ramses called the troops to a halt, jumped down from his chariot and followed the scouts into the desert.

An enormous beast bellowed in anguish. Thrashing its snakelike snout, it tried to work loose a spear tip. The scouts identified the spear as the southern tribes' assegai. Ramses recognized the animal as the legendary elephant, long since vanished from the southern borders of Egypt and the Isle of Elephantine where it had roamed. He had never seen a live one.

'A big bull,' one of scouts declared. 'Those tusks must weigh close to a couple of hundred pounds apiece. Keep clear of him!'

'But he's hurt.'

'The Nubians tried to kill him. We've got them on the run.'

Confrontation grew more imminent. While a scout headed back to inform the king, Ramses approached the elephant. At fifty paces he halted and made eye contact. The wounded animal stopped thrashing and stared back.

Ramses raised his hands. The big bull waved his trunk as if to show he understood the two-legged creature's peaceful intentions. The prince slowly drew nearer. One of the scouts opened his mouth to scream, but his neighbour silenced him. With the slightest provocation, the elephant might trample Pharaoh's son.

Ramses felt no fear. In the beast's eyes, he read instant

comprehension. A few more steps and he was only an arm's length from the wounded elephant, its tail thumping its hindquarters. The prince reached out and the elephant lowered its trunk.

'This will hurt,' he announced. 'But it's the only way I can help you.' Ramses gripped the shaft of the spear. 'Will you let me?'

The huge ears flapped, as if in agreement. The prince yanked the spear tip out on his first try. The beast trumpeted in relief. The scouts stared, aghast. Ramses would never survive. Even now the elephant was wrapping its bloody trunk around his waist. In a few seconds, the bull would crush him to pieces, then come after them. They'd better run.

'Look, men, look!'

The prince's triumphant voice stopped them. They turned to see him straddling the elephant's neck, where the wounded trunk had ever so delicately placed him.

'The view from up here is great,' Ramses laughed. 'I can see any move the enemy makes.'

The prince's exploit galvanized the army. He must have supernatural powers, they reasoned, to impose his will on the mightiest of all animals. The elephant's wound was dressed with cloths soaked in oil and honey. The prince and the pachyderm communicated effortlessly. One spoke with his mouth and hands, the other with his trunk and ears. The beast guided them down a beaten path to a village of mud-walled, palm-thatched huts.

Scattered all around were the bodies of old men, children and women, some of them speared in the stomach, others with their throats slashed. To one side lay a mutilated heap of adult males who had tried to resist capture. Crops had been burned, livestock slaughtered.

Ramses felt sick. So this was war, this carnage and boundless cruelty that made man the most feared of predators.

'Don't drink the well water!' cried one veteran scout. Two younger men, thirsty from their march, had tried it. Two minutes later they had died, screaming in pain. The rebels had poisoned the well to punish the villagers for remaining loyal to Egypt.

'Can't do a thing for them,' lamented Setau. 'I have a lot to learn about herbal poisons. Good thing I have Lotus to teach me.'

'What are you doing here?' Ramses asked in amazement. 'I thought you were guarding the fort!'

'Too boring. There's so much to explore out here!'

'Massacred villages, for instance?'

Setau laid a hand on his friend's shoulder. 'Do you see why I prefer snakes? The way they kill is nobler, and their venom is strong medicine.'

'There's more to mankind than this horror.'

'Are you so sure?'

'Ma'at is on one side, chaos on the other. We're put on earth to do Ma'at's work and fight evil, time after time.'

'Only a pharaoh thinks like that. You're just a young commander convincing yourself that one good massacre deserves another.'

'And not sure who will get it this time.'

'Lotus knows a brew that can ward off the evil eye. Come along and try some. You'll be invincible.'

Seti was sombre. He had called Ramses and the other officers to his tent and asked for their recommendations.

'Let's keep advancing,' said one experienced officer. 'We'll go past the Third Cataract into Irem. A swift strike will do the trick.'

'They might be lying in wait for us,' said a junior man. 'The Nubians know we favour moving fast.'

'True,' said Pharaoh. 'To avoid a trap, we have to learn

the enemy positions. I need volunteers to go under cover of darkness.'

'Risky,' the veteran observed.

Ramses stood up. 'I volunteer.'

'So do I,' said the veteran, 'and I know three more men as brave as the prince.'

31

The prince removed his headdress, his leather vest, his uniform kilt and sandals. For his night mission in the Nubian desert, he would blacken his body with coal and bring only a dagger. Before taking off, he stopped in Setau's tent.

The snake charmer was boiling down a yellowish liquid; Lotus's hibiscus brew was red.

'A red-and-black snake crawled under my sleeping mat. What a stroke of luck! Another new specimen, another good harvest. The gods are with us, Ramses! Nubia is a paradise. I wonder how many kinds of snake live here?'

Finally noticing Ramses's skin, he took a long look at the prince.

'Where are you going in that disguise?'

'To reconnoitre the rebel camps.'

'What's your plan?'

'I'll head straight south. There's no way to miss them.'

'Just make sure you come back.'

'I'll trust my luck.'

Setau nodded. 'Try some of Lotus's brew with us. At least you'll taste a delicious new drink before the savages get you.'

The red liqueur had a fruity, refreshing taste. Lotus refilled his cup three times.

'In my opinion,' Setau declared, 'you're being foolish.'

'I'm doing my duty.'

'Big words! What if you're only acting like a daredevil?'

'I'm not, I . . .'

'Feeling all right?'

'Yes, of course . . .'

'Sit down.'

'I have to go.'

'In this condition?'

'I'm fine, I . . .' Ramses slumped into Setau's arms. His friend laid him on a reed mat by the fire and left his tent. Although he had been expecting the Pharaoh, Seti's presence impressed him.

'Thank you, Setau.'

'Lotus says it's a harmless potion. Ramses will be back to normal in the morning. Don't worry about the scouting mission: Lotus and I will go. She knows this country.'

'What can I do to thank you?'

'Nothing. I only want to keep your son from risking your neck.'

Seti left, and Setau felt a quiet pride. How many men earned Pharaoh's personal thanks?

A ray of sunshine filtered into the tent, rousing Ramses. For a few minutes, he was in a fog. Then the truth dawned. Setau and his Nubian sweetheart had drugged him!

Furious, he ran outside, right into Setau, sitting cross-legged and breakfasting on dried fish.

'Hey there! You almost made me choke.'

'Well, you knocked me out.'

'Knocked some sense into you, I'd say.'

'I had a mission and you interfered.'

'Go and say thank you to Lotus. In fact, a kiss wouldn't hurt. Last night she scouted the location of the main enemy camp.'

'But she's one of them!'

190

'Her relatives were slaughtered in that village.'

'Is she really with us?'

'Are you getting sceptical in your old age? Yes, she'll be loyal. That's why she decided to help. The rebels are from a rival tribe and they're ruining the most prosperous region in Nubia. Now stop feeling sorry for yourself. Go and wash, dress and have breakfast: your father is expecting you.'

The Egyptian force marched off in the direction Lotus indicated, with Ramses in front, perched on the elephant. For the first two hours, the beast walked easily, almost playfully, nibbling branches along the way. Then he grew more intent, staring straight ahead, moving slowly, quietly, light as a feather on his mammoth feet. Suddenly his trunk disappeared into the top of a palm tree, plucked out a black man armed with a slingshot, and smashed him against the tree trunk, breaking his back.

Had this lookout had time to warn the rebel army? Ramses looked back, awaiting Pharaoh's order. The signal was unequivocal: deployment and attack. The elephant forged ahead.

He had barely pushed through to the other side of the palm grove when Ramses saw them: hundreds of Nubian warriors, black as night, with pushed-in noses, full lips, ritual scars on their cheeks, gold hoops in their ears, heads shaved in front but with feathers in their nubbly back hair. The soldiers wore spotted fur loincloths, the chiefs white robes with bright red sashes.

There was no need to call for their surrender. As soon as they saw the elephant in the Egyptian army's vanguard, they grabbed their bows and started firing. Their haste proved fatal; they scattered in all directions, while the Egyptian assault troops advanced in an orderly column, wave after wave.

Seti's archers picked off the Nubian bowmen. Then the

lancers came from behind to attack the slingshot brigade. The Egyptian foot soldiers used their shields to fight off a desperate hatchet charge, then stabbed the rebels.

The survivors threw their arms down in a panic, got to their knees and begged for mercy. Seti raised his right hand, and the battle ended only a few minutes after it had begun. The victors tied their captives' hands behind their backs to lead them away.

The elephant's battle was not over. He walked to the biggest hut, brushed the roof away, and kicked in the mud walls, exposing two Nubians. One was tall and distinguished-looking, with a wide red sash across his shoulder. The other, shorter man, crouching nervously behind a straw basket, was the one who had speared the elephant's trunk.

Now he used that trunk to pluck the man like a piece of ripe fruit and hold him in the air for a long moment. The small black man shouted and flailed, trying in vain to break the iron grip. The beast set him down. Before he had time to run for his life, a huge foot landed on his head. Unhurriedly, the elephant snuffed out the man who had caused him so much pain.

Ramses addressed the tall Nubian, who had quietly observed the scene, arms crossed.

'Are you their chief?'

'Indeed I am, and you are very young to be dealing us such a blow.'

'The glory is Pharaoh's.'

'Ah, your king is here. That must be why the medicine men said we couldn't win. I should have listened.'

'Where are the other tribes involved in the uprising?'

'I'll give you their positions. I'll go to them myself and tell them to surrender. Will Pharaoh spare them?'

'Only he can say.'

Seti was relentless, attacking two more rebel camps the same day. Neither of them would heed the captive chief's advice.

As before, the engagements were brief. The Nubians battled disjointedly. At the thought of their sorcerers' predictions, at the sight of Seti's blazing eyes, their fighting spirit fled. In their minds, the war was doomed from the start.

At dawn the next day, the remaining tribes laid down their arms. They had heard about the king's terrifying son, who rode a bull elephant trained to trample Nubians. Nothing could stop Pharaoh's army.

Seti took six hundred prisoners. Along with them came fifty-five under-age males, sixty-six girls, and forty-eight small children who would be educated in Egypt and then sent back to Nubia, indoctrinated in a culture that complemented their own, championing peace with their powerful neighbour.

The king satisfied himself that the whole province of Irem had been liberated and that the wells seized by the rebels again served the rich farmland. From now on, the Viceroy of Kush would tour the region at regular intervals to watch for signs of unrest. If the people had complaints about the government, he would listen and try to resolve them. In the case of a serious disagreement, Pharaoh himself would intervene.

Ramses felt nostalgic: he was sad to be leaving Nubia. He wanted to ask his father for the post of viceroy and was sure he could do the job. When he next saw Seti, however, his father's expression discouraged him from speaking. Then he told Ramses he planned to leave the current viceroy in place, though under threat of recall at the first sign of trouble.

The elephant's trunk stroked Ramses's cheek. Ignoring the pleas of his men, who would have loved to see the beast parade through the streets of Memphis, Ramses decided to leave him free to roam. Ramses stroked the healing scar. The elephant's trunk gestured towards the open plains, as if in invitation. But here the prince and the elephant parted ways.

For a while, Ramses stood there, missing his unexpected ally. He would have liked to go with him, discover the grasslands, learn the wisdom of the elephants. But the dream was over, and it was time to go home. The prince swore he would return to Nubia.

The Egyptians broke camp, singing. They had the highest praise for Seti and Ramses, who had turned a treacherous expedition into a resounding triumph. They left no ember of revolt for the natives to rekindle.

Passing some brush, the prince heard a moan. Had some wounded man been left behind by accident?

He parted the branches and found a frightened lion cub, struggling for breath. Its right leg was stiff and swollen; it whimpered feverishly. Ramses lifted the cub and felt its heart pounding erratically. Without treatment, the cub would surely die.

Luckily, Setau's boat hadn't left yet. Ramses brought him the patient. His examination left no room for doubt. 'Snakebite,' Setau concluded.

'The prognosis?'

'Grim. Look here: three holes, for the two main fangs and a backup, plus twenty-six tooth marks. A cobra. This is a special cub, or it would be dead already.'

'Special?'

'Look at the paws: they're twice as big as usual. This would have been a giant.'

'Will you try to save it?'

'One thing going for this little fellow: it's winter. Cobra venom's less potent at this time of year.'

Setau ground up some snakewood root from the eastern desert and mixed it with wine. He got some down the cub, then crushed the snakewood leaves into powder, mixed it with oil, and rubbed it on the little animal to stimulate its circulation.

On the voyage home, Ramses cared for the lion cub,

applying plasters of dampened desert sand and leaves from the castor-oil plant. The lion hardly moved now; without its mother's milk, it was growing weak. Yet it looked up gratefully when the prince petted it, and purred.

'You'll live,' Ramses promised, 'and we'll be friends.'

32

At first, Wideawake was wary. Then he inched closer.

Finally the yellow dog timidly sniffed the lion cub, which stared at him in wonder. Though still weak, the cub was ready to play; it pounced on Wideawake, nearly crushing him. The dog yelped and got away, but not quickly enough to escape a swat at his hindquarters.

Ramses took the cub by the neck and gave him a thorough lecture. Ears perked, the lion listened. Then the prince checked his dog, found only a scratch, and tried putting the two animals together again. Wideawake pawed the lion's face, somewhat spitefully. Setau called the cub 'Invincible'. It beat a cobra's venom, he said, which almost always meant certain death. The name would bring him luck, and besides, this cub was strong. Setau wondered aloud: a tame elephant, an oversized lion . . . Perhaps Ramses only knew how to think big.

The lion cub and watchdog quickly sized each other up. Invincible was more careful and Wideawake less teasing. They fast became friends, running and playing to their hearts' content. After meals, the dog curled up against the cub for a nap.

The court was abuzz with news of Ramses's exploits. A man who could control an elephant and a lion had magical powers that must be taken seriously. Iset the Fair was truly proud, Shaanar deeply bitter. How could such sophisticated people be so naive? Ramses had been lucky, that was all. No one could communicate with wild animals. One day soon the lion would tear him to pieces.

Nevertheless, the king's older son deemed it wise to maintain excellent outward relations with his brother. Along with the rest of Egypt, Shaanar applauded Seti for quashing the Nubian revolt, then made sure to stress Ramses's contribution. He praised Ramses's military valour and recommended official recognition.

During a banquet for veterans of the Asian campaign, during which Shaanar handed out rewards as the king's delegate, the heir apparent asked to speak to his brother in private. Ramses waited until the end of the ceremony and the two men repaired to Shaanar's office, newly redecorated with amazingly lifelike murals of flower beds and flitting butterflies.

'Wonderful, isn't it? I find I work better in beautiful surroundings. Would you care for some new wine?'

'No, thank you. Official ceremonies wear me down.'

'Me, too, but someone has to do it. Our men need recognition. They risked their lives to protect our country, the same as you did. Outstanding performance in Nubia, after that rough beginning.'

Shaanar had put on more weight. He loved good food, avoided exercise, and was beginning to look like a portly provincial official, old beyond his years.

'Pharaoh ran a masterful campaign. His mere presence was decisive.'

'Of course, of course. But having you ride in on an elephant must have helped. I hear you were quite taken with Nubia.'

'Yes, I'd go back.'

'What do you think of the viceroy?'

'Worthless.'

'But Pharaoh let him keep the job.'

'Seti knows what he's doing.'

'The situation can't last. The viceroy is bound to have more trouble.'

'Unless he's learned from experience.'

'Not awfully likely, brother dear. People tend to repeat their mistakes, and the viceroy is no exception, mark my words.'

'Then what will be will be.'

'It could have something to do with what *you* will be.'

'How so?'

'Don't feign innocence. You'd like to spend time in Nubia and being appointed viceroy would be perfect. I can help you get the job.'

This was a prospect Ramses had not considered. Shaanar noted his discomfiture.

'You have a valid claim to the post. Having you on the scene would discourage even the thought of further revolt. It would be a chance to serve your country in a setting you love.'

A dream, an impossible dream. Life in the open with his lion and his dog, the Nile, the cliffs, the golden sands . . . The thought was too much.

'You're joking,' he said finally.

'The king has seen you in action; he'll listen when I explain why you're cut out for the job. With the support I can orchestrate, it's a certainty.'

'If you say so.'

Shaanar applauded his brother's good judgement.

In Nubia, Ramses would be out of his way.

Ahsha was bored.

Working at the State Department had grown stale after just a few weeks. Office work had no appeal for him: he needed to out in the field. Making contacts, talking with people from every walk of life, detecting lies and secrets, important or petty, negotiating obstacles and getting to the heart of the matter – that was what he enjoyed.

Still, there was work to be done here in Memphis. Buckling under as he waited for an opening in Asia, a chance to understand what made Egypt's enemies tick, Ahsha followed the time-honoured diplomatic tradition of snooping. Never asking favours, polite, cultured, discreet, he wheedled secrets out of senior men who were tight-lipped and suspicious. Little by little, he learned the content of their confidential files without ever having to read them. Careful flattery, judicious compliments, articulate comments and pertinent questions helped make Ahsha's reputation at the highest levels of the State Department.

Shaanar heard nothing but good reports on his young contact. Recruiting Ahsha had been a master stroke. During their frequent behind-the-scenes meetings, Ahsha spelled out the latest foreign-policy secrets. Shaanar checked the information against his own facts. It was all part of his constant and methodical preparation for the task of ruling.

Since his return from Nubia, Seti seemed tired. Several of his advisers urged moving up Shaanar's appointment as regent, to ease the burden of power. Since it was a foregone conclusion and there could be no objection, why wait any longer?

Shaanar, however, shrewdly backed off. His youth and inexperience worked against him, he insisted. Pharaoh, in his wisdom, would know the proper timing.

Ahmeni was back on the attack after being laid low by a chest cold. He was ready to show Ramses that the ink investigation was getting somewhere. Overwork had compromised his health, but he returned to his secretarial work as diligently as ever, apologizing for falling behind. Although Ramses had never said a word, Ahmeni felt guilty. Taking a day off seemed like an unforgivable sin.

'I went through all the waste dumps and I found evidence.'

'Admissible in court?' asked Ramses.

'Two scraps of limestone that fit together perfectly, one with the address of our factory, the other with the name of the owner – chipped, unfortunately, but ending in R. I'm fairly sure it points to your brother.'

In Nubia, Ramses had virtually forgotten the loose ends he had left behind. The groom, the charioteer who had died twice, the counterfeit ink cakes . . . It all seemed so far away and hardly worth worrying about any more.

'Good work, Ahmeni, but no judge will prosecute with so little to go on.'

The young scribe hung his head. 'I was afraid you'd say that. Isn't it worth a try, though?'

'It would be a lost cause.'

'I'll get more evidence.'

'Is that possible?'

'Don't let Shaanar fool you. He's only trying to have you named Viceroy of Nubia to get you away from Memphis. His dirty tricks will be forgotten and it will be clear sailing for him.'

'I'm aware of that, Ahmeni, but Nubia attracts me. You can come with me and see what a wonderful place it is, so far from palace infighting and pettiness.'

The prince's private secretary did not respond, convinced that Shaanar's new-found helpfulness concealed another plot. As long as he stayed in Memphis, Ahmeni would keep trying to track down the truth.

Dolora lazed by the pool where she soaked during hot afternoons, before her facial and massage. Since her husband's promotion, she did nothing all day long and felt more and more fatigued. Hairdresser, manicurist, steward, cook . . . they all exhausted her.

Despite expensive face creams, her complexion only got worse. She ought to take better care of her health, it was true, but her social obligations consumed the greater part of her time. Keeping abreast of all the latest gossip required her attendance at the endless round of receptions and ceremonies defining Egyptian high society.

For the past few weeks, Dolora had been worried. Shaanar's close associates were less confiding, almost as if avoiding her, a fact she felt compelled to share with Ramses.

'Now that you two have made up,' she ventured, 'you may have some influence with him.'

'What do you want from me?'

'Shaanar will be at the centre of power when he becomes regent. I'm afraid he'll overlook me. I'm already being pushed aside. Soon I'll be no better than a provincial house-wife.'

'I doubt there's anything I can do.'

'Remind Shaanar I'm alive and I have connections. They could be useful to him in the future.'

'He'll laugh in my face. As far as my brother is concerned, I'm Viceroy of Nubia and out of the picture.'

'So your reconciliation is only for show?'

'Shaanar is trying to be fair to me.'

'And you'll settle for exile in darkest Nubia?'

'I like it there.'

Dolora sprang suddenly to life. 'Don't let him do this to you, please! There's no excuse for your attitude. If we join forces, you and I can take on Shaanar. We'll make him see he can't treat his family like so much trash!'

'Sorry, big sister, I'm not one for palace plots.'

She got to her feet, furious now.

'Ramses, don't abandon me.'

'I think you can take care of yourself, Dolora.'

The Temple of Hathor was silent. The priestesses had finished singing and Queen Tuya had performed the evening rites. Now she meditated. Serving the goddess helped the queen distance herself from human baseness. It gave her a clearer vision of the right direction for Egypt.

She and her husband had long discussions. When she expressed her doubts about Shaanar's leadership ability, Seti had listened attentively, as ever. He knew, of course, about the attempt on Ramses's life by a person or persons unknown and unpunished, unless the charioteer who died at the turquoise mines was the mastermind. Although Shaanar no longer seemed antagonistic towards his brother, could he be considered blameless? It was horrifying even to voice such suspicions with nothing to back them up; at the same time, it was true that an appetite for power could change a man into a raging beast.

Seti weighed each detail. His wife's opinion counted more than anything he heard from palace insiders, who were apt to be yes-men or members of Shaanar's faction. Together Seti and Tuya examined their two sons' behaviour and listed the pluses and minuses.

Reason helped to sort and analyse facts, but reason alone could not lead to a decision. *Sia*, the lightning bolt of intuition, the direct knowledge transmitted from one Pharaoh's heart to the next, would be Seti's guide.

Opening the door to Ramses's private garden, Ahmeni encountered an amazing object: a magnificent acacia-wood bed. Most of their countrymen slept on simple reed mats; a piece of furniture like this one cost a small fortune.

Flabbergasted, the young scribe ran to shake the prince awake.

'A bed? Impossible.'

'Come and see for yourself. A masterpiece!'

The prince agreed with his private secretary: this was the work of an exceptionally gifted craftsman.

202

'Shall we bring it inside?' asked Ahmeni.

'I should say not! Keep an eye on it.'

Jumping on his horse, Ramses galloped to Iset the Fair's parents' house. She made him wait as she dressed and primped.

As always, Ramses was struck by her beauty.

'I'm ready,' she said, smiling.

'Iset . . . then the bed was from you?'

Radiant, she put her arms around him.

'Who else would have dared?'

The 'gift of the bed' put Ramses in a difficult position. He would have to offer her one in return, even more elaborate, a lifetime gift, implying an official engagement.

'Do you accept my gift?'

'I left it sitting outside.'

'A grave insult,' she whispered cajolingly. 'Why delay the inevitable?'

'I need my freedom.'

'I don't believe you.'

'Would you like to live in Nubia?'

'What a dreadful idea!'

'That's where they'll probably want me to go.'

'Say no!'

'I can't.'

Wrenching loose, she ran from Ramses.

Ramses was in a roomful of people assembled to hear Pharaoh's latest official appointments. The older ranking bureaucrats and civil servants were calm, at least outwardly; the younger ones fidgeted. Seti tolerated no delays in meeting his deadlines and was quite impervious to elaborate excuses.

In the weeks preceding the ceremony, activity was at a fever pitch, with each administrator posing as a zealous and unconditional upholder of Seti's policies, the better to protect his department's interests and his own job.

When the scribe assigned to the task began reading the decree, a hush fell. Ramses, who had dined with his older brother the evening before, was quite at ease. For him, there was no suspense; he thought instead of his friends and acquaintances.

He watched faces light with hope, go blank, or grimace; whatever the case, it was respected as Pharaoh's decision.

Finally it was time for Nubia, eliciting only limited interest; after recent events there, as well as Shaanar's overt manoeuvring, Ramses was the obvious choice.

When the current viceroy was reappointed, it came as no small surprise.

33

Iset the Fair exulted. Despite Shaanar's campaigning, Ramses had not been named Viceroy of Nubia. The prince would stay in Memphis, with nominal duties. This would be her final chance to catch him, and she would make the most of it. The more he resisted the pull of her passion, the more he attracted her.

Her parents' please to consider Shaanar notwithstanding, Iset still had eyes only for his brother. Since his return from Nubia, he was even handsomer and more appealing. He had filled out, his splendid body was more imposing, his natural nobility even more apparent. A head taller than average, he looked as if nothing could touch him.

Sharing his life, his feelings, his desires – it was all she dreamed of. Nothing and no one would keep Iset the Fair from marrying Ramses.

A few days after the announcement, she called on the prince. Going too soon would have been intrusive. Now that the shock had worn off, Iset would offer him her pretty shoulder to cry on.

Ahmeni, whom she disliked, greeted her deferentially. How could the prince put so much stock in this puny specimen, always sniffling and hunched over his scribe's palette, with no social position at all? Sooner or later she would persuade her future husband to replace him with someone more presentable. Ramses should have no use for anyone as insignificant.

'Tell your master I'm here.'

'Sorry, he's gone again.'

'For how long?'

'I don't have that information.'

'Where is he?'

'I don't have that information.'

'Are you fooling me?'

'That's the last thing I'd do.'

'Then tell me what you do know. When did he leave?'

'The king came to fetch him yesterday morning. Ramses got in his chariot and headed for the river.'

The Valley of the Kings lay in stony silence. The sages called it 'the great meadow', a paradise for the reborn souls of the pharaohs. From the river landing on the West Bank of Thebes to this sacred site, Seti and his son had followed a winding road between high cliffs. Above the Valley loomed the pyramid-shaped Peak, home of the goddess of silence.

Ramses was rigid with suspense.

Why had his father brought him to this mysterious place, where the only mortals allowed were the reigning pharaoh and the workmen assigned to build his eternal dwelling? Because of the treasures amassed in the tombs, archers were stationed with orders to shoot any unidentified person on sight and without warning. Any attempt at theft was considered a breach of national security and incurred the death penalty. But there was also talk of knife-wielding spirits who cut off the heads of unauthorized visitors.

Riding next to Seti was reassuring, but Ramses would have preferred ten armed encounters with the Nubians to this trip through the valley of fear. His strength and bravery would be of no help to him. He felt diminished, easy prey to unknown powers he was unsure how to combat.

Not one blade of grass, no bird, no insect – the Valley seemed to have rejected every life form. There was only stone, symbolizing the victory over death. The farther Seti drove their chariot, the closer they came to the towering walls of the monuments. The heat grew stifling, the sensation of leaving the human world behind was oppressive.

A narrow passage appeared, a sort of door cut in the stone face; on either side, armed soldiers. The chariot halted. Seti and Ramses got out. The guards bowed; they knew their sovereign by sight, since he regularly came to inspect the work on his tomb, dictating which hieroglyphs were to be carved on the walls of his eternal dwelling.

When they passed through the door, Ramses's heart stopped.

The 'great meadowland' was a boiling crucible, boxed in by tall cliffs and capped with a bright blue sky. The Peak imposed an almost total silence, providing rest and peace for the souls of the pharaohs. The prince's fear had given way to wonderment. Absorbed by the light in the Valley, he felt both insignificant and elevated. He was one small man, a speck in comparison to all this grandeur and mystery. He was also aware of an otherworldly presence that did not destroy, but nourished.

Seti led his son to a stone portal. He pushed open the gilded cedar door and walked up a steep ramp into a small room with a sarcophagus on a central platform. The king lit smokeless torches. The splendour and perfection of the wall paintings dazzled Ramses, brilliant shades of gold, red, blue and black. He lingered over a picture of the huge serpent Apophysis, monster of the netherworld and devourer of light, subdued yet not destroyed by the Creator, with his white staff. He admired the Barque of the Sun steered by *Sia*, the spirit of intuition, the only means of successfully navigating the netherworld. He stood awestruck before the mural of the pharaoh being magnetized by falcon-headed Horus and jackal-headed Anubis, then admitted into paradise by the goddess Ma'at, the Universal Law. The king was depicted as young, strikingly handsome, dressed in the traditional head-dress, golden collar and loincloth. He appeared serene, eyes raised towards eternity, opposite Osiris or Nefertum, the god crowned with a lotus representing life renewed. A hundred other details caught the prince's attention, particularly an enigmatic text about the gates to the netherworld, but Seti would not give him time to finish reading it. He made Ramses lie face down in front the sarcophagus.

'The king who lies here shared your name, Ramses. He was the founder of our dynasty. After years of dedicated service to his country, he had just retired when Horemheb named him as his successor. What energy the old man had left, he spent in governing Egypt. He lasted only two years, but he justified his coronation titles: He Who Confirms Ma'at throughout the Two Lands; Divine Light Brought Him Forth; Stable Is the Power of Divine Light; Elect of the Creator. Such was this wise and humble man, whom we must honour, asking him to help us see more clearly. Pray to him, Ramses, honour his name and his memory, for we must follow in the footsteps of our illustrious ancestors.'

The prince felt the spiritual presence of their dynastic founder. A palpable energy emanated from the sarcophagus, which bore the designation 'Purveyor of Life'. It felt like warm sunshine.

'Rise, Ramses,' his father said. 'Your first journey is over.'

The Valley was scattered with pyramids. The most impressive was Pharaoh Djeser's — a stairway to the sky. His father brought him to another burial ground, Saqqara, where the Old Kingdom pharaohs had built eternal resting places for themselves and their faithful servants.

Seti drove towards the edge of the desert plateau, over-looking palm groves, green fields, the Nile. For nearly a mile stretched tomb after rough-brick tomb, a hundred and fifty feet long, the sides like palace façades. Twenty feet high, the walls were painted in vivid hues.

One monument stunned Ramses with three hundred terra-cotta bull's heads jutting from its perimeter. Equipped with real horns, they formed an invincible army guarding the tomb from harm.

'The pharaoh who lies here is named Djet,' revealed Seti. 'The name means "eternity". Around him are the other the kings of the First Dynasty, our most distant ancestors. They were the first to establish the earthly reign of Ma'at, bringing order out of chaos. Every reign must be rooted in the garden of their planting. Do you remember the wild bull you faced? This is his birthplace. This is where power has been reborn again and again since the beginning of our civilization.'

Ramses stopped to look at each bull's head. Not one wore the same expression. They represented each facet of the art of leadership, from strict authority to benevolence. Once Ramses had toured the perimeter, Seti got back in the chariot.

'Now your second journey is finished.'

They had sailed north, then ridden down narrow trails between newly green fields, to a little town where the arrival of Pharaoh and his son was greeted enthusiastically. In this Delta backwater, such an occurrence should pass for a miracle, yet the villagers seemed quite familiar with the king. The local police made feeble attempts at controlling the crowd while Seti and Ramses made their way into the utter darkness of a small shrine. They sat facing each other on stone benches.

'Do you know the name of Avaris?'

'The dreaded capital of the Hyskos invaders?'

'You're sitting in the middle of Avaris.'

Ramses was dumbfounded. 'I thought it was destroyed.'

'What man can destroy a divine presence? This is the domain of Set, the god of thunder and lightning, who gave me my name.'

Ramses was terrified. He sensed that Seti might annihilate him with a mere touch, a single glance. Why else would he have brought him to this cursed place?

'You're afraid. That's good. Only the vain and the foolish know no fear. Your dread must give rise to a strength that can overcome it: that is the secret of Set. Anyone who denies it, as Akhenaton did, is commits a fatal error and endangers Egypt. A pharaoh must embody the firestorm of the cosmos, the relentlessness of thunder. He is the arm that guides, and sometimes strikes in punishment. No king should be deluded into believing in the goodness of man. Such an error would bring ruin to his country and misery to his people. Can you stand up to Set?'

A ray of light pierced the chapel roof, illuminating the statue of an upright figure. The eerie head had a long snout and two big ears: the fiendish face of Set.

Ramses rose and marched towards the statue.

He collided with an invisible barrier and could go no further. He tried again, but could not go beyond it. On the third try, he broke through. The statue's red eyes blazed like twin flames. Ramses looked directly into them, although he felt a burning, as if tongues of fire danced over his body. The pain was sharp, but he held fast. He would not back down to Set, even if it meant the end of him.

It was the decisive moment, an unfair duel he was not allowed to lose. The red eyes burst from their sockets. Ramses was wrapped in flames, devouring his head, consuming his heart. But he stayed on his feet, challenging Set and willing his spirit away, deep into the shrine.

Thunder crashed, and a torrential rain broke over Avaris. Hailstones pounded the walls of the shrine. The red glow dimmed. Set returned to the underworld. He was the only god who had no son, but Pharaoh Seti, the earthly heir of Set, recognized his own son as a man of power.

'Your third journey has ended,' he murmured.

34

The entire court had travelled to Thebes for the grandiose feast of Opet in mid-September. This was when Pharaoh communed with Amon, the hidden god, who renewed the *ka* of his son and representative on earth. The two weeks of festivities in the great southern city were not to be missed. Attendance at religious ceremonies was restricted to initiates, but the people celebrated in the streets and the rich held society receptions in their elaborate villas.

For Ahmeni, it was no holiday. He had to pack up his scrolls and writing gear, throwing his orderly work habits into upheaval. Despite his obvious distaste for the expedition, he had made meticulous preparations, to please Ramses.

Since returning from his last mysterious journey, the prince had changed. He had become more sombre, often slipping away to meditate in silence. Ahmeni left him alone except to present a daily account of his activities. As a royal scribe and commanding officer, the prince had a number of administrative responsibilities, which his private secretary took care of, naturally.

At least, on the river journey to Thebes, Ahmeni would not have to deal with Iset the Fair. Every single day that Ramses was gone, she had come to insist he give her information that he simply did not possess. Since he was immune to her charms, their exchanges often became rather heated. When

Ramses returned and Iset demanded the dismissal of his private secretary, the prince had unceremoniously dismissed her and the couple had not spoken for several days. The pretty young noblewoman seemed to have difficulty digesting the fact that Ramses was always loyal to his friends.

In his cramped cabin, Ahmeni composed letters for Ramses to stamp with his private seal. The prince came to sit on a reed mat beside the scribe.

'How can you stay out in the hot sun like that?' Ahmeni exclaimed. 'In less than an hour, I'd be fried.'

'The sun and I understand each other. I worship him, he nourishes me. Why don't you take a break and enjoy the scenery?'

'Sitting around makes me sick. And I must say your last trip didn't seem to do you much good.'

'Is that a complaint?'

'You keep to yourself these days.'

'It could be your influence.'

'Don't make fun of me. Just go ahead and keep your secret.'

'All right. I do have a secret.'

'So you won't confide in me any more.'

'In fact, you're the only one who might understand what I can't explain.'

'Your father initiated you into the mysteries of Osiris?' Ahmeni asked, wide-eyed.

'No, but he took me to meet his ancestors – all his ancestors.'

Ramses's tone was so serious as he said those words that the young scribe was flooded with emotion. He realized that the experience must have been a turning point in the prince's life. He could not help blurting out the question, 'Has Pharaoh changed his mind about you?'

'I don't know, but he changed me. I faced the god Set with him.'

213

Ahmeni shivered.

'And you're . . . alive!'

'Touch me.'

'If it were anyone else claiming to meet Set, I wouldn't believe him. With you, it's different.'

Haltingly, Ahmeni reached for Ramses's hand, squeezed it, and sighed in relief. 'So you didn't turn into an evil spirit . . .'

'Who can be sure?'

'I can. You don't look anything like Iset!'

'Don't be too hard on her.'

'She tried to have me fired.'

'Did I let her?'

'Just don't expect me to be nice to her.'

'Perhaps you're the one who needs a little more company.'

'Women are dangerous. I prefer my work. And you should be thinking about your role in the festival of Opet. You're to march in the first third of the procession, wearing a new linen robe, very fine, so be careful not to tear it. Stand up straight and walk slowly.'

'You're asking a lot of me.'

'A trifle for someone in touch with the power of Set.'

With Canaan and Syro-Palestine pacified, Galilee and Lebanon subjugated, the Bedouins and Nubians defeated, the Hittites contained beyond Oronte, there was no shadow over Egypt and Thebes. The most powerful country on earth had reasserted its control on both the northern and southern fronts. In the eight years of his reign, Seti had established himself as a great Pharaoh, to be venerated by future generations.

Court gossip maintained that Seti's eternal home in the Valley of the Kings would be the largest and most beautiful ever built. Several architects were also at work at Karnak, where the Pharaoh was personally directing a huge construction project. There was nothing but praise for the West Bank temple at Gurnah, where the cult of Set, his *ka* or spiritual essence, would be celebrated for all eternity.

The more restive elements now admitted that the sovereign had been correct not to launch a risky war against the Hittites; it was wiser to channel the country's resources into building places of worship, testaments in stone to the divine presence. However, as Shaanar pointed out to his business contacts, the potential for developing trade relations was being neglected during this period of truce, and the best guarantee of future peace was international commerce.

Many aristocrats and officials looked forward to the day when Shaanar came to power, for he was like them. Seti's austerity and secretive ways were unpopular; some resented the extent to which he kept his own counsel. Shaanar was more open. Charming, pleasant, he knew how to make all parties to a discussion come away satisfied, telling each and every one what they wanted to hear. For Shaanar, the festival of Opet would be a perfect opportunity to extend his influence, winning over the high priest of Amon and his coterie.

The fact that Ramses would be at the festival was irksome to Shaanar. However, his worst fears had not been confirmed: after Seti's incomprehensible refusal to appoint Ramses governor of Nubia, Pharaoh had done nothing to enhance the status of his younger son. Like so many other royal offspring, Ramses was enjoying a life of wealth and ease.

It had been a mistake to fear Ramses and consider him a rival. His energy and physical presence were only a front: he had no breadth of vision. It would not even be necessary to have him appointed to Nubia, which might prove too great a responsibility. Shaanar would think of some honorary post, lieutenant in the charioteers, perhaps. Ramses would have the finest mounts and take charge of a troop of thick-witted horsemen, while Iset the Fair sighed over her rich prince's bulging muscles.

No, the danger lay elsewhere. How could he persuade Seti to spend more time in the temples and concentrate less on affairs of state? The king might insist on his prerogatives and interfere with his co-regent's initiatives. Shaanar would have to sweet-talk his father and steer him gently towards a life of meditation. Then, cultivating his contacts in the world of commerce, Shaanar would gradually take over. There would be no direct confrontation: Seti would be simply be immobilized in the web of influence his son slowly wove.

He must also neutralize his sister Dolora. Talkative, nosy and fickle, she would be of no use whatsoever in his future plan. In fact, she would resent being left out and might go so far as to plot against him with several wealthy and therefore indispensable courtiers. Shaanar had considered offering Dolora a huge villa, livestock and an army of servants, but she would never be satisifed. Like him, she had a taste for intrigue. No swamp was big enough for two crocodiles, and he knew he was stronger than his sister.

Iset the Fair tried on her fifth dress of the morning. It was no better than the first four. Too long, too full, not enough pleats . . . Irritated, she ordered her chambermaid to find another dressmaker. For the banquet marking the close of the festivities, she had to find something special – special enough to make Shaanar feel envious and Ramses excited.

Her hairdresser came in, panting.

'Hurry, hurry, my lady. Let me do your hair and put on a dress wig.'

'Why all the rush?'

'There's a ceremony this morning at the temple of Gurnah, on the West Bank.'

'What? The opening rites are tomorrow. I haven't heard about this.'

'But there is something going on. The whole town's in an uproar. We have to hurry.'

Vexed, Iset had to settle for a simple dress and plain wig that did nothing to accent her youth and beauty, but she could not afford to pass up this added event.

The temple of Gurnah, once it was finished, would be consecrated to the cult of Seti's immortal spirit, when he had returned to the ocean of energy after his brief incarnation in human form. Sculptors were still completing the inner sanctum, where the king was represented performing traditional religious rites. Nobles and dignitaries had flocked to the main façade, gathered in a huge open courtyard that would soon become a covered colonnade. Despite the early hour, most of them carried portable rectangular parasols to ward off the hot sun. Amused, Ramses observed these important personalities parading their elaborate outfits: long dresses, puffy-sleeved tunics and black wigs made them look stiff and uncomfortable. As soon as Seti appeared, however, they would stop strutting and begin to grovel.

The best-informed courtiers insisted that the king, after celebrating the morning rites at Karnak, was coming here to make a special offering to the god Amon in the room where his barque would be kept. Seti would pray for the strength of his *ka* and the continuation of his life force. That was the reason for this delay, which was physically very trying for the older members of the audience. Seti often lacked the human touch. Shaanar vowed he would do better, exploiting everyone's weaknesses to his best advantage.

A priest, his head shaven, wearing a plain white robe, emerged from inside the temple. Using a long staff, he made his way through the crowd. The guests stepped aside, wondering what would come next at this strange and unanticipated ceremony.

The priest stopped in front of Ramses.

'Follow me, prince.'

Many women remarked on Ramses's looks and presence as he passed. Iset nearly swooned in admiration. Shaanar smiled. So this was it: his plan had worked after all, and his brother would be named Viceroy of Nubia before the feast of Opet. In no time, Ramses would be far, far away.

Perplexed, Ramses stepped inside the temple, following his guide towards the left side of the building.

The cedar door swung shut behind them and the guide placed the prince between two columns, opposite three darkened chapels. From the central chapel came a deep voice, belonging to Seti.

'Who are you?'

'My name is Ramses, son of the pharaoh Seti.'

'In this secret place, untouched by the profane, we celebrate the eternal presence of Ramses, our ancestor and the founder of our dynasty. Carved in these walls, his likeness will live for ever. Will you undertake to honour the cult of Ramses and venerate his memory?'

'I will.'

'I speak as Amon, the hidden god. My son, come forward.'

The chapel was illuminated.

Seated on thrones were Pharaoh Seti and Queen Tuya. He wore the crown of Amon, with its signature of two tall plumes; she wore the white crown of his consort, Mut. They were king and queen; they were god and goddess. Ramses was their son and their divine offspring, completing the sacred trinity.

Confused, the young man could not fathom this myth come to life, a myth whose meaning was revealed only in the holy of holies. He knelt before the two enthroned beings, discovering that they were far more than his father and mother.

'My beloved son,' declared Seti, 'receive the light from me.'

Pharaoh laid his hands on Ramses's head; the Great Royal Wife did the same.

At once, the prince felt a gentle warmth that eased away his nervousness and tension, filling him with an unknown energy that penetrated every fibre of his being. From now on, he would be nurtured by the spirit of the royal couple.

A hush fell when Seti appeared in the temple doorway, with Ramses on his right. Pharaoh wore the double headdress symbolizing the union of upper and lower Egypt; on Ramses's head sat a simple crown.

Shaanar was jolted awake. The Viceroy of Nubia wore no crown. There must be some mistake. This was madness!

'I appoint my son to join me on the throne,' declared Seti in his deep and powerful voice, 'so that I may witness his achievement in my lifetime. I name him co-regent of the kingdom. From this day forward, he will take part in all my decisions. He will learn to govern the country, to keep it united and strong. He will be at the head of the people and care more for them than for himself. He will fight enemies from within and without, enforcing the law of Ma'at by protecting the weak from the strong. I so proclaim, for great is the love I bear towards Ramses, son of light.'

Shaanar pinched himself. It was only a bad dream. Seti would retract his decree. Ramses would shy away from a responsibility too overwhelming for a boy of sixteen . . . But then the high priest, at a nod from Pharaoh, fastened a golden uraeus on Ramses's crown. The royal insignia bore a cobra ready to strike at the enemies, seen or unseen, of Egypt's new regent and future pharaoh.

The brief ceremony was over. Cheers rose high in the luminous sky above Thebes.

35

Ahmeni was checking the protocol directives. On the procession from Karnak to Luxor, Ramses would be placed between two old dignitaries and must take care not to rush them. Keeping a slow and solemn pace would be taxing for the prince.

Ramses walked into the office, leaving the door open behind him. A draft swept in, causing Ahmeni to sneeze.

'Close the door after you,' Ahmeni demanded crossly. 'Other people can catch colds, even if you never do.'

'Sorry,' said Ramses. 'But is that any way to address the co-regent of the kingdom of Egypt?'

The young scribe stared at his friend, wide-eyed. 'What regent?'

'Unless I was dreaming, that's what my father just named me, in a special ceremony with the whole court in attendance.'

'Tell me you're joking!'

'I accept your congratulations.'

'Regent, oh my goodness! Just think of the work!'

'Your job description is about to get longer, my friend. My first official act is to name you my sandal-bearer. That way you won't be able to leave me and I'll profit from your advice.'

In a daze, Ahmeni's slight figure slumped forward in his

chair. 'Sandal-bearer and private secretary . . . What do the gods have against a poor young scribe like me?'

'Check the protocol again before tomorrow, will you? I'm not in the middle of the procession any more.'

'Let me see him at once!' Iset the Fair demanded sharply.

'Quite impossible,' answered Ahmeni, polishing a fine pair of white leather sandals for Ramses to wear during the imminent ceremonies.

'This time you know where he is, at least.'

'I do.'

'Then tell me!'

'It won't do you any good.'

'I'll decide that!'

'You're wasting your time.'

'A miserable little scribe has nothing to say about that!'

Ahmeni set the sandals down on a reed mat.

'A miserable scribe is what you call the prince regent's private secretary and sandal-bearer? Please be a bit more civil, my good woman; Ramses wouldn't think highly of you for abusing me.'

Iset the Fair came close to slapping him, but checked herself. The impudent boy was right. The high esteem in which the prince regent held him made Ahmeni an official personage she could no longer heap with scorn. Grudgingly, she changed her tone.

'Would you be so kind as to tell me where the regent can be reached?'

'As I was trying to tell you, it can't be done. The king has taken him to Karnak, where they will spend the night in meditation before leading the procession to Luxor in the morning.'

Iset left, feeling chastened. Now that a miracle had happened, would Ramses slip out of her grasp? No, she loved him and he loved her. Her instinct has steered her correctly,

222

away from Shaanar and close to the new prince regent. Next she would be Great Royal Wife and Queen of Egypt!

The thought sent a sudden chill through her. Thinking of Tuya, she realized how great a responsibility that meant. She clung to Ramses not out of ambition, but passion. She was mad about the *man*, not the reigning prince.

Ramses as heir apparent . . . Was it a miracle or a curse?

In the uproar following Seti's proclamation, Shaanar had seen his sister Dolora and her husband Sary elbow their way to the front of the crowd of well-wishers surging forward to congratulate the new regent. Still too stunned to react, Shaanar's supporters had not openly sworn allegiance to Ramses, but he knew their defection was only a matter of time.

He was obviously beaten, obviously out of the running. It was time for a gesture of conciliation. What more could he expect from Ramses than some honorary post with no real power?

Shaanar would pay lip service, but no more. He would not give up. The future might have a few more surprises in store, and Ramses wasn't pharaoh yet. In the country's history more than one regent had died before the reigning monarch who had chosen him. Seti's strong constitution meant he might live for years, delegating only a tiny portion of his powers, leaving his regent hanging. Shaanar would be able to push him over the brink, steer him into fatal errors.

In truth, nothing was lost.

'Moses!' exclaimed Ramses, finding his friend on Seti's vast construction site at Karnak. The Hebrew left the team of stone-cutters he was directing and came to greet the new prince regent.

'I bow to you, Prince . . .'

'Get up, Moses.'

They congratulated each other, glad of this unexpected meeting.

'The first site you've managed?' Ramses asked.

'The second. I learned brick-making and stone-cutting techniques on the West Bank, then was sent here. Seti wants to build a huge colonnade with papyrus flowers carved in the capitals, alternating with lotus buds. The walls will be like mountainsides with murals of Egypt's glories. There's never been anything like it.'

'You're proud of your project.'

'A temple must be the embodiment of all the wonders of creation. Yes, I love this work. I think I've found my calling.'

Seti joined the two young men and spelled out his plans for the temple. The covered colonnade built by Amenhotep III, with sixty-foot columns, no longer suited the grandeur of Karnak. He pictured a dense forest of pillars pierced with light from strategically placed windows. When the hall was completed, it would be a place of perpetual worship, with the gods and Pharaoh carved into the column shafts. The stone would contain the primeval light, the source of Egypt's nourishment. Moses raised some technical questions about stress and support; the king referred him to a master builder from 'the place of truth', Dier el-Medina, the West Bank village where trade secrets were handed down from generation to generation of workmen.

Night was falling on Karnak. The workmen had laid down their tools; the site was empty. In less than an hour, astronomers and astrologers would climb up to the temple roof to look for messages in the stars.

'What is a pharaoh?' Seti asked Ramses.

'The happiness of his people.'

'To that end, do not seek human happiness, but act in a way that befits the gods and the Creative Principle. Build temples reflecting the divine and offer them to their heavenly master. Your quest must be for the essential. The rest will fall into place.'

'The essential, meaning Ma'at?'

'Ma'at gives direction. She is the rudder of the ship of state, the base of the throne, the perfect measure, the source of rectitude. Without her, nothing just can be accomplished.'

'Father . . .'

'What worries you so?'

'Will I be equal to my task?'

'If you cannot rise to it, you will be crushed. The world cannot remain in balance without Pharaoh's acts, his word, the rites he celebrates. If the rule of the pharaohs ever falters, because of human stupidity and greed, Ma'at will no longer prevail and the earth will once again be plunged into darkness. Man will destroy everything around him, including his fellow man; the strong will crush the weak, injustice will triumph, violence and ugliness will flourish. The sun will no longer rise, even if his golden disc remains in the sky. Left on his own, man tends towards evil; Pharaoh's role is to straighten the twisted bough, to work towards bringing order out of chaos. Any other form of government is doomed to failure.'

Insatiable, Ramses asked his father a thousand questions; the king evaded none of them. It was well into the warm summer night when the regent lay down on a long stone bench, his heart full, his eyes searching the starry heavens.

Seti's order officially opened the ritual celebration of the feast of Opet. Priests brought out the sacred barques of the Theban trinity: Amon the hidden god, Mut the cosmic mother, and their son Khonsu, incarnated by Ramses. Before they left the temple, Seti and his son placed bouquets of flowers on the divine vessels and poured a drink in their honour. Then the barques were covered with cloth for the procession, so that profane eyes could view them, yet not see them.

On this nineteenth day of the second month of the season of inundation, a large crowd had gathered on the outskirts of the Temple of Karnak. When the huge gilded doors parted to make way for the procession the king and his son were to lead, cheers filled the air. The gods were present on earth. It would be a good year.

There would be two processions. One took the overland route, following the Way of the Sphinx from Karnak to Luxor. The second would sail the Nile between the two temple landings. All eyes would be on the royal barque, covered with gold and precious stones, dazzling in the sunlight. Seti himself headed the flotilla, while Ramses walked the road with protective sphinxes lined up on either side.

Acrobats and dancers moved to the sound of trumpets, flutes, tambourines, sistra and lutes. On the banks of the Nile there were food stands, with beer to wash down snacks of grilled fowl, cakes and fruit.

Ramses tried to ignore the commotion and concentrate on his ritual role: leading the gods to Luxor, the temple where the royal *ka* was renewed. The procession stopped at several shrines to leave offerings. Slowly but surely, it arrived at the doors of Luxor at the same time as Seti.

The barques of the gods entered the temple building, where the throng was not allowed to follow. While outside the feasting continued, it was time for the ritual rebirth of the hidden force that was the basis of all life. For eleven consecutive days, in the Holy of Holies, the three sacred barques would be recharged with new power.

The priestesses of Amon danced, sang and played instruments. The sacred dancers had long hair and firm breasts; anointed with laudanum and scented with lotus, wearing woven crowns of fragrant reeds, they moved solemnly and with a compelling charm.

Among the lute players sat Nefertari, a little apart from the others, intent on her music and seemingly aloof from the outside world. How could such a young girl be so serious? Attempting to go unnoticed, she only called attention to herself. Ramses tried to catch her eye, but her blue-green gaze was focused on the lute strings. No matter how she sat, Nefertari could not conceal her beauty. She outshone all the other celebrants, attractive as they were.

Finally silence fell. The temple musicians went off, some of them satisfied with their performance, others eager to exchange impressions. Nefertari remained collected, as if she wished to let the ceremony echo deep inside her.

The prince regent watched until her slim silhouette, clad in spotless white, withdrew into the blinding summer sunlight.

36

Iset the Fair snuggled against Ramses and sang a familiar
love song:

> *Why am I not your servant, following behind?*
> *I could dress and undress you, be the hand*
> *that combs your hair and bathes you.*
> *Why am I not the one who washes your dress*
> *and rubs you with perfumed oils?*
> *Why am I not your bracelets and the jewels*
> *that touch your skin and know your scent?*

'Those are the verses the lover sings, not his mistress,'
Ramses told her.

'No matter. I want you to hear them over and over.'

Iset the Fair managed to combine tenderness and abandon
in her lovemaking. Her bold, inventive young body amazed
and delighted him with endless new games.

'I wouldn't care whether you were prince regent or a poor
farmer! It's you I love, your strength, your beauty.'

Iset's sincerity and passion touched Ramses. Her eyes
were clear and honest. He answered her naked need with
his sixteen-year-old's ardour, until they reverberated with
pleasure.

'Give it up,' she suggested.

'What?'

'Being crown prince, your future as pharaoh. Give it up, Ramses, and we can be happy.'

'When I was younger, I wanted to be king, so badly I couldn't sleep. Then my father showed me it was an unreasonable ambition, madness, in fact. I gave up the whole idea. Now Seti has made me heir apparent, it's like a river of fire roaring through my life, and I'm not sure where it's leading.'

'Then don't jump in. Stay safe on the riverbank.'

'Am I free to choose?'

'Trust me to help you.'

'No matter what you do for me, I'm alone.'

Tears streamed down Iset's cheeks. 'You mustn't think that! Together you and I can take on the world.'

'I can't refuse my father.'

'At least don't abandon me.'

Iset the Fair knew better than to mention marriage. If necessary, she would let things remain as they were.

Setau handled the regent's crown and uraeus gingerly, as an amused Ramses looked on.

'Does that snake scare you, Setau?'

'I have no cure for its bite, and there's no antivenom.'

'Are you going to tell me I shouldn't be regent, too?'

'I'm not the only one who thinks so?'

'Iset the Fair would prefer a less public existence.'

'Who can blame her?'

'And you, with your taste for adventure? You're preaching the quiet life?'

'The road you're heading down is dangerous.'

'We all promised one another to try to find our true calling. You risk your life every day. Why should I be timid?'

'I only handle reptiles. You'll have to deal with men, a much more lethal species.'

'Can I count on you to work with me?'

'I'd make a strange adviser for a regent . . .'

'I trust Ahmeni and you.'

'What about Moses?'

'He needs to go his own way, but I'm sure that one day the two of us will build wonderful temples.'

'And Ahsha?'

'I'll talk to him.'

'I'm honoured by your offer, but I decline. Did I mention that I'm marrying Lotus? Women are trouble, I agree, but she's an assistant I can't afford to lose. Good luck, Ramses.'

Within less than a month, Shaanar had lost half of his friends. His situation, then, was far from desperate: he had expected almost total desertion, but quite a number of influential people had no faith in Ramses, despite Seti's proclamation. When the pharaoh died, perhaps his regent would realize he was out of his depth and step aside in favour of a more experienced man.

An injustice had been done him, Shaanar felt. *He* was the older son, *he* had been brushed callously aside without the least word of explanation. How had Ramses worked his way into Seti's good graces, if not by slandering his older brother?

There was a certain satisfaction in posing as a victim. He would make careful use of this unexpected advantage, slowly feeding the rumour mill and positioning himself as a sane alternative to Ramses's excesses. The plan would take time, a great deal of time, and require inside knowledge of the opposition. Shaanar's first step would be to request an audience with the prince regent in his new quarters, near the Pharaoh's in the main building of the royal palace

He would have to get past Ahmeni, Ramses's henchman. Was there any way to tempt him? He cared nothing for women nor for revelry, spent all his time toiling away in his office, and had no apparent ambition outside of serving Ramses. However, every man had a chink in his armour, and Shaanar was confident he could identify Ahmeni's.

He addressed the regent's sandal-bearer deferentially and praised his organizational skills, with twenty scribes busily carrying out his orders in this new establishment. Immune to flattery, Ahmeni wasted no compliments on Shaanar, merely showing him into the prince's reception room.

Sitting on the steps to a platform where a throne sat, Ramses was playing with his dog and his nearly grown lion cub. The two animals were a happy pair; the lion curbed his strength, the dog refrained from teasing. Wideawake had even taught the cub how to filch meat from the palace kitchens, and no one got near the dog without Invincible's approval.

Shaanar was aghast. A poor excuse for a crown prince! This muscle-bound boy, wrestling with his pets – how could he be next in line to the throne? Seti had made a horrible mistake. Seething with indignation, Shaanar controlled himself with some effort.

'I beg leave to address His Excellency.'

'Such high-flown language! Come and sit down, Shaanar.'

The yellow dog had rolled on his back, begging, in a show of submission to Invincible. Ramses admired the ruse. The lion never noticed how Wideawake ran the show and orchestrated all their games. Observing them taught the prince a great deal: they symbolized the joined forces of strength and intelligence.

Hesitantly, Shaanar sat down on a step some distance from his brother. The lion growled.

'Don't be afraid. He won't attack unless I tell him to.'

'The beast is becoming dangerous. Suppose it wounded a state visitor . . .'

'Not a chance.'

Wideawake and Invincible stopped their game and watched Shaanar, resenting the intrusion.

'I've come to offer you my services.'

'I thank you kindly.'

'What do you have in mind for me?'

'I have no experience of public life or the workings of government. How could I be sure of assigning you the correct role?'

'But you're the regent!'

'Seti is the sole master of Egypt. He and he alone makes the essential decisions. He has no need of my opinion to govern.'

'But—'

'I'm the first to admit my incompetence and I have no intention of pretending I'm in charge. My job, as I see it, will always be to serve the king and obey him.'

'You'll have to take *some* initiative.'

'Not if it goes against Pharaoh. I'll do the work he gives me and try my hardest. If I fail, he'll dismiss me from my duties and name another regent.'

Shaanar was nonplussed. He had expected someone arrogance and swagger, and instead met with meekness and servility. Had Ramses grown more cunning? Was this all an act intended to confound his opponent? There was one simple way to find out.

'I suppose you've become acquainted with the hierarchy.'

'It would take me months, if not years, to figure out the fine points. Is it really indispensable? Ahmeni will take the administrative details off my hands, so I can spend time with my pets.'

There was nothing ironic in Ramses's tone. He seemed incapable of understanding the scope of his power. Ahmeni, gifted and industrious as he might be, was only a seventeen-year-old scribe; the inner workings of the court would not be

232

an open book to him. Rejecting the help of more experienced men, Ramses would appear a flighty outsider.

Where Shaanar had feared open warfare, he found smooth sailing.

'I thought Pharaoh might have given you some directives concerning me.'

'You're right.'

Shaanar stiffened. At last, the moment of truth! He was right: Ramses *had* been putting on a show and now would deal his brother the blow excluding him from public life for good.

'What are Pharaoh's wishes?'

'For his elder son to carry out his duties as before and for him to become chief of protocol.'

Chief of protocol – a plum appointment. Shaanar would organize official ceremonies, see that decrees were carried out, and be intimately involved in royal policy-making. Far from being excluded, he would be in a key position, even if it did have a lower profile than the regent's. With what he already knew, he could weave himself a nice, solid web.

'Will I be reporting to you, brother?'

'No, directly to Pharaoh. I wouldn't be able to evaluate your performance.'

He knew it! Ramses was only a sham regent. Seti would still rule with an iron hand and continue to rely on his first-born son.

In the centre of the holy city of Heliopolis stood the immense temple of Ra, the god of divine light who had created life. In November, as the nights grew cool, the priests were preparing for the festivals honouring Osiris, the hidden face of Ra.

'You know Memphis and Thebes now,' Seti told Ramses. 'It's time for you to see Heliopolis, where our ancestors' guiding philosophy took shape. Do not neglect to honour this holy place; at times, too much emphasis is placed on Thebes.

Ramses, the founder of our dynasty, advocated that power be divided equally among the high priests of Heliopolis, Memphis and Thebes. I have respected his vision, and you should do so as well. Submit to no single dignitary, but be the link that connects and controls them all.'

'I find myself thinking of Set's city, Avaris,' Ramses confessed.

'If it is your fate to become a pharaoh, you will return there to commune with the secret power when I am dead.'

'You'll never die!'

The words burst out of him, so heartfelt that Seti's lips curved in a smile.

'Perhaps not, if I am so fortunate as to have a successor who maintains my *ka*.'

Seti led Ramses into the sanctuary of the great temple of Ra. In the centre of a courtyard rose a might obelisk, its golden tip glinting towards the sky to ward off evil influences.

'This monument symbolizes the primordial stone emerging from the original ocean at the dawn of time. It anchors the creative principle on this earth.'

Still in shock, Ramses was next led towards a giant acacia where two priestesses worshipped, dressed as Isis and Nephtys.

'This tree,' explained Seti, 'is where the invisible powers conceive a pharaoh, nurse him on star milk, and choose his name.'

There were more surprises in store. The next thing the crown prince saw was a scale made of gold and silver. On a stuccoed wooden base, it was seven feet tall with a span of six feet. On top sat a golden baboon representing the god Thoth, master of hieroglyphs and measurement.

'The scale of Heliopolis weights the heart and soul of every being, every entity. It is the symbol of Ma'at. May your thoughts and acts be inspired by her always.'

At the close of their day in the city of light, Seti took

Ramses to a construction site where the workers had left for the day.

'A new chapel is being built here, for sacred places must always be under construction. Building temples is a pharaoh's first responsibility. Through them, he will build his people. Kneel down, Ramses, and lay your first stone.'

Seti handed his son a mallet and chisel. Beneath the soaring obelisk, beneath his father's watchful gaze, the prince regent cut the chapel's cornerstone.

37

Ahmeni had a boundless admiration for Ramses, but acknowledged his faults. For one, he was too quick to forgive; for another, he too easily forgot important matters that concerned him, like the mystery of the counterfeit ink cakes. The crown prince's sandal-bearer, however, had a long memory. His new position had certain prerogatives, and he exploited them.

His twenty employees sat cross-legged on reed mats, in the classic scribe's position, as he outlined the case, then filled in every detail as he knew it. Although Ahmeni was not much of a speaker, they were spellbound.

'The next step?' asked one of the new scribes.

'We have better access to the archives now. Somewhere there has to be a copy of the original document giving the full name of the workshop's owner. I'll assign each of you to a section. Whoever finds the information should bring it here without delay and without a word to anyone. There will be a reward from the regent.'

An investigation of this scope would have to succeed eventually. When he had concrete proof, he would take it Ramses. Once the case of the ink fraud was settled, Ahmeni would persuade him to try again to track down the mastermind who had hired the two would-be assassins. No crime so serious should go unpunished.

As regent, Ramses received many petitions and a great deal

of official mail. Ahmeni discarded what was worthless and drafted answers two which the crown prince affixed his seal. The private secretary read each letter, pursued each official matter. The regent's office must perform flawlessly, even if it cost Ahmeni what little strength he had left.

Although only eighteen, Ahsha seemed mature and worldly-wise. Elegant and refined, he changed his outfit daily, followed Memphis fashion, and took pains with his grooming. Scented, close-shaven, he sometimes covered his naturally wavy hair with a costly wig. His thin moustache was perfectly trimmed and combed. His fine features bore the stamp of his proud aristocratic lineage.

There was general agreement on Ahsha's merits. Senior diplomats could not find enough good things to say about him, and no one understood why Pharaoh hadn't yet assigned him to a high-level diplomatic post. Ahsha, unruffled as ever, made no complaint. With his inside knowledge of State Department workings, he knew that his turn would come soon.

Nevertheless, he was surprised when the prince regent called on him. He immediately felt he was on the wrong footing: he should have been the one to pay a congratulatory call on Ramses.

'Accept my excuses, Prince Regent of Egypt.'

'There's no need for excuses between friends.'

'I neglected my duty.'

'Are you satisfied with your work?'

'More or less, though I'd like a more active life.'

'Where would you like to go?'

'To Asia. That's where the fate of the world will be settled. Without accurate intelligence, Egypt will be at a serious disadvantage.'

'Does our diplomacy seem out of step to you?'

'From what I gather, yes.'

'What do you suggest?'

'We shoulds pend more time in the field, get a better understanding of how our allies and enemies think, take stock of their strengths and weaknesses, stop thinking that we're invulnerable.'

'Are the Hittites really a threat?'

'There are so many conflicting rumours. Who can really gauge the size or strength of their military? So far, direct conflict has been avoided.'

'Do you regret that?'

'Of course not, but you have to agree the situation is equivocal.'

'Aren't you happy in Memphis?'

'A rich family, a nice place to live, a Promising career – is that happiness? I speak several languages, including Hittite; why not use my talents?'

'I can help you.'

'How so?'

'As regent, I'll suggest that the king appoint you to one of our Asian embassies.'

'I can't thank you enough!'

'Hold on, now. It's still up to Seti.'

'I appreciate the offer.'

'Let's hope we get results.'

Everyone who was anyone was invited to Dolora's birthday party, though since his coronation Seti no longer attended such events. Leaving the arrangements to Shaanar, Ramses hoped he could also find a way out of it, but on Ahmeni's advice he made an appearance before dinner.

Paunchy and jovial as ever, Sary steered the new regent clear of well-wishers and, most of all, favour-seekers.

'It's an honour to have you here. You make your old teacher feel proud – proud and a little jaded.'

'Why is that?'

'I won't have another chance to educate a future regent. Next to you, the students at the *Kap* will seem a bit dull, I'm afraid.'

'Are you saying you want to change jobs?'

'I admit that managing the granaries would be more interesting and leave me more time to spend with Dolora. But don't think I'm one more petitioner asking you for a favour! Just your old friend and teacher.'

Ramses nodded. His sister hurried over, heavy make-up adding ten years to her age. Sary took his leave.

'Did my husband speak to you?'

'He did.'

'I'm so glad that you've taken Shaanar's place. He's an evil little worm who was working against us.'

'What harm did he ever do you?'

'No matter. You're the regent now, not him. Stick with your real supporters.'

'You and Sary overestimate my influence.'

Dolora batted her eyes at him. 'Meaning?'

'I don't hand out government appointments. My job is to study my father's approach to the kingship so that I can follow in his footsteps, if the gods so desire.'

'Don't be so holier-than-thou! Anyone as close as you are to the throne is only concerned with building influence and consolidating support. Sary and I want to be part of your inner circle. We deserve it, and besides, we have a lot to contribute.'

'You're misjudging me and our father. Egypt isn't run by interest groups. Being regent gives me a chance to observe how Pharaoh rules and draw lessons from it.'

'You're not talking sense. All that counts on this earth is ambition. You're like everyone else, Ramses. Face facts, or else you won't survive long.'

Alone beneath the colonnade in front on his residence,

Shaanar drew conclusions from the latest batch of information reaching him. Luckily, his network of connections had not come unglued, nor had the number of Ramses's enemies decreased. They reported everything the crown prince said and did, since they considered Shaanar a more likely prospect to become pharaoh once Seti died. The new regent's almost passive behaviour, his unconditional allegiance and blind obedience to Seti, lent him little credibility as a leader.

Shaanar was less optimistic, in view of a recent catastrophic event: Ramses's short trip to Heliopolis. That was where a pharaoh was acknowledged as a pharaoh, where the first kings of Egypt had been crowned.

It was a clear stamp of approval from Seti, the more so since Ramses had been shown the sacred scale, as one loose-tongued priest reported. The reigning pharaoh thus recognized the regent's capacity for rectitude and ability to implement the law of Ma'at. This crucial step had been taken in secret, of course, and so far had only magical value, but Seti's intention was clear, and nothing would change his mind.

Chief of protocol . . . a farce! Seti and Ramses hoped he would settle into this cosy position and forget his dreams of glory, while the regent little by little seized of the reins of power.

Ramses was more devious than he appeared. His humble exterior cloaked a fierce ambition. Treading softly around his older brother, he had tried to pull the wool over his eyes, but the trip to Heliopolis revealed his true plans. Shaanar would have to change his strategy. Waiting for Ramses to trip himself up would never work. It was time to go on the offensive and consider Ramses a tough competitor. Attacking from the inside would not be enough. Strange thoughts ran through Shaanar's mind, so strange they frightened him.

His desire for revenge won out in the end. Life as Ramses's

subject would be unbearable. No matter the consequences of this surreptitious battle he was launching: he would proceed.

The boat sailed down the Nile with stately elegance, its broad white sail unfurled. The captain knew the river's every current and used them to his advantage. Shaanar was seated in his cabin, out of the sun. He was avoiding heatstroke, but also wanted to keep his complexion white, to differentiate himself from the lower classes.

Sitting across from him, sipping carob juice, was Ahsha.

'No one saw you come on board, I trust?'

'I took care not to be seen.'

'You're a wise man.'

'I'm mainly curious. Why all the secrecy?'

'While you were a student at the *Kap*, you were friends with Ramses.'

'We were classmates.'

'Since he was named regent, have you been in touch?'

'He's trying to have me named to a post in Asia.'

'I helped your request along, believe me, even if I no longer have the means to grant your request directly, now that I'm in disgrace.'

'Disgrace? Isn't the term a bit strong?'

'Ramses hates me and cares little for the good of the country. His only goal is absolute power. If no one stops him, the country is heading for ruin. It's my duty to help prevent it, and I'm not the only one who thinks so.'

Ahsha remained impassive.

'I knew Ramses well,' he objected, 'and he was nothing like the future tyrant you describe.'

'He's playing a very clever game, posing as a good son and Seti's obedient disciple. Nothing goes down better with the court and the people. He even had me fooled for a while. His real aim, however, is to be Lord of the Two Lands as soon as possible. Did you know he went to Helopolis to be approved by the high priest there?'

The argument was not lost on Ahsha. 'That does seem premature.'

'Ramses has a negative influence on Seti. As I see it, he is trying to persuade the king to step down and hand the power over to him.'

'Is Seti that easily manipulated?'

'If not, why would he have chosen Ramses as regent? I'm the older, and better equipped to help him run the government.'

'And make sweeping changes?'

'Only because they're necessary! Too many old ways are outdated. The great Horemheb's wisdom was applauded when he revised the legal code. The old laws had grown unjust.'

'Do you plan to open Egypt to the outside world?'

'I did. International trade seemed the only real guarantee of prosperity.'

'And now you're not so sure?'

Shaanar grew sombre. 'The prospect of Ramses's reign has forced me to modify my plans. That's why I wanted to keep our conversation confidential. What I need to discuss with you is of the gravest importance. Since I want to save my country, I must undertake a secret war against Ramses. If you join me, you will have a major role to play, and when we take over, you will be compensated accordingly.'

Ahsha, unreadable, sat and thought.

If he refused to play along, Shaanar mused, the young diplomat would have to be eliminated; he already knew far too much. But the prince needed good men, and there was no other way to recruit them. Ahsha would be one of the best.

'Tell me more,' Ahsha said finally.

'Trade relations with Asia won't be enough to overthrow

Ramses. Given the circumstances, we will have to go much farther.'

'Do you envision some other . . . some sort of agreement with foreign powers?'

'When the Hyskos invaded and governed the country, centuries ago, they were helped by several provincial chiefs in the Delta who preferred collaboration to death. Let's go ahead of history, Ahsha, and use the Hittites to get rid of Ramses. Let's form a group to keep our country going in the right direction.'

'The danger would be considerable.'

'Should we just give Ramses carte blanche, then?'

'Tell me exactly what you have in mind.'

'Your Asian appointment will be the first step. I know all about your exceptional gift for making contacts. You'll need to win the enemy's friendship and persuade them to help us.'

'No one knows what the Hittites' real intentions are.'

'We'll find out, though, thanks to you. Then we'll adapt our strategy and manipulate Ramses into committing fatal errors that can be turned to our advantage.'

Coolly, Ahsha crossed his fingers. 'A surprising plan, in all honesty, but quite risky.'

'Nothing ventured . . .'

'Suppose the Hittites really want only one thing: to make war.'

'In that case, we'll arrange for Ramses to lose and appear as the saviours of our country.'

'It will take several years to prepare.'

'You're right. We start today. First, we use every means we can find to keep Ramses off the throne. If we fail, then he'll have to be overthrown, attacked from within and without. I consider him a strong opponent who will only get stronger. That's why everything must be so carefully planned.'

'What are you offering in exchange for my help?'

'Would you settle for Secretary of State?'

The diplomat's slight smile showed Shaanar he had hit his mark.

'While I'm still cooped up in Memphis, I won't be able to do much.'

'You have a fine reputation, and Ramses will help us without even knowing it. I'm convinced it's only a matter of time before you're named to Asia. We won't meet again before you leave, and afterward our contact must remain a secret.'

The boat docked well outside the main harbour. On the riverbank, one of Shaanar's allies waited to drive Ahsha home in his chariot.

The pharaoh's older son watched the young diplomat fade into the distance. Several men would be shadowing him. If tried to inform Ramses, he would not have long to live.

38

The mastermind who had tried to have Ramses killed, using the services of the groom and charioteer, had known it all along: the king's younger son was born to succeed him. Many of his traits were like his father's. His apparently inexhaustible energy, his enthusiasm and intelligence, seemed capable of surmounting any difficulty. An inner fire predestined him to supreme power.

Despite his repeated predictions, no one would listen to him. Now that the prince had been chosen as regent, the mastermind's associates had finally seen the light. They expressed regret that his earlier initiative had failed. Fortunately, the groom and charioteer were dead. He had never met them face to face. The agent he had used to contact them had been silenced. The investigation had reached a standstill; there was no trail leading back to him and no means of proving his guilt.

Given his plans, which were kept strictly secret, he could not afford any slip-ups. A hard and accurate strike was the only solution, even if Ramses's new position made it more difficult to proceed. The crown prince was rarely alone. Ahmeni screened his visitors. The lion and watchdog provided excellent security. Any action inside the palace seemed impossible.

On the other hand, it would be quite easy to arrange an

accident in the course of an official visit or expedition, under the right conditions. He had a sudden flash of inspiration. If Seti fell for the trick and took his son to Aswan, Ramses would never return.

In Year Nine of Seti's reign, Ramses celebrated his seventeenth birthday with Ahmeni, Setau and his Nubian wife Lotus. They were sorry Moses and Ahsha could not be with them. Moses was still directing work on Karnak; Ahsha had just left for Lebanon on an information -gathering mission for the Secretary of State. It would be harder and harder to arrange regular reunions, unless the regent could make all of his old friends into close associates. However, they were too independent-minded and tended to go their own way. Only Ahmeni refused to leave Ramses; his excuse was that the prince regent would not be able to run his office and keep his work up to date without his secretary's services.

Lotus had catered for the party herself, refusing help from the palace kitchens. They ate grilled lamb with raisins and chickpeas.

'Delicious,' the regent admitted.

'Let's not stuff ourselves,' recommended Ahmeni. 'Some of us have work to do.'

'How can you stand this finicky little grouch?' asked Setau, feeding titbits to the dog and the lion, which had grown to an impressive size.

'Not everyone has time to chase snakes in the desert,' Ahmeni retorted. 'If I didn't write down the remedies you test, your research would all be for nothing.'

'Where have you newlyweds settled?' asked Ramses.

'On the edge of the desert,' answered Setau, eyes sparkling. 'At nightfall, the reptiles come out, with Lotus and me on their tails. I wonder if we'll live long enough to identify and study every kind there is.'

'Your house is no hovel,' said Ahmeni. 'It's more like a

laboratory. And you keep adding on to it. With all the money you make selling your potions to the hospitals, that's hardly surprising.'

The snake charmer shot a curious glance at the young scribe. 'Where did you learn all that? You never set foot outside your office!'

'Isolated or not, your house is in the registry and you pay for waste disposal. It's my job to procure information that might be useful to the regent.'

'You're spying on us! You're worse than a scorpion, you little wretch.'

The yellow dog barked merrily, not believing in Setau's anger as he continued his mock sparring with Ahmeni. Suddenly there was a real intruder to worry about: a messenger from Pharaoh asked Ramses to drop everything and follow him.

Seti and Ramses walked slowly down the path winding between huge blocks of pink granite. Arriving that very morning in Aswan, the sovereign and his son had gone at once to the quarries. Pharaoh wanted to see for himself what truth there was to the alarming report he had received. Furthermore, he wanted to introduce his son to the primary source of obelisks, colossal statues, doors and thresholds of temples, and other masterpieces carved from this incomparable stone.

The missive had detailed serious conflict involving the foremen, workers and soldiers in charge of transporting enormous monoliths on huge, linked barges, constructed especially for the purpose. Another, even more serious, problem was mentioned: experts estimated that the main quarry was mined out. Supposedly, there were only limited veins of stone left, too short to yield good-sized obelisks or giant statues.

The message was signed by a certain Aper, the head

quarryman, and had not come through the usual official channels. Fearing his superiors' wrath if they learned of his revelations, the quarryman had decided to go straight to the king. His staff, judging the report to be balanced and realistic, had passed it on to Seti.

Ramses felt at ease in the sun-baked rock. He sensed the stone's everlasting strength, waiting to be unleashed by sculptors. The huge Aswan quarry had provided a solid foundation for Egypt since the days of the First Dynasty. It represented continuity, work spanning generations and outlasting time.

The quarrying operation was carefully organized. Teams of granite-cutters identified the best blocks, tested and approached them respectfully. Their work must be perfect; Egypt's survival depended on it. Their hands gave birth to temples sheltering the forces of creation, statues containing the souls of the resurrected.

Each pharaoh took a personal interest in the quarries and the working conditions that prevailed in them. The team leaders were happy to see Seti again and meet the prince regent, who seemed more like his father every day. They did not even know Shaanar by name.

Seti called the head quarryman. Stocky, broad-shouldered, square-jawed, thick-fingered, Aper bowed low before the king, wondering whether he had come to praise or criticize.

'The quarry seems quiet.'

'Everything is in order, Majesty.'

'Not what you claimed in your letter.'

'My letter?'

'Do you deny that you wrote to me?'

'Writing . . . not my strong point. Don't do it often, and I usually hire a scribe.'

'Then you didn't alert me to a conflict between the workmen and soldiers?'

'Uh . . . there's a little friction, but we work things out.'

'And the foremen?'

'We respect one another. They're not city folk: they're men who've come up through the ranks. They've worked with their hands and they know the trade. If one of them gets big ideas, we take him down a peg.' Aper rubbed his hands together, ready to deal with any abuse of authority.

'And the main site – isn't it nearly quarried out?'

The head stone-cutter gaped. 'Uh . . . who told you?'

'Is it the truth?'

'More or less. Good blocks are getting harder to find. We have to dig deeper; in two or three years, we'll need to move on. If you already know that, you're a mindreader.'

'Show me the section we're talking about.'

Aper led Seti and Ramses to the top of a small hill with a view of nearly the whole operation.

'There, to your left,' he pointed. 'We're having trouble cutting an obelisk.'

'Let us have silence,' demanded Seti.

Ramses saw his father's face change. He stared at the rock walls with an extraordinary intensity, as if seeing inside them, as if his flesh were turning to granite. An almost unbearable heat seemed to blast from Seti. Gaping, the quarryman backed away. Ramses stayed at the king's side, trying, like him, to see beyond outward appearances. His mind collided with solid rock; he felt a blow to the solar plexus, but stubbornly tried again. Ignoring the pain, he eventually pictured the different veins of stone. They seemed to surge up out of the earth, reaching towards the air and sun, taking on a specific form, then solidifying into pink granite, sprinkled with stars.

'Leave the main site,' ordered Seti, 'and move towards the right. Dig wide. We'll find enough granite for decades to come.'

Aper hurried to the spot the pharaoh had indicated. His pick broke off an unpromising chunk of dark and worthless gangue. Digging deeper, he found that Seti was not mistaken: a beautiful and unusual new shade of granite came to light.

'You saw it too, Ramses. Keep at it, look into the heart of stone, and you will know.'

In less than fifteen minutes, news of Pharaoh's miracle had spread through the quarry, the dockyard, the town. It meant continued life for the quarrying operation and guaranteed prosperity for Aswan.

'Aper didn't write that letter,' Ramses concluded. 'What do you think is behind it?'

'I wasn't lured here to relocate the quarry,' Seti agreed. 'Whoever sent the letter had something else in mind, I'm sure.'

'But what?'

Perplexed, the king and his son headed down the narrow path carved in the hillside. Seti, sure-footed, walked in front.

A low rumble caught Ramses's attention. As he turned to look, two small rocks bounced down the hillside like panicked gazelles, grazing his leg. They were followed by a shower of stone, then a huge block of granite hurtling towards them. Blinded by a cloud of dust, Ramses yelled 'Move, Father!' The young man jumped aside and stumbled.

Seti's strong grip pulled him clear. The granite careened down the hill. Shouts rang out. Quarrymen and stone-cutters spotted a man on the run.

'That's him, over there! He pushed the block!' Aper cried. They were after him.

Aper caught up with the man, stopping him cold with a blow to the back of the head. Unfortunately, the head quarryman underestimated his strength: a dead body was all he had to show the pharaoh.

'Who is he?' asked Seti.

'I don't know,' answered Aper. 'Not from the quarry.'

250

The Aswan police had no trouble identifying the corpse: a boatman who hauled pottery, a childless widower.

'You were the target, Ramses,' his father told him. 'But death had not written your name on that block of stone.'

'Will you grant me the right to find out who's responsible?'

'I insist on it.'

'Good. I know the perfect investigator.'

39

Ahmeni was apprehensive and overjoyed.

He was apprehensive after hearing Ramses's account of his narrow escape from a dreadful death, the latest in a string of attempts on his life. He was overjoyed because the crown prince had just produced a remarkable piece of evidence: the letter sent to lure Seti to Aswan.

'Beautifully written,' he noted. 'Someone upper-class, cultured, accustomed to composing letters.'

'So Pharaoh knew that it didn't come from a quarry foreman and that there was something behind it?'

'In my opinion, they were targeting both of you. Accidents have been known to happen in quarries.'

'Will you help me investigate?'

'Of course. But . . .'

'But what?'

'I have a confession to make. I never gave up trying to find the owner of the counterfeit ink factory. I wanted to find proof that Shaanar was behind it, but I couldn't. Now you're offering me something better.'

'Let's hope so.'

'Did they learn anything more about the boatman?'

'No. There's no way to trace whoever hired him.'

'A real snake. We should get Setau to help us.'

'Why don't we?' asked Ramses.

'I confess: I already asked him.'

'What did he say?'

'Since it concerns your safety, he agreed to lend me a hand.'

Shaanar was not at all fond of the south. The heat was oppressive and no one seemed to care what was going on in the world. The huge temple at Karnak, however, was such a rich and influential economic entity that no pretender to the throne could fail to curry the high priest's favour. Shaanar had paid a courtesy call on the pontiff, during which they exchanged no more than platitudes. Still, it was gratifying to feel no ill will from this important religious leader, who observed political power struggles from a distance and would throw his support behind the strongest candidate when the time came. The fact that he offered nothing positive about Ramses was an encouraging sign.

Shaanar asked to be allowed to spend some time in meditation at the temple, a retreat from public life. His request was granted. A priest's cell was not his idea of adequate lodging, but he would put up with it to achieve his goal of meeting with Moses.

During a break at the work site, he found the Hebrew examining a column. It was carved with scenes depicting worship of the divine eye, which represented every means of apprehending the world.

'Marvellous work! You're a gifted builder.'

Moses, leaner and tougher than ever, glanced at the man who spoke to him, noting his flabbiness with distaste.

'I'm learning my trade. Any credit goes to the architects.'

'Don't be so modest.'

'I have no use for flattery.'

'I don't think you care much for me.'

'I hope it's mutual.'

'I came to Karnak to gather my thoughts and find some

peace. Having Ramses named prince regent was a shock, I can tell you, but I'll have to come to terms with reality. The quiet here is a help.'

'I'm so glad for you.'

'Don't be blinded by your friendship for Ramses. My brother does not have good intentions. If you love order and justice, you'd better stay alert.'

'Are you questioning Seti's decision?'

'My father is an exceptional man, but everyone makes mistakes. I've lost any claim to the throne, and I don't regret it. My new position is satisfying. But what will happen if Egypt falls into the hands of someone inexperienced and power-hungry?'

'What exactly are your intentions, Shaanar?'

'Just to let you know what's going on. I see great things in your future. Backing Ramses could be a disastrous error. By the time he comes to power, he'll have alienated everyone. You'll be forgotten.'

'What are you suggesting?'

'Let's take matters into our own hands.'

'And make you the next pharaoh, I suppose.'

'I have no personal ambition.'

'I find that hard to believe.'

'Then you're mistaken. Serving my country is my only goal.'

'The gods can hear you, Shaanar. You know how the gods hate lies.'

'Egypt is run by men, not gods. I rely on your support, Moses. Together we can make it work.'

'You couldn't be more wrong. Now leave me alone.'

'You'll regret this.'

'I don't want to raise my voice or my fists in this holy place, but if you like, we can continue the discussion outside.'

'That won't be necessary. But remember my warning. One day you'll thank me.'

Moses's angry face kept Shaanar from going any farther. As he had feared, his mission was a failure. The Hebrew would be much harder to win over than Ahsha. But even Moses must have his weaknesses. Time would tell.

Dolora shoved Ahmeni rudely aside, rushing into her younger brother's office like an ill wind.

Ramses, sitting cross-legged on a reed mat, was copying out one of Seti's decrees on forestry.

'Aren't you ever going to do anything?' Dolora screamed.

'I'm doing something right now, dear sister. May I ask why you're calling?'

'You know very well what I'm talking about!'

'Refresh my memory.'

'Sary is still waiting for his new appointment.'

'See Pharaoh about that.'

'He says he can't give family members an unfair advantage! Of all the—'

'The subject is closed, then.'

Dolora grew even more furious. 'This decision is what's unfair! My husband deserves a promotion, and as regent you should name him to oversee the granaries!'

'Would a regent go against Pharaoh's wishes?'

'Don't behave like a coward.'

'I won't commit high treason.'

'You can't be serious!'

'Please calm down.'

'Give us what we deserve.'

'I can't.'

'You think you're so perfect, but you're like everyone else, Ramses. You need friends. Why not keep the few you have?'

'You're not yourself today, sister.'

'I thought Shaanar was bad. You're ten times worse! Why won't you help me?'

'Be content with what you have, Dolora. Greed is a deadly sin.'

'Spare me your old-fashioned sermons,' she said, storming out.

Majestic sycamores grew in the garden of Iset the Fair's family mansion. The young woman basked in their refreshing shade, while Ramses transplanted young shoots in the loamy, well-worked soil. Above, the leaves rustled in a light north wind. This was the tree of the goddess Hathor. Its green branches were outstretched to the netherworld, offering shelter and sustenance to the souls of the just, wrapping them in the divine fragrance that charmed the master of eternity.

Iset picked lotus flowers and tucked them in her hair.

'Would you care for some grapes?'

'In twenty years, another tall sycamore will make this garden even more pleasant.'

'In twenty years, I'll be old.'

Ramses looked at her attentively. 'Keep taking care of yourself, and you'll look even better than you are now.'

'Will I finally be married to the man I love?'

'I'm no fortune teller.'

She slapped him on the chest with a flower. 'I hear you had a close call in the quarry at Aswan.'

'With Seti to protect me, I'm invulnerable.'

'But it was another attempt on your life.'

'Don't worry. This time we'll find out who did it.'

She took off her wig, undid her long hair and let it spill over Ramses, her warm lips covering him with kisses.

'Is it so complicated to be happy?'

'If you know how, go ahead.'

'All I want is to be with you. When will you understand that?'

'Any moment now.'

Clinging together, they rolled to one side. Iset welcomed her lover's desire like a blessing.

Papyrus production was a major economic activity. The price varied according to the length and quality of rolls. Some, bearing passages from *The Book of Coming Forth by Day* (also known as *The Book of the Dead*), was destined for tombs; some was sent to schools and universities; most was reserved for government use. Without papyrus, it would be impossible to run the country.

Seti had given the crown prince responsibility for inspecting papyrus production at regular intervals and making sure it was fairly distributed. Each sector complained of receiving inadequate supplies and pointed a finger at greedy neighbours.

Ramses had uncovered excess consumption by Shaanar's scribes. Hoping to correct the situation, he called his brother in for a talk.

Shaanar seemed in excellent spirits. 'If there's anything at all I can do for you, Ramses, let me know.'

'Do your scribes report directly to you?'

'Yes, but I can't say I watch them too closely.'

'For instance, how do you purchase papyrus?'

'Is something wrong?'

'In fact, for no apparent reason your scribes have consistently requisitioned large quantities of first-quality papyrus.'

'I like to use the finest writing materials, but I admit that stockpiling is an unfair practice. Whoever is responsible will be severely punished.'

No arguing, even admitting he was in the wrong: Shaanar's reaction surprised the regent. 'Absolutely the right approach,' declared Shaanar. 'A new broom sweeps clean, as they say. Not even the slightest government corruption should be tolerated. I'm sure I can be of help to you in the matter: as chief of protocol, I keep a close watch on what's happening at court, and I can detect irregularities. Merely reporting them won't be enough; seeing them rectified is indispensable.'

Ramses wondered if this could really be his older brother talking. What benevolent god had turned the crafty courtier into a seeker of justice?

'I gladly accept your proposal.'

'Nothing could please me more than working hand in hand with you! I'll start by putting my own house in order; then we'll get to work on the rest of the kingdom.'

'Are things as bad as all that?'

'Seti is a great ruler, whose name will go down in history, but he can't be everywhere and do everything. Let's say you're a nobleman, like your father and grandfather before you. It's easy to take more than your due, trampling the rights of others, without even realizing it. As regent, you can put an end to this laxity. I know I overstepped my bounds in the past, but those days are over. We're brothers. Pharaoh has given each of us his rightful place. We must live according to that truth.'

'Is this a truce or an armistice?'

'A peace agreement, signed, sealed and delivered,' Shaanar affirmed. 'We've had our conflicts, and each of us has been partly responsible for them. Brother against brother no longer makes sense. You're the regent, I'm chief of protocol. Let's work together for the good of the country.'

When Shaanar left, Ramses was troubled. Was he laying a trap, changing strategy, or could he really mean it?

40

Pharaoh's advisory body met immediately after the morning rites. The sun beat down; shade was at a premium. Overweight courtiers sweated copiously, calling to be fanned each time they moved.

Fortunately, the king's audience chamber was well designed for the heat, with high windows allowing cool air to circulate. Unconcerned with fashion, the king wore only a simple white robe, while several ministers were elaborately dressed. The vizier, the high priests of Memphis and Heliopolis and the chief of the desert patrol had been called to this special session.

Ramses, seated at his father's right, observed them. The fearful, the nervous, the vain, the level-headed – so many different types of men were gathered together here, under the supreme authority of the pharaoh. Without him, they might have torn each other apart.

'The chief of the desert patrol has some bad new for us,' Seti revealed. 'We'll hear him first.'

The police chief, in his early sixties, had worked his way up to the top of his profession. Calm, competent, he knew every turn in every desert trail, both east and west of the Nile, and maintained security for the caravans and mining convoys that crossed the vast empty spaces. No higher office tempted him; he looked forward to a quiet retirement on his property at Aswan. He was rarely asked to address such a high-level gathering, which made his audience all the more attentive.

'The gold-mining expedition that left a month ago for the eastern desert has disappeared,' he began.

A long silence greeted his blunt and horrifying statement. Set himself could not have left them more thunderstruck. The high priest of Ptah asked for the floor, and the king granted it, according to council ritual. No member spoke otherwise, and there were never interruptions. No matter how grave the subject under discussion was, one voice was heard at a time. The search for a just solution began with respect for the views of others.

'Are you certain of this information?'

'Alas, yes. Ordinarily, a relay of messages keeps me informed of an expedition's progress, problems it encounters, even its failure. For several days now there has been no news whatsoever.'

'Has this never happened before?'

'Yes, in times of trouble.'

'A Bedouin attack?'

'Highly unlikely in the area in question. The police patrol it aggressively.'

'Unlikely, but not unheard of?'

'No known tribe could have interfered with the expedition to the point of reducing it to silence. A squadron of experienced policemen was guarding the prospectors.'

'What's your theory?'

'I have none, but I am very worried.'

Gold from the deserts was used in decorating temples. Called 'flesh of the gods', this enduring metal was a symbol of eternal life as well as giving a peerless brilliance to the temple artists' work. Gold was also important to the government as a means of payment for certain imports or as a diplomatic peace offering to foreign rulers. No disturbance in mining operations could be tolerated.

'What are your recommendations?'

'Acting without delay and sending in the army.'

'I'll take command,' announced Seti, 'and the prince regent will go with me.'

The council approved the decision. Shaanar, who had made sure to say nothing, encouraged his brother and promised to start work on the government watchdog programme they would implement as soon as Ramses returned.

In the Year Nine of Seti's reign, the twentieth day of the third month of the year, the expeditionary force of four hundred soldiers, commanded by Pharaoh in person and his son and heir, marched through the blazing desert north of the town of Edfu and some sixty miles south of the trail to the quarries of Wadi Hammamat. They were nearing Wadi Mia, from where the prospectors had sent their last message to Memphis.

It was an unremarkable message. The expedition's morale seemed to be high, their health holding up well. The scribe who wrote reported no alarming incidents.

Seti maintained his troops on alert, night and day. Despite reassurances from the desert patrol chief, who rode along with them and had brought a hand-picked squadron, the king feared a surprise attack from Bedouins sweeping down from the Sinai peninsula. Pillage and murder were the order of the day with them; whipped into a sudden frenzy, their chiefs were capable of the worst barbarities.

'What are you sensing, Ramses?'

'The desert is magnificent, but I feel uneasy.'

'What do you see there, beyond the dunes?'

The prince concentrated. Seti's face wore the same strange, almost supernatural expression as when he had found the new veins of granite at Aswan.

'My view is blocked. I see nothing but a blank.'

'Yes, emptiness. The emptiness of an awful death.'

Ramses shivered.

'Bedouins?'

261

'No, a more insidious and far more pitiless assailant.'

'Should we prepare for combat?'

'No use.'

Ramses mastered his fear, although it nearly choked him. What attack had befallen the gold-mining expedition? If there were spirit monsters in the desert, as most of the soldiers believed, no human army could overcome the winged beasts and their long, curved claws that tore a man to shreds without even giving him time to react.

Before scaling the sand dune, the horses, donkeys and men stopped to drink. The desert heat necessitated frequent rest stops, and their water supply would soon be depleted. They were less than two miles from one of the region's main wells, where they could refill their water skins.

Three hours before sunset, they set off again, crossing the dune without difficulty. Soon the well was in view. The stone housing was set into a mountainside, and deep within the mountain there was gold.

The prospectors and their armed guards had not disappeared at all. They were there in plain sight, in the burning sand around the well, lying prone or exposed to the sun, with black, blood-tinged tongues protruding.

Not one had survived.

If not for the pharaoh, most of the soldiers would have bolted in horror. Seti gave the order to set up the tents and mount a guard, as if the encampment were under threat of an imminent attack. Then he had graves dug for the ill-fated prospectors and their escort. Their sleeping mats would serve as shrouds. The king himself would say the prayers for the dead, the prayers for resurrection.

The funeral rites, in the peace of the desert sunset, calmed the soldiers. The medical officer then approached Seti.

'Cause of death?'

'Thirst, Your Majesty.'

The king immediately headed for the entrance to the

well, which was being patrolled by his personal guardsmen. In the encampment, the men had been hoping for cool, refreshing water.

The large well was filled to the rim with stones.

'Let's empty it,' suggested Ramses.

Seti agreed. His guardsmen went to work: it was better not to alarm the main detachment. The relay they organized was remarkably efficient. Ramses set the pace and kept up their sometimes flagging spirits.

When the full moon shone on the bottom of the well, the elite troops, exhausted, watched the crown prince lower a heavy jar with a rope. Despite the suspense, he manoeuvred the jar slowly, taking care not to break it.

Hoisting the filled jar, the regent presented it to the king, who sniffed the water, but did not drink it.

'Let one of you go down into the well.'

Ramses tied the rope under his armpits, made a solid knot, and asked four soldiers to hold tight to the end. Then he straddled the rim and used stone toeholds to climb down inside. It was quite simple. Six feet above water level, the moonlight gave him a clear view of several floating donkey cadavers. Shuddering, he climbed back to the top.

'The well is polluted,' he murmured.

Seti emptied the water jar into the sand.

'Our countrymen were poisoned drinking water from this well; then the small group of assassins, probably Bedouins, finished them off with rocks.'

Now the king, the regent and every member of their own expedition would also perish. Even if they departed that very moment for the Valley, they would die of thirst before reaching arable land.

This time the trap was a tight one.

'Let's get some sleep,' ordered Seti. 'I'll pray to our mother, the starry sky.'

* * *

At dawn, the news of their situation spread. No soldier would be allowed to refill his bone-dry water skin.

One man loudly tried to incite his comrades. Ramses blocked his path. Panicking, the foot soldier swung at the prince, who blocked his punch and held him by the wrist until one knee was on the ground.

'Losing your head will only hasten your death, soldier.'

'There's no more water . . .'

'Pharaoh is among us; we have hope.'

The men made no further move to revolt. Ramses addressed them.

'We have a map of the region, a classified document, showing secondary trails that lead to old wells, some of which may still be viable. While Pharaoh remains with you, I will explore these trails and bring back enough water to see us halfway home. Our strength and our courage will do the rest. In the meantime, stay out of the sun and take care not to waste your energy.'

Ramses left with ten men and six donkeys, water skins strung on their saddles. One prudent veteran had saved a small part of his ration. After wetting their lips with morning dew, the exploratory force was given his last few swallows.

Before long, each step they took was a source of pain. The heat and dust scorched their lungs. But Ramses marched steadily, fearing that otherwise they would all falter. Their only thought must be of a fresh-water well.

The first trail shown on the map had been buried in the sand. Continuing the same direction would have been suicidal. The second track came to a dead end at a dry river bed; the map-maker had done his job poorly. The third track took them to an empty circle of weathered stones. The men ran up and collapsed the rim of the well, long since filled in with sand.

The 'top-secret' map was a joke. Ten years earlier, it might have been accurate. Some lazy scribe had simply made a copy, without checking its validity. Then another scribe had copied his work.

Reporting back to Seti, Ramses wasted no time in explanation. His crestfallen face spoke for him.

The soldiers had not drunk a single drop for the last six hours. The king addressed his officers.

'The sun is at its highest point,' he noted. 'Ramses and I will go to look for water. When the shadows begin to lengthen, I will be back.'

Seti climbed the hill. Despite his youth, Ramses at first found it hard to keep up. Then he imitated his father's gait. Like the ibex, the hieroglyphic symbol of nobility, the king moved purposefully, without squandering the least bit of energy. He carried only one object: a rod whittled from two acacia branches, polished and tied together at one end with tight linen bands.

The rock crunched beneath their feet, releasing hot dust. Ramses, near asphyxiation, joined his father at the top of the dune. The desert panorama was spectacular. The crown prince enjoyed it for a few seconds before his obsessive thirst reminded him that the expanse could become their final resting place.

Seti held the two acacia branches apart in front of him, bending them easily. He walked them slowly around, until the divining rod suddenly jumped and tumbled a few yards in front of him.

Ramses, feverish, fetched the forked stick and handed it back to his father. Together they walked down the slope. Seti stopped in front of some heaped flat stones with thorny plants growing out of them. The rod again leaped in his hands.

'Go get the quarrymen and have them dig here.'

His fatigue vanished. Ramses ran as fast as he could, jumping over rocks, and brought back forty men who went set to work at once.

The soil was loose. Ten feet down, they hit water.

One of the soldiers fell to his knees.

'God guided the king's spirit – the water is running like the Nile at flood stage.'

'My prayer was answered,' said Seti. 'The name of this well will be May the Truth of Divine Light Shine For ever. When all the men have drunk their fill, we will begin construction of a mining camp and a temple for the gods. Their presence will guard this well and open the way for those seeking the light of gold to shine for ever in sacred objects.'

Under the leadership of Seti, called Good Shepherd, Father and Mother of All Men, Confidant of the Gods, the rejoicing soldiers were transformed into master builders.

41

In Memphis, the Great Royal Wife was presiding at the temple of the goddess Hathor, where female novices were being inducted into the priesthood. Young women singers, dancers and musicians from all over the country had been chosen for this honour through a rigorous selection process.

Tuya's large eyes were serious and attentive, her cheek-bones prominent, nose straight and delicate. Wearing a wig in the form of a vulture carcass, symbolic of motherly protection, Tuya made such an impression on the candidates that many of them were unable to perform. Having gone through the ordeal herself when she was young, the queen was not about to coddle them. Self-control should be first and foremost in anyone wishing to enter the divine ministry.

She was not overly impressed with the artistic technique displayed. She made a note to speak to the harem music and dance masters about this recent lapse. The only outstanding performance was from a young woman who wore a serious, somewhat withdrawn expression on her amazingly beautiful face. When she played the lute, her concentration was so intense that the outer world clearly ceased to exist for her.

After the auditions, refreshments were offered to all the candidates, winners and losers alike. Some of them were tearful, others giggly, still part child, part woman. Only the lovely young lute player seemed unaffected by the day's events, even though the board of retired priestesses had decided to name her the temple's new director of women's music.

The queen walked up to her. 'You were brilliant.' The girl bowed to Tuya. 'What is your name?'

'Nefertari.'

'Where do you come from?'

'I was born in Thebes and sent to study in the harem at Merur.'

'And now Memphis, though you don't sound particularly thrilled with your accomplishments.'

'I had hoped to return to Thebes and find a place at the temple of Amon.'

'To live in the cloister?'

'My dearest wish is to be initiated into the mysteries of Amon, but I'm still too young for that.'

'It's not a wish many women your age would share. Has life disappointed you, Nefertari?'

'No, Majesty, but the religious life attracts me.'

'You don't want to marry and have children?'

'I haven't given it much thought.'

'The temple life is an austere one.'

'I like being surrounded by the eternal stones, their secrets and their call to contemplation.'

'Nevertheless, would you agree not to answer that call for the time being?'

Nefertari bravely raised her eyes to meet Tuya's; the Great Royal Wife appreciated her clear, direct gaze.

'Being the women's music director of this temple is a special job, but I have something else in mind for you. Would you become mistress of my household?'

Mistress of the Great Royal Wife's household! It was an appointment noble ladies dreamed of, with the status of being the queen's confidante attached to it.

'The old friend who worked with me died last month,'

Tuya revealed. 'There have been many contenders at court, and it hasn't been pretty.'

'I have no experience, I—'

'You don't belong to the nobility. You don't feel anything is owed to you, or that your family's illustrious status should make up for your lacklustre efforts.'

'Couldn't my background prove too much of a handicap?'

'All that interests me is a person's worth. There is no handicap that cannot be overcome by inner worth. What do you say?'

'May I think it over?'

The queen was amused. No noble lady would ever have asked such a question. 'I'm afraid not. If I let you inside the temple, I'll never get you out.'

Hands folded on her breast, Nefertari bowed.

'At Your Majesty's service.'

An early riser, Queen Tuya loved the predawn quiet. The instant when the first ray of light pieced the darkness was a daily re-enactment of the mystery of life. To her great satisfaction, Nefertari was also a 'lark'. They went over the new housemistress's assignments during breakfast.

Three days after impulsively hiring Nefertari, Tuya knew it had not been a mistake. The girl was as astute as she was lovely, with an astonishing ability to get to the heart of every matter. From their first planning session, the queen and the mistress of her household worked together beautifully. They communicated in sentence fragments, sometimes with no words at all. When their morning business was concluded, Tuya went to be dressed for the day.

As the queen's hairdresser was scenting her wig, Shaanar arrived to see his mother.

'Ask your servant to leave,' he demanded. 'What I have to say is for your ears only.'

'Is it that serious?'

'I'm afraid so.'

The hairdresser withdrew. Shaanar seemed genuinely upset.

'Speak to me, son.'

'I was hoping I wouldn't have to.'

'Now that you've made up your mind, don't keep me in suspense.'

'Well, I . . . I'd hate to cause you pain.'

'Now Tuya was worried. 'Has something happened?'

'Seti, Ramses and their search party have disappeared.'

'Do you have any details?'

'It's been some time since they left for the desert, in search of the missing gold-mining party. The rumours are dire.'

'Don't pay any attention. If Seti were dead, I'd know it.'

'How?'

'There are invisible bonds between your father and me. Even when we're apart, we remain connected. So please don't worry.'

'Still, consider the evidence. The king and his army should have returned by now. We can't simply let the country slide.'

'The vizier and I are handling day-to-day matters.'

'Would you like my help?'

'Do your own job and be content with it: there is no greater happiness on this earth. If you're still worried, why not form your own expedition to look for your father and brother?'

'Strange things happen in the desert, with monsters devouring prospectors who come to steal their gold. As the surviving heir, my duty is to stay put, don't you think?'

'Listen to your conscience,' said the queen.

Neither of Seti's two messengers, leaving four days apart, made it back to Egypt. On the trail to the Valley, desert trappers lay in wait to kill them, steal their clothing, and break the wooden writing boards with Ramses's message to the queen: that the prospecting had been successful and the troops were laying the foundations for a temple and a mining town.

The trappers sent a man to tell Shaanar that the Pharaoh and the crown prince were alive and well after the king had found a new source of water deep in the desert, thanks to divine intervention. The Bedouins had poisoned the district's main well in vain.

The majority opinion at court was that some evil had befallen Seti and Ramses. How best to make use of the king's absence? Tuya kept a firm grip on the reins of power. Only physical proof of her husband and younger son's death would have forced her to name Shaanar as co-regent.

In a few weeks, at the latest, the expedition would return home and Shaanar would miss his best chance yet to mount the throne. There was still a slim chance that the unbearable heat, the snakes and scorpions would do what the fierce Bedouins had been unable to accomplish.

Ahmeni was losing sleep.

Every day, the rumour grew stronger that the search party led by Seti and Ramses had also perished in the desert. At first, the young scribe shrugged it off as foolishness. Then he checked with the royal dispatch service and learned the upsetting truth.

There was indeed no news of Pharaoh and the crown prince, and no one was doing anything about it!

Only one person, he knew, could break the deadlock and dispatch an emergency force into the eastern desert. Ahmeni went to call on the Great Royal Wife and was admitted by an unusually lovely young woman. Wary as he was of the opposite sex, of feminine wiles, the young scribe took note of the young woman's perfect face, deep blue-green gaze, soft voice.

'I wish to see Her Majesty.'

'She has much to do in Pharaoh's absence. May I ask the reason for your visit?'

'Excuse me, but have we met?'

'My name is Nefertari. The queen has named me mistress of her household. I promise to report to her accurately anything you may tell me.'

For a woman, she sounded sincere. Ahmeni grudgingly yielded to her charm.

'As the crown prince's private secretary and sandal-bearer, I believe that an elite search party should be sent to the desert immediately.'

Nefertari smiled. 'Have no fear. The queen is informed about her husband and son.'

'Informed . . . but that's not enough!'

'Pharaoh is in no danger.'

'Then why have no messages reached the court?'

'I'm afraid I can say no more, but please have faith.'

'I beg you to present my request to the queen.'

'She is just as concerned as you are, believe me; if they were in any danger, she would act.'

Ahmeni hated to travel, and trotting along on the back of a spirited donkey compounded the torture, but he had to get to Setau. The snake charmer lived on the edge of the desert, far out of Memphis. The dirt track along an irrigation ditch seemed endless. Fortunately, a few of the local people had heard of Setau and his Nubian bride and pointed the way to his house.

Safe at his destination, Ahmeni felt as if his back was broken. He was sneezing his head off from the dust and rubbing his bloodshot eyes.

Lotus was at work outside the house, mashing some horrid-smelling mixture that almost made Ahmeni swoon. She stopped and asked him inside, but he backed away from the doorstep, where a hooded cobra loomed.

272

'A harmless old thing,' Lotus assured him. When she stroked the snake's head, it swayed appreciatively from side to side. Ahmeni seized the opportunity to slip into the house.

The main room was full of vials of all sizes and strangely shaped objects used to process venom. Crouching, Setau was decanting a thick, reddish liquid.

'Are you lost, Ahmeni? Seeing you outside your office amounts to a miracle.'

'More like a disaster.'

'So what magic enticed you out of your den?'

'A plot against Ramses.'

'Your imagination is playing tricks on you.'

'He's lost in the eastern desert, tracking some prospectors with Seti.'

'Ramses, lost?'

'No word for more than ten days.'

'That's just a missed relay or two.'

'No, I checked myself with the dispatch service. And that's not all.'

'What else, now?'

'Queen Tuya is at the bottom of it.'

Setau nearly upended his venom flask. He looked hard at the young scribe.

'Have you lost your mind?'

'I asked for an audience and she refused to see me.'

'Nothing unusual in that.'

'I found out that the queen thinks everything is quite normal, has no fears for their safety and no intention of sending out a search party.'

'Is that hearsay?'

'No, direct from Nefertari, the new mistress of her household.'

Setau looked thoroughly sorry. 'You think Tuya's trying to get rid of her husband and seize power? It's hardly likely.'

'Facts are facts.'

'Seti and Tuya are such a close couple.'

'Then why won't she send help? Consider the evidence: she sent him towards certain death to clear her path to the throne.'

'Even if you're right, what can we do about it now?'

'Go and find Ramses?'

'Did you bring a search party?'

'A party of two: you and me.'

'Setau got to his feet. '*You* plan to hike through the desert? You really have lost you mind this time, friend.'

'Will you go with me?'

'Of course not.'

'You give up on Ramses?'

'If your hypothesis is correct, he's already dead. Why should we risk our lives?'

'I have a donkey and water. Just give me something to help with snakes.'

'You wouldn't know how to use it.'

'Thanks for everything.'

'Ahmeni, this is madness. Sheer madness!'

'I took a vow to serve Ramses. I have to keep my word.'

The scribe climbed back on his donkey and rode east. Before long he had to stop and lie down on his back, hugging his knees to ease the pain, while the donkey munched tufts of dried grass in the shade of a persea tree.

Half asleep, he considered finding a stick. Would he need one?

'Had enough now?'

Ahmeni opened his eyes and sat up.

He saw Setau leading a team of five donkeys, laden with water and all the equipment required for a trek through the desert.

42

Shaanar had several important luncheon guests. As they were exclaiming over the excellent grilled beef with spicy sauce, Iset the Fair burst in.

'How can you think of food when the country is in peril?'

Shaanar's companions were shocked. The prince rose, excused himself, and led the young woman out of the dining room.

'What is the meaning of this outburst?'

'Let go of my arm!'

'You're going to ruin your reputation. You know that my luncheon guests are influential people, don't you?'

'I don't care who they are!'

'Why are you acting like this?'

'Because no one seems upset that Seti and Ramses have gone missing in the eastern desert.'

'That's not what the queen thinks.'

Iset the Fair was disarmed. 'The queen?'

'My mother is convinced that Pharaoh is in no danger.'

'But no one has heard from them!'

'That's hardly news.'

'You should go and look for them!'

'And contradict my mother? Would that be wise?'

'Is she relying on another source of information?'

'Her intuition.'

The young woman gazed at him, round-eyed. 'Tell me you're joking.'

'It's the truth, my dear, nothing but the truth.'

'What on earth is she thinking?'

'When Pharaoh is gone, ours is not to reason why.'

Shaanar felt quite satisfied with himself. With Iset the Fair so distraught, he knew he could count on her to spread the worst rumours about the queen. The council would have to request an explanation, her judgement would be questioned, and he would be called on to handle affairs of state.

Ramses marched at the head of the expedition returning from the eastern desert. They had built a chapel and suitable housing for the gold miners. The water source Seti had divined provided a well that would last for years. And on this return trip, the donkeys were laden with sacks of the finest gold.

Not one man had died. Pharaoh and the crown prince were proud to be bringing back their full complement. A few of the weaker men lagged behind, looking forward to a long leave at the end of their march. One quarryman, suffering from a scorpion bite, was carried on a litter. His high fever and chest pains alarmed the medical officer.

At the top of a hill, Ramses spotted a speck of green.

The first green fields at the edge of the desert! The regent turned around and shouted the good news, which was greeted with cheers.

A sharp-eyed patrolman pointed towards an outcropping.

'Caravan heading our way. Small one, though.'

Ramses looked hard. At first he saw only rocks, then slowly made out a few donkeys and two riders.

'Suspicious,' said the patrolman. 'Could be thieves hiding

out in the desert. Let's bring them in.' A posse was dispatched, quickly bringing two prisoners back to the crown
prince.

Setau sputtered in anger. Ahmeni was close to faint-
ing. 'I knew I'd find you,' he murmured in Ramses's ear,
while Setau was taken to consult on the case of scorpion bite.

Shaanar was the first to congratulate his father and brother.
The story of their exploit would be passed down through history, and he personally offered to put it in writing. Seti, however, assigned the task to Ramses. With Ahmeni's advice on
style and vocabulary, he set to work. The soldiers gave them
a wonderful account of the miracle of Pharaoh's divining rod
and their narrow escape from death.

However, the prevailing atmosphere of good cheer seemed
lost on the young scribe. Ramses speculated that the desert
trek had put a serious strain on Ahmeni's health, but he
needed to make a clean breast of it.

'What's worrying you?' Ramses asked finally.

The scribe was prepared. Painful as the truth was, he knew
he must make a clean breast of it.

'I thought your mother was plotting a coup.'

Ramses roared.

'You've got to stop working so hard, my friend. I'm going
to make you get outside and exercise more.'

'Well, she wouldn't send out a search patrol.'

'Don't you know about the invisible connection between
Pharaoh and the Great Royal Wife?'

'I do now, believe me.'

'Another thing I've been wondering about: did you finally
scare off Iset? I thought she would have come running to see
me by now.'

Ahmeni hung his head. 'She . . . we were both guilty.'

'Of what?'

'She was suspicious of your mother, too, but she decided to go public with her criticism.'

'Send for her.'

'But we were misled by appearances, she—'

'Send for Iset.'

Iset the Fair, who had even done her face, threw herself at Ramses's feet.

'Forgive me, I beg of you!'

Her hair undone, she shakily grasped the prince regent's ankles.

'I was sick with worry . . .'

'Is that any reason to suspect my mother of wrongdoing and, even worse, to go around spreading slander?'

'Forgive me,' Iset wept.

Ramses lifted her up. Still trembling, she cried on his shoulder.

'Who did you talk to?' he asked harshly.

'I can't remember. Anyone who'd listen. I was beside myself, I wanted them to go out and search for you.'

'Unfounded accusations could land you in court, Iset. If the verdict is high treason, you'll be sent to prison or exiled.'

Iset the Fair broke out in sobs, clinging desperately to Ramses.

'I'll plead for mercy,' he told her, 'because you're truly sorry.'

Pharaoh lost no time in taking the helm again. Tuya had steered a steady course in his absence; high-ranking officials trusted her to focus on matters at hand, not the power struggles that wasted so much of most noblemen's time. When Seti was forced to leave Memphis, he could rest assured that his wife would never betray him and would govern with wisdom and lucidity.

Of course, he could have involved Ramses more directly

in government matters, but the king preferred to proceed by a sort of psychic osmosis, transmitting his experience mystically, rather than sending his son unarmed into the political fray.

Ramses was a person of strength and scope. He had all the qualities necessary to rule and overcome obstacles of any nature, but how would he adapt to a pharaoh's overwhelming solitude? To prepare him, Seti had made the crown prince travel, both physically and mentally. They still had a long way to go.

Tuya introduced Nefertari to the king. Awed, the young woman said not a word, but bowed low. Seti studied her closely for a few seconds and urged her to carry out her duties with the utmost care. Directing the Great Royal Wife's household demanded a firm hand and sealed lips. Still unable to look up at the Pharaoh Nefertari withdrew.

'You were rather hard on her,' observed Tuya.

'She's very young.'

'Don't you think she's capable?'

'She has exceptional gifts.'

'I found her in the temple, where she wanted to stay for ever.'

'I can understand that. The palace must be a terrible ordeal for her.'

'True.'

'Then why did you bring her here?'

'I don't quite know. As soon as I saw Nefertari, I sensed how special she was. The religious life clearly suited her, but my instincts tell me she has another mission in life. If it turns out I'm wrong, she can go her own way.'

Ramses lunched with his mother, bringing Wideawake and introducing the Nubian lion Invincible, now grown to alarming proportions. As if aware they were honoured to be in their presence, the two pets were on their best behaviour. After a meal prepared by the queen's personal chef, they curled up head to toe for the ineffable pleasure of a nap in the shade of a palm tree.

'This has been pleasant,' Tuya conceded, 'but I'm sure you've come for a reason. What is it?'

'Iset the Fair.'

'Is your engagement off?'

'She's done something very wrong.'

'How bad can it be?'

'She slandered the Queen of Egypt.'

'How so?'

'She thought you arranged the king's disappearance and were to seize the throne.'

To Ramses's amazement, his mother seemed amused. 'Almost every last person at court would have agreed with her. I was criticized for not sending out a search party, when all along I knew you and Seti were perfectly safe. For all our temples and rites, few people understand that psychic communication is possible.'

'At court . . . will you be bringing charges?'

'Iset's reaction was nothing unusual.'

'Doesn't it bother you that everyone was so ungrateful, so unfair to you?'

'It's the way of the world. We must only take care not to run the country that way.'

A young woman laid some documents on a low table to the queen's left, then slipped silently away. Her brief appearance was like sunshine through leafy branches.

'Who was that?'

'Nefertari, the new mistress of my household.'

'I've met her before. How did she end up in such an important position?'

'Circumstances. She was called to be a priestess in the temple of Hathor. I picked her out at the induction ceremony.'

'You took her away from the temple?'

'A harem education is excellent preparation for all kinds of work.'

'But she's so young. It's so much responsibility.'

'You're only seventeen yourself. In the king's eyes, and mine, what a person is and does are all that matter.'

Nefertari's otherworldly beauty had stirred Ramses; her brief appearance was stamped in his mind like a miracle.

'Tell Iset not to worry,' Tuya continued. 'There will be no repercussions. But she must learn not to get so carried away, or at least to hold her tongue if she can't help it.'

43

In ceremonial dress, Ramses paced the landing stage of Memphis's main harbour, known as 'Safe Journey'. His entourage included the mayor, the head of the harbour patrol, the Secretary of State and an impressive security force. The fleet of ten Greek boats was due to arrive any time now.

At first, the coastal patrol had thought it was an attack. Part of the Egyptian fighting fleet had been dispatched in answer. But the foreigners had displayed peaceful intentions and expressed a wish to sail on to Memphis and meet the pharaoh.

Under close escort, they came up the Nile and reached the capital late on a windy morning. Hundreds of curious onlookers crowded the banks. This was not the time of year when shipful after shipful of foreign dignitaries came to pay tribute. However, these imposing vessels were obviously from some rich land. Had they also come with costly offerings for Seti?

Patience was not Ramses's strong point, and he was afraid his diplomatic skills were close to nonexistent. Welcoming this foreign delegation was a chore. Ahmeni had written out some sort of official greetings, so dull and boring he could not even recall the first sentence. It made him miss Ahsha – just the man for the job.

The Greek ships had suffered heavy damage and would

need major repairs before heading out to sea again. Some even had burned timbers; they must have run into pirates on their way across the Mediterranean.

The lead ship steered skilfully into harbour, although a part of its rigging was missing. A gangway was thrown aboard and silence fell. What would these strangers be like?

Out stepped a man of medium height, broad-shouldered, blond, with a rugged face, who looked about fifty. He wore a breastplate and leg armour, but held his brass helmet against his chest, as a sign of peace.

Behind him stood a tall and beautiful woman with bare white arms, a purple cloak and tiara attesting to her noble lineage.

They descended the gangway and halted in front of Ramses.

'I am Ramses, Prince Regent of Egypt. In the name of the Pharaoh, I bid you welcome.'

'I am Menelaus, son of Atreus, King of Sparta, and this is my wife Helen. We come from the ill-fated city of Troy which we have conquered and destroyed after ten years of hard fighting. Many of my friends have died, and the taste of victory is bitter. As you see, my remaining ships are in poor repair. My soldiers and sailors are exhausted. Will Egypt permit us to stop and recuperate before returning home?'

'The answer depends on Pharaoh.'

'Putting me off, are you?'

'No, telling the truth.'

'Good. I'm a warrior and I've killed men before. I'll wager you haven't.'

'I wouldn't be so sure.'

Menelaus's small dark eyes glinted with anger.

'If you were one of my subjects, I'd cut you down to size.'

'Lucky for me I'm Egyptian.'

Menelaus and Ramses locked eyes. The King of Sparta was first to look away.

'I'll wait on board for my answer.'

Ramses's negative recommendation did not meet with unanimous approval at the limited council session. Certainly Menelaus and the remnants of his armed forces posed no immediate or future threat to Egypt. Furthermore, he was a king and deserved to be treated accordingly. Ramses listened but remained unconvinced. The man was a roughneck soldier, a bloodthirsty Spartan warrior hell-bent on pillaging and razing cities. Offering hospitality to such an outlaw did not seem appropriate.

The secretary of state, Meba, departed from his habitual reserve. 'The regent's stance seems dangerous to me,' he said. 'Menelaus must not be turned away lightly. Our foreign policy is based on maintaining good relations with many countries, large and small, to discourage potential alliances against us.'

'The Greek is a scoundrel,' declared Ramses. 'You can tell from his eyes.'

Meba, a fine-looking man of sixty with a broad, reassuring face and soft voice, smiled indulgently at the prince. 'Diplomacy cannot have its basis in feelings; at times we're forced to deal with people we dislike.'

'Menelaus will betray us,' continued Ramses. 'He is not a man of his word.'

'The regent's youth may incline him to make snap judgements,' protested Meba. 'Menelaus is a Greek; we know them to be sly. Perhaps he hasn't told the whole truth. We must proceed slowly and find out what is behind this visit.'

'We will invite Menelaus and his wife to dinner at the palace,' declared Seti. 'Their behaviour will dictate our response.'

Menelaus presented the pharaoh with beautifully worked metal vessels and bows made from a combination of woods, which had proved most effective in warfare with the Trojans. The Spartan officers wore boots, coloured skirts with geometric trim, and flowing waist-length hair.

Nectar wafted from Helen's green dress and the white veil that covered her face. She sat at Tuya's left, while her husband Menelaus was to the right of Seti. Pharaoh's stern face inhibited the visitor; Meba carried the conversation. Oasis wine loosened the Spartan's tongue to the point where he lamented the long years spent besieging Troy, related his exploits, extolled his friend Ulysses, deplored the cruelty of the gods, and vaunted the charms of the homeland he so longed to see again. The secretary of state, who spoke flawless Greek, seemed swayed by his guest's jeremiad.

'Why do you hide your face?' Tuya asked Helen in her own language.

'Because no one can stand the sight of it. So many brave men have died because of my face! When Paris, the Trojan prince, made off with me, I never dreamed that his rash act would lead to ten years of bloodshed. A hundred times I wished I could be blown away by the wind or washed out to sea. Too much misery . . . I've caused too much misery.'

'But now you're free, aren't you?'

Beneath the white veil, a pathetic smile. 'Menelaus can't forgive me.'

'Time will ease your pain, now that you're back together.'

'It's worse than that . . .'

Tuya let Helen keep her grave silence. She would speak if she wished.

'I hate my husband,' said the beautiful white-skinned woman.

'A passing resentment?'

'No, I never loved him. I even hoped Troy would win. Your Majesty?'

'Yes, Helen?'

'Please let me stay here as long as you can. I dread returning to Sparta.'

Shaanar, as chief of protocol, had cautiously placed Ramses at a distance from Menelaus. The crown prince's dinner partner was an ageless man with a white beard flowing from his lined, craggy face. He ate slowly and sprinkled all his food with olive oil.

'The key to good health, my prince!'

'My name is Ramses.'

'Mine is Homer.'

'Are you a general?'

'No, a poet. My eyesight is bad, but my memory is excellent.'

'A poet, with a brute like Menelaus?'

'I happened to hear he was sailing for Egypt, the land of wisdom and letters. After all my roaming, I'd like to settle here and work in peace.'

'Menelaus won't be here long, if I have anything to say about it.'

'And your opinion counts?'

'It should. I'm the pharaoh's co-regent.'

'You're so young . . . and you hate us Greeks.'

'I was talking about Menelaus, not you, sir. Where would you plan to stay?'

'Somewhere more comfortable than a boat! It's cramped, my gear is stowed belowdecks, and I can't stand sailors. The howling wind and the waves don't inspire me, either.'

'Would you accept my help?'

'Your Greek is good.'

'A friend of mine taught me, mostly. He speaks every language; now he's a diplomat.'

'Do you like poetry?'

'I'll introduce you to our great authors.'

'If we share the same tastes, we may get along after all.'

*   *   *

The secretary of state relayed Pharaoh's decision to Shaanar: Menelaus had been granted permission to stay in Egypt. His fleet would be repaired, he would live in a centrally located Memphis mansion, his troops would be placed under Egyptian command and must adhere to the strictest discipline.

Pharaoh's older son was appointed to show the Spartan king around Memphis. Day after tiring day, Shaanar tried to give Menelaus a rudimentary understanding of Egyptian culture, but his efforts were frustrated by the Greek's indifference, so marked that it bordered on rudeness.

Architecture, on the other hand, excited him. He could not conceal his amazement when they visited temples.

'First-rate forts! It must not be easy to storm those walls.'

'They're dwelling places for our divinities,' Shaanar explained.

'Warrior gods?'

'No, Ptah is the patron of the all the arts, the creative urge. Hathor is the goddess of joy and music.'

'Why do they need such thick walls around them?'

'The sacred cults are placed in the hands of experts who shelter and feed the divine energy. No one may enter the enclosed sanctuary without first being initiated into certain mysteries.'

'In other words, as the king of Sparta, son of Zeus, and conqueror of Troy, I have no right to pass through those golden doors.'

'Correct. Though on feast days, with Pharaoh's permission, you might be allowed in the outer courtyard.'

'And what secret rites would I witness?'

'The great offering to the god who resides in the temple and enriches the earth with divine energy.'

'Humph!'

Shaanar showed infinite patience. Although Menelaus was rather crude of manner and speech, he felt a certain bond with this shrewd-eyed stranger. His intuition told him that unfailing courtesy would wear down the Greek's defences.

Menelaus returned again and again to his ten years of warfare, ending in Troy's defeat. He deplored the cruel fate of his allies who fell to the enemy, criticized Helen, hoped that Homer soon would write of the Greeks' high deeds and be sure to show him in a good light.

Shaanar tried to learn exactly how Troy fell. Menelaus described fierce engagements, feats of bravery from Achilles and the other heroes, their firm resolve not to leave without Helen.

'In such a long war,' hinted Shaanar, 'surely your strategy must have included a trick or two.'

Hesitant at first, Menelaus opened up to him. 'Ulysses hit on the idea of building a big wooden horse and hiding our soldiers inside it. The Trojans were foolish enough to let it through their gates, and we were able to launch a surprise attack within their own walls.'

'I'm sure Ulysses didn't think of it all alone.'

'We discussed it together, but—'

'He was only interpreting your thoughts, I'm sure of it.'

Menelaus puffed with pride. 'Yes, it's quite possible he was.'

Shaanar spent the greater part of his time cementing his friendship with the Spartan king. He had a strategy in mind as well – a new way to eliminate Ramses and regain his rightful place as sole heir to the throne of Egypt.

44

In his garden, beneath the grape arbour, Shaanar entertained Menelaus royally. The Greek admired the dark-green leaves and the laden vines, feasting on the plump blue-black fruit before their meal was served. Pigeon stew, roast beef, quails with honey, delicately seasoned pork chops, pork kidneys – all delighted his palate. He never tired of watching the scantily clad young women who played lovely tunes on their woodwind instruments and strings.

'Egypt is quite a country,' he admitted. 'Better than the battlefield.'

'Is the residence we chose for you acceptable?'

'Acceptable? It's a palace! When I get home, I'll have my architects build me one just like it.'

'The servants?'

'Very attentive.'

At the Spartan's request, a granite tub had been installed in the mansion. He had it filled with warm water and soaked there endlessly. His steward judged the process unhygienic and enervating; like his fellow Egyptians, he preferred showers. But he followed Shaanar's instructions, and had a masseuse come daily to rub the Greek hero's scar-covered body with oils.

'But those slave girls of yours aren't very cooperative,' he complained to Shaanar. 'At home, they'd never make such a fuss, and do whatever I dream up during my bath.'

'There are no slaves in Egypt,' Shaanar explained. 'These women are paid workers.'

'No slaves? We could teach you a thing or two, then.'

'Yes, Egypt needs men of your stature.'

Menelaus pushed aside his alabaster dish of honeyed quail. Shaanar's remark had ruined his appetite.

'What are you insinuating?'

'Egypt is a rich and powerful country, but we might benefit from a more forward-looking government.'

'The way I understand it, Pharaoh *is* the government, and you're his son.'

'That makes me proud, but not necessarily blind.'

'Seti is an impressive figure. Not even Agamemnon had as much authority. If you're plotting against him, give up. You'll never win. He has supernatural powers. I'm no coward, but I'm afraid to look him in the eye.'

'Who said anything about a plot? The entire population worships Seti, but he is also a man and no longer in the best of health, apparently.'

'Isn't that why he named a regent? He's grooming his successor.'

'If Ramses comes to power, Egypt is done for. My brother is incompetent.'

'But if you oppose him, it would mean going against your father's wishes.'

'Ramses has the pharaoh fooled. If you side with me, your future will be assured.'

'My future is sailing home as fast as I can! Yes, Egypt has offered me more hospitality than I ever thought possible, but here I'm a guest, not a ruler. Forget your crazy schemes, my friend.'

Nefertari had taken beautiful, blonde Helen to see the harem at Merur. The white-skinned woman was enthralled with the land of the pharaohs. Bruised and weary, she still responded to the pleasure of walking in gardens and listening to music. The refined climate of Tuya's household had been a balm to her spirit over the past few weeks. The latest news, however, had plunged her into despair again: two Greek ships were already seaworthy. She would soon be leaving.

Sitting by a pond where blue lotus flowers drifted, Helen gave in to her tears.

'Forgive me, Nefertari.'

'When you go home, won't you be a queen again?'

'Menelaus will keep up appearances. The great warrior, who destroyed a city, burned and slaughtered to win his wife back and avenge the stain on his honour. For me, it will be a living hell. Death would be easier.'

Nefertari said no empty words of comfort. Instead, she taught Helen to weave. Helen took to it immediately, spending her days by the looms, picking the brains of more experienced weavers. Soon she was designing her own luxury fabrics. Her nimble touch won the admiration of the professionals. The craft took her mind off Troy, Menelaus and the inevitable return to Sparta, until the evening when Queen Tuya's sedan chair was borne through the harem gates.

Helen ran to her room and lay sobbing on the bed. The fact that the Great Royal Wife had arrived meant the end of a happy interlude that would be her last. She regretted not having the strength to kill herself.

Gently, Nefertari tried to rouse her.

'The Queen is asking for you.'

'Don't make me go.'

'Tuya must not be kept waiting.'

Helen yielded. Once again, she was not mistress of her destiny.

Menelaus was unprepared for the skill of the Egyptian shipbuilders. The rumour that Pharaoh's boats could sail for months at a time seemed plausible, given the speed with which the Memphis naval yard had reconditioned the Greek fleet. He had seen huge barges that could carry an entire obelisk, clippers and warships he would not care to meet in battle. Egyptian defence forces more than lived up to the stories about them.

Well, no need to suffer by comparison. He was going home! This stop in Egypt had allowed him to regain his usual energy. His soldiers had received medical attention and an improved diet. Now the boats were ready to sail.

Marching briskly, Menelaus headed for the Great Royal Wife's residence, where Helen had been staying since her return from Merur. Nefertari showed him in.

He found his wife wearing an Egyptian-style linen gown with shoulder straps. She looked almost indecent. Fortunately, no local Paris would think of kidnapping her! It would be strictly against pharaonic law, and furthermore the women here seemed much more independent than they were in Greece. They were not confined to their quarters, but went about freely, their faces uncovered; they resisted men and even held government posts. Erroneous ways, and one practice Menelaus would be sure not to take back to Greece.

When her husband walked in, Helen neglected to stand, her attention focused on her loom.

'It's me, Helen.'

'I know.'

'Is that all the greeting I get?'

'How should I greet you?'

'Why, as your lord and master!'

'The only master here is Pharaoh.'

'We're leaving for Sparta.'

'I still have a long way to go on this fabric.'

'Get up and come with me.'

'I'm not going with you, Menelaus.'

The Greek king pounced on his wife, trying to drag her

by the wrist. The dagger she waved in his face made him back off.

'Don't attack me, or I'll call for help. In Egypt, rape is punishable by death.'

'But you're my wife! You belong to me.'

'Queen Tuya has put me in charge of her dressmakers. It's an honour, and one I intend to live up to. My shop will weave the fabrics worn by all the noblewomen of Egypt. When I'm tired of it, we can leave. If you can't wait that long, don't let me keep you.'

Menelaus had broken two swords and three lances over the millstone at his mansion. The baker and the other servants were so alarmed that they were about to fetch the police when Shaanar stepped in. Pharaoh's older son kept a careful distance until the Greek's fury was spent. When the hero's sword arm finally grew tired, Shaanar brought him a cup of strong beer.

The King of Sparta gulped it down and sat heavily on the millstone.

'The bitch! Up to the same old tricks again.'

'I understand your anger, but it serves no purpose. Helen is free to choose where she lives.'

'Free! A culture that gives so much freedom to women deserves to perish!'

'Will you stay in Memphis?'

'Do *I* have any choice? If I go back to Sparta without Helen, I'll be a laughing stock. My people won't respect me and one of my faithful officers will slit my throat while I'm sleeping. I have to have that woman!'

'The job Tuya's given her is no mere token; the queen has a very high opinion of your wife.'

'My wife. Damn her!' He pounded his fist on the millstone.

'It's no use lamenting. You and I have better things to do.'

The Greek listened closely. 'If I become pharaoh, I'll deliver Helen to you.'

'What do I have to do?'

'Help me get rid of Ramses.'

'Seti could live to be a hundred!'

'Nine years on the throne have begun to take their toll, and constant work has undermined his health. Our preparations, though, will take time. Once the throne is officially vacant, while the country is in mourning, we must be ready to move, strike hard and fast.'

Menelaus slumped forward. 'How long will we have to wait?'

'Our luck will turn, believe me. In the meantime, there's a much to be done behind the scenes.'

Leaning on Ramses, Homer explored his new surroundings, a tidy villa set in a garden, only a short distance from the regent's wing of the palace. A cook, a chambermaid and a gardener formed the poet's staff. His sole requests were a good supply of olive oil and some full-bodied wine, with anise and coriander to spice it.

Nearly blind, Homer bent close to each tree, each flower. He seemed to sense something missing. Ramses worried that he might not find his quarters adequate, fine and new though they were. Suddenly, the poet halted, inhaling deeply.

'At last! A lemon tree, creation's masterpiece! An absolute requirement for writing poetry. Let me sit down!'

Ramses fetched a three-legged stool, which seemed to satisfy Homer.

'Have some dried sage leaves brought to me.'

'Are you sick?'

'You'll see. Now tell me, what do you know about the Trojan War?'

'It was long and deadly.'

'Not a very poetic summary! What I have in mind is a long

narrative to sing the deeds of Achilles and Hector. Ah, it will go down through the ages.'

The crown prince regarded Homer as a bit pretentious, but admired his spirit.

A black-and-white cat came out of the house and stopped just short of the poet, hesitating only briefly before it jumped in his lap and began to purr.

'A cat, a lemon tree, a cup of spiced wine! I knew I should come here. My poem will be a masterpiece. I'll call it the *Iliad*.'

Shaanar was proud of Menelaus. The Greek hero, making the best of it, had decided to play along. To win the good graces of the king and the priestly caste, he had made an offering at the temple of Gurnah, dedicated to the Pharaoh's *ka*. The beautiful Greek amphorae, banded in yellow with a frieze of lotus buds at the bottom, were added to the temple's treasure.

The Greek soldiers, learning their stay was indefinite, settled in the Memphis suburbs and began to barter, trading salves, perfume and silver pieces for food. Eventually, the government authorized them to open their own shops.

The officers and crack troops were integrated into the Egyptian army. They would perform community service such as canal maintenance and dyke repair. Most of them would marry, have children, build a house, and blend into Egyptian society. Neither Seti nor Ramses thought anything of it, but a new 'Trojan Horse', much more subtle than the original, had just been introduced into Egypt.

Menelaus paid another call on Helen, this time supervised by Tuya. He behaved respectfully as a husband should, informing her that from now on they would meet only if she wished it and he would no longer trouble her in any way. Helen was cynical about this change of heart, but was glad to see that Menelaus, like a wildcat caught in a net, had at least stopped struggling.

The King of Sparta was next assigned another, even more delicate, task: appeasing Ramses. He was granted an official audience and made sure to hold his temper, as did Ramses. As an honoured guest, Menelaus would adhere to court etiquette and maintain the best possible relations with the crown prince. Despite his cool reception, open conflict was avoided. Shaanar and his Greek friend would weave their web in peace and quiet.

Looking better than ever with his perfect clothing, neat moustache, new manicure, and sparkling, intelligent eyes, Ahsha sat in the cabin of Shaanar's boat, thanking him for the excellent beer. As always, their meetings were held in secret.

The king's older son explained the standoff between Menelaus and Helen, without revealing how he planned to exploit it.

'Tell me about developments in Asia,' he said.

'It gets more complicated by the day. The smaller states are in constant conflict; each petty king dreams of heading a federation. It's the most propitious situation for us, but it won't last. Unlike my colleagues, I do believe that the Hittites will rally the most disgruntled leaders to their own cause. When that happens, Egypt will be in grave danger.'

'How long do you think it will take them?'

'A few years; a coalition takes some time to build.'

'Will Pharaoh hear about it?'

'Yes, but not in the correct perspective. Our ambassadors in the field are too old-fashioned, with no clear view of the future.'

'And you have your own sources?'

'Not yet, but I've made some important contacts. We see each other socially, and I hear things.'

'On my end, I've got closer to the secretary of state; we're almost friends. If things work out as I plan, he'll advance your career.'

'Your reputation in Asia is solid, Shaanar. Ramses is an unknown quantity.'

'As soon as anything important happens, let me know.'

45

In the tenth year of his reign, Seti decided it was time he led Ramses through a crucial rite of passage, although the crown prince was only eighteen. He would never be able to rule until he was initiated into the mysteries of Osiris. Pharaoh would have preferred to wait and watch his son mature, but fate might not permit him that luxury. So, despite the potential shock to the young man's system, Seti decided to take him to Abydos.

Abydos was where Seti had built the largest temple in all of Egypt, a monument to Osiris, murdered by his brother Set. Being named for Set associated Seti with terrifying forces of destruction, which he transformed into the power of resurrection, just as the murderous Set carried the divine light of Osiris on his back for all eternity.

Walking behind his father, Ramses went through the first monumental gateway. In the courtyard, two priests purified his hands and feet in a stone basin. They passed a sacred well, then came to the façade of the inner sanctuary. Before each sculpted likeness of the king as Osiris were floral arrangements and baskets full of food.

'This is the home of light,' Seti revealed.

The cedar doors, gilded with electrum, seemed like a barrier.

'Do you wish to go farther?'

Ramses nodded.

A white-robed priest with a shaved head bade him on. As soon as his feet touched the silver floor, he felt himself glide on a wave of incense into another world. Seti had placed a statue of the goddess Ma'at before each of the seven chapels, symbolizing the sum of all offerings. He led his son down the Gallery of Lists, where the name of every Pharaoh was carved, beginning with Menes, the unifier of the Two Lands.

'They are dead,' said Seti, 'but their *ka* lives on and will guide your actions. As long as heaven exists, so will this temple. Here, you will commune with the gods and learn their secrets. Take care of their dwelling place. Make their light shine.'

Father and son read the columns of hieroglyphs. They ordered the pharaoh to draw up plans for temples, the kingly prerogative since the dawn of time. When the gods were happy with their places of worship, the earth would reflect their joyous light.

'The names of your ancestors live in the starry sky,' declared Seti. 'Their annals are the millions of years. Govern according to the Rule, place it in your heart, for it is what binds all forms of life.'

One scene stunned Ramses: an adolescent boy roping a wild bull, with Pharaoh's help! The decisive moment in his life had been captured in stone, and experience each heir apparent had shared, unaware he was stepping into his limitless destiny.

The prince followed Seti out of the temple and up a slope to a grove of trees.

'The tomb of Osiris; few people have ever seen it.'

They went down an underground flight of stairs, through a long, arched passageway whose inscriptions named the gates to the netherworld. A sharp bend to the left brought them to an extraordinary sight: ten massive pillars supporting the roof of the shrine rose from an artificial island in a subterranean lake.

'Osiris is reborn each year when his mysteries are celebrated, within this giant sarcophagus. It is identical to the primeval mound emerging from the ocean of energy when the One became Two, taking thousands of shapes while remaining One. This invisible ocean gave rise to the Nile, the inundation, the dew, the rain, the wellspring. It surrounds the universe, surrounds our world, so the barque of the sun may sail in it. Immerse yourself in this ocean, that your spirit may step beyond the visible world and draw strength from that which has no beginning nor end.'

The next night, Ramses was initiated into the mysteries of Osiris.

He drank cool water from the invisible ocean and ate wheat that sprang from the risen body of Osiris, then was dressed in fine linen for the procession of the faithful, led by a priest in a jackal mask. Set's henchmen blocked their way, determined to slay them and do away with Osiris for good. A ritual battle ensued, to eerie music. In the role of Horus, Osiris's son and heir, Ramses enacted the son of light beating back the hounds of hell, though his father died in the fighting.

His faithful carried him at once to the sacred mound and began a vigil led by priestesses, including Queen Tuya, who embodied Isis, called 'Great of Magic'. Her incantations would retrieve the scattered remnants of her husband's body so the slain god could be resurrected.

Each word that came from her mouth on this night like no other was stamped in Ramses's heart. It was not his mother officiating, but a goddess. His spirit was drawn into the heart of the mysteries of resurrection, and several times he wavered on the brink of losing all contact with the human world, dissolving into the great beyond. But he emerged victorious from this inconceivable combat, his body and soul intact.

Ramses stayed several weeks in Abydos. He meditated

beneath tall trees by the sacred lake. Here the barque of Osiris, built not by human hands but by light, would sail during his Mysteries. The crown prince spent hours at the 'Stairway of the Great God'. Nearby stood stones bearing the names of those Osiris found to be just when he passed judgement over them. Their souls took the form of human-headed birds and made the pilgrimage to Abydos, where they enjoyed daily offerings.

He was allowed to view the temple's hoard of gold, silver, royal linen, statues, holy oils, incense, wine, honey, unguents and vases. Ramses was intrigued by the storerooms, where food produced on the temple's dependent estates were received and ritually cleansed before it was redistributed to the general population. Steers, fattened cows, calves, goats and fowl were also blessed. Some animals were kept for the temple barnyard, most sent back to the neighbouring villages.

It had been decreed in Year Four of Seti's reign that each man employed by the temple must know his duty and never veer from it; consequently, every worker at Abydos was protected from abuses of power, forced labour and the conscription into the army. The vizier, judges, ministers, mayors and provincial officials had been ordered to respect and enforce this decree. All that belonged to Abydos – boats, livestock, land – could never be taken away. The local farmers, stockmen, vintners and other growers lived in peace under the twofold protection of Pharaoh and Osiris. Seti published his decree all over the country, even as far as Nauri in the Nubian desert, where it was strikingly carved on a stone twice as tall as a man. Whoever tried to encroach on temple lands or commandeer its personnel would have his nose or ears cut off and receive two hundred lashes.

Taking part in the daily life of the temple, Ramses noted that religious and economic activity were distinct but intertwined. When Pharaoh communed with the divine presence in the inner sanctum, the material world no longer existed, but it had taken talented architects and sculptors to build the shrine and make the stones speak. When Pharaoh made offerings of the choicest foodstuffs, it was thanks to the temple farmers.

No absolute truth was taught here, no dogma translated spiritual yearning into fanaticism. The temple was a container for divine energy, a stone vessel that was only apparently motionless; its function was to purify, transform, make sacred. It fed on the connection between the living pharaoh and divine love and fed every level of Egyptian society with that love.

Ramses returned several times to the Gallery of Lists and made out the names of kings who built the country according to the Law of Ma'at. Near the temple were the tombs of the earliest rulers, the resting place not of their mummies – entombed in the eternal dwellings at Saqqara – but their invisible, immortal bodies, without which Pharaoh could not exist.

He was suddenly overwhelmed. He was only a young man of eighteen, in love with life, burning with a powerful fire, perhaps, but no match for these giants. How could he be so impudent and vain to think he could ever take Seti's place?

Ramses had been living in a dream world, and Abydos brought him back to reality. That was the main reason his father had brought him here. There was nothing better than this holy place to show him how small he was.

The crown prince left the temple enclosure and walked towards the river. The time had come to return to Memphis, marry Iset the Fair, enjoy the town with his friends, and tell his father he no longer wanted to be regent. Since his older brother wanted nothing more than to succeed Seti, why not let him?

Lost in thought, Ramses wandered into the marshlands bordering the river. Parting the scratchy reeds, he saw it.

The drooping ears, legs thick as pillars, black-and-brown coat, stiff beard, pointed helmet of backward-curving horns, intense and hostile stare were all the same as four years earlier.

Ramses stood firm. He would let the bull dictate his destiny. If the king of the beasts and most powerful force in nature decided to charge, gore and trample him, Egypt would have one fewer prince and easily find a replacement. If the bull spared him, his life would no longer be of his own choosing, but a gift and a calling.

46

Menelaus was the guest of honour at a variety of banquets and festivities. Helen consented to appear at his side and won unanimous approval. The Greek military men became law-abiding citizens and caused little comment.

Shaanar was credited with this satisfactory outcome. The court applauded his diplomatic gifts, implicitly criticizing the crown prince's overtly hostile attitude towards the King of Sparta. Ramses's lack of flexibility and disregard for social conventions were cited as proof that he was unfit to rule.

Week by week, Shaanar regained lost ground. His brother's extended stay at Abydos left the field clear for him. He may have lost the title of heir apparent, but he still knew how to act the part. Although no one dared challenge Seti's decision, some factions wondered whether he might have made a mistake. Ramses was much more dashing, but would personal presence be enough to rule a great nation?

There was no solid opposition as yet, only rumbles of protest that could turn into a groundswell, one more strategic weapon he could use when the time came. Shaanar had learned his lesson well: Ramses would be a tough opponent. He would need to be attacked simultaneously on several fronts, without giving him time to recover between blows. Patiently, tirelessly, Shaanar wove his secret web.

One crucial step in his plan had just been accomplished,

with two Greek officers appointed to the palace guard. They would slowly recruit other foreign mercenaries already on the force and prepare to strike a decisive blow from within. By then, perhaps one of them might even be in the regent's personal bodyguard! With Menelaus's help, it could be arranged.

Since the King of Sparta's arrival, the future looked rosier. Next on his agenda was persuading one of Pharaoh's doctors to provide reliable information about his state of health. While Seti certainly looked unwell, Shaanar knew he must not jump to conclusions.

He hoped his father would not die suddenly; his master plan was not quite ready. Ramses, the hothead, might think time was on his side, but he was mistaken. Given time, Shaanar's sturdy web would strangle him to death.

'It's good,' agreed Ahmeni, skimming the first part of the *Iliad* he had transcribed for Homer, sitting beneath his lemon tree.

The poet with flowing white locks sensed a slight reservation in the scribe's voice.

'What's your objection?'

'Your gods are too much like humans.'

'It isn't that way in Egypt?'

'In folk tales, sometimes, but that's only for entertainment. What's taught in the temple is quite another matter.'

'And I suppose a young scribe would know all about it.'

'Of course I don't, but I do know that our gods represent the forces of creation and their energy must be carefully handled by experts.'

'I'm writing an epic here! Forces of creation don't make good characters. My gods are up against heroes like Achilles and Patrocles. When you read about their exploits, you won't be able to put it down.'

Ahmeni kept his thoughts to himself. Homer's wild claims

fitted with what he knew about Greek poets. Classic Egyptian authors wrote about wisdom, not warfare, no matter how grand in scale; however, it was not his place to lecture an older guest.

'It's been a long time since the crown prince called on me,' complained Homer.

'He's spending some time in Abydos.'

'The Temple of Osiris? I've heard great mysteries are taught there.'

'It's true.'

'When will he be back?'

'I don't know.'

Homer shrugged and sipped his heady wine, spiced with anise and coriander. 'Must mean exile.'

Startled, Ahmeni cried 'What?'

'Consider this scenario: Pharaoh has decided his son isn't fit to rule, so he's sent him to Abydos to become a priest, locked away in the temple for life. In a country as religious as this, isn't that the best place for a castoff?'

Ahmeni was depressed. If Homer's analysis was correct, he would never see Ramses again. He would have liked to consult with his friends, but Moses was at Karnak, Ahsha in Asia, Setau in the desert. Alone, in anguish, he tried to steady himself with work.

His staff had produced an impressive stack of inconclusive reports on the counterfeit-ink case. Their thorough research had turned up no new clue to the identity of either the factory owner or the letter-writer who had lured the king and his son to Aswan.

Ahmeni felt a rising anger. Why should so much work result in nothing but frustration? No one could vanish without a trace. He took the documents off the shelf and sat on the floor. He would read the whole case file again, beginning from his initial search of the waste dumps.

When he came to the draft deed containing the letter R, the

last letter in Shaanar's name, he suddenly had an idea. The idea became a theory of how the mastermind could have done it. The theory became a certainty when he double-checked the handwriting.

It was all clear to him now. But Ramses, confined in the temple, would never know the truth, and the culprit would go unpunished.

Ahmeni was outraged. He and his friends would never rest until the villain was brought to trial.

Iset the Fair told Nefertari she must see the queen, she must see the queen at once. Since Tuya was discussing details of an imminent religious festival with the chief priestess of Hathor, Iset was forced to wait. Fidgeting, she twisted one long sleeve of her linen dress until it tore.

Finally Nefertari opened the door to the audience chamber. Iset the Fair stumbled in to throw herself at the feet of the Great Royal Wife.

'Your Majesty, please, won't you do something?'

'Whatever is the matter?'

'Ramses has no wish to be a priest, I'm sure of it! What has he done to deserve such punishment?'

Tuya lifted Iset the Fair and asked her to be seated on a low-backed chair.

'Does the cloistered life seem that awful to you?'

'Ramses is only eighteen! It might be all right for an old man, but being sent away to a temple, at his age . . .'

'Who told you he was staying?'

'His private secretary, Ahmeni.'

'My son is a resident at Abydos, but not on a permanent basis. A future pharaoh must be initiated into the mysteries of Osiris and understand the inner workings of a temple in detail. He will return when his education is complete.'

Iset the Fair felt both shamefaced and deeply relieved.

*   *   *

A shawl thrown over her shoulders, Nefertari was the first one up, as usual. She mentally ran through her daily tasks and reviewed the queen's schedule, without a thought for herself. Running the Great Royal Wife's household demanded a great deal of work and constant attention to detail. Different as it was from the structured religious life of her dreams, she soon found her position as housemistress rewarding because of her deep admiration for the queen. Holding herself to the same high standards she demanded of others, steeped in Egypt's grandeur, devoted to traditional values, Tuya was truly a living goddess, embodying the rectitude of Ma'at. Nefertari sensed the scope of the Great Royal Wife's responsibilities and realized that her own role had added significance: the royal household must serve as an example of harmonious management.

The kitchen was empty. The servant girls must have slept in. Nefertari went to knock on each door: no answer. She reversed direction and looked in each room: all empty.

What had got into her usually reliable and punctual staff? It was not a religious holiday, not a day of rest. Even then, there would be staff to cover. No fresh bread, cakes or milk in the usual places. And the queen would need her breakfast within ten minutes!

Nefertari was distraught. Could the palace be under a spell?

She hurried out to the millstone. Perhaps the fleeing staff had left some food there. But all that she found was wheat; she would never have time to grind it, mix the dough, bake bread. With good reason, Tuya would accuse her housemistress of negligence and unpreparedness; her dismissal would be immediate.

On top of the humiliation, there would be the pain of leaving the queen. Nefertari realized how deeply attached she had grown to the Great Royal Wife. No longer serving her would bring heartbreak.

'It will be a great day,' prophesied a low voice. Nefertari slowly turned around.

'You, the prince regent of the realm, at the millstone?'

Ramses was leaning against a wall, arms crossed.

'Is my presence here unseemly?'

'No, I . . .'

'As far as my mother's breakfast is concerned, don't worry. Her maids will serve it at the usual time.'

'But the place is deserted!'

'I believe your favourite maxim is "A perfect word is rarer than green stone, yet the servant girl grinding wheat at the millstone may possess it"?'

'Am I to understand that you banished the household staff to lure me here?'

'I expected that you'd come.'

'Would you like me to grind you some wheat for your trouble?'

'No, Nefertari. A perfect word is what I'm after.'

'Sorry to disappoint you, but I have none.'

'I'm convinced that you have.'

She was lovely, radiant; her eyes had the depth of heavenly waters. 'Perhaps I ought not to say so, but I find your practical joke in the worst of taste.'

The prince seemed less sure of himself. 'Say the word, Nefertari.'

'Everyone thinks you're to stay at Abydos permanently.'

'I came back yesterday.'

'And your most pressing business is interfering with the Queen's servants?'

'By the Nile at Abydos, I met a wild bull. We were face to face, my life hung on his horns. In the few seconds he stared at me, I reached some serious decisions. Since the bull didn't kill me, I need to take charge of my life.'

'I'm glad that you lived and I hope you become king.'

'Is that my mother's opinion, or your own?'

'I'm not in the habit of lying. May I take my leave now?'

'I know that you can say that word, Nefertari, the one more precious than green stone. It would bring me such happiness to hear it.'

The young woman bowed. 'I am your humble servant, Regent of Egypt.'

'Nefertari!'

She raised her proud eyes to his once more. Her nobility was dazzling.

'The Queen expects me for our morning conference. Tardiness is a grave infraction.'

Ramses took her in his arms.

'What must I do to make you say you'll marry me?'

'Ask me,' she softly replied.

47

Seti began the tenth year of his reign by making an offering to the Great Sphinx of Giza, guardian of the plateau where Pharaohs Cheops, Khephren, and Mycerinus had their pyramids. The Sphinx's vigilance kept intruders off this holy ground, an energy source for the entire country.

As prince regent, Ramses accompanied his father into the small temple erected in front of the colossal lion with the head of a king, eyes raised heavenward. A stela beside it showed Seti killing an oryx, the animal associated with his evil namesake, Set. Representing a victory over the forces of darkness, the hunt scene showed Pharaoh in his most important role: bringing order out of disorder.

The site impressed Ramses, its power seeping into each fibre of his being. Everything was immutable; the pyramids would outlast time. Next to intimate, reflective Abydos, Giza bore the most striking testimony he had seen to the presence of *ka*, the invisible and ubiquitous life force; in the animal world, it inhabited the wild bull.

'I met the bull again, by the Nile,' Ramses whispered to his father. 'We were face to face, and he stared me down, like the first time.'

'You wanted to renounce your right to the throne,' said Seti, 'and he wouldn't let you.'

His father had read his mind. Perhaps Seti had even

changed into a wild bull to make his son face up to his responsibilities.

'Not all the secrets at Abydos were clear to me, but the long retreat there did teach me that mystery is at the heart of life.'

'Go back often and watch over the temple. Celebrating the mysteries of Osiris is a key to maintaining the country's equilibrium.'

'I made one other decision.'

'Your mother approves, and so do I.'

In a less solemn setting, the prince would have jumped for joy. One day would he be able to see into people's hearts the way Seti did?

Ramses had never seen Ahmeni so excited.

'I know everything and I've identified our villain! It's unbelievable, but there's no room for any doubt. Look, look here!'

The young scribe, ordinarily so fastidious, was surrounded by a genuine jumble of papyri, fragments of wooden writing boards, shards of limestone. He had gone over every scrap of evidence collected over the months, then done it again to make sure.

'It's him,' he stated flatly, 'and that's his writing. I can even link him to the chariot driver, who worked for him, and from the driver to the groom. Can you imagine, Ramses? A thief and a criminal, that's what he is! Why would he act like that?'

At first incredulous, the crown prince yielded to the evidence. Ahmeni had put together a remarkable case; there were no loose ends.

'I don't know,' said Ramses. 'But I plan to ask him.'

Dolora and her husband Sary, plumper than ever, were busy feeding the exotic fish that splashed in their garden pool.

Dolora was feeling testy; the heat made her tired and her oily complexion only seemed to get worse. She would have to change doctors and face creams again.

A servant announced Ramses.

'Finally showing us some respect!' exclaimed Dolora, kissing her brother. 'Do you know that at court they thought you were in Abydos for good?'

'Wrong again, but then the court doesn't run the country.'

His authoritative tone surprised the pair. Ramses had changed. This was not merely a privileged young man speaking, but the prince regent of Egypt.

'I hope you're here to give Sary the granary job.'

'I'll need to speak to him alone.'

'There are no secrets between my husband and me,' fumed Dolora.

'Are you certain of that?'

'Absolutely!'

Sary's customary good cheer was nowhere in evidence. He looked tense and nervous.

'Do you recognize this handwriting?' Ramses asked his old teacher, producing the letter that had lured Seti and his son to the granite quarries at Aswan.

Sary and his wife were dead silent.

'The signature is an alias,' Ramses said at length, 'but the writing is easy enough to identify. It's yours, Sary. Comparison with other documents in your hand is conclusive.'

'It's a forgery, a fake . . .'

'Teaching wasn't enough for you, so you devised a way to sell cheap ink cakes as the top-quality product. When you sensed trouble, you decided to cover your tracks. Given your inside knowledge of the archives and your experience as a scribe, there was nothing simpler. The one thing you missed was a fragment of a draft-copy deed that my secretary dug out of a waste dump, *after* his private investigation almost cost him his life, mind you. For a long time, we both suspected

313

Shaanar. Then Ahmeni realized where he'd gone wrong. All that was left of the owner's name on the deed was the letter R. It wasn't the last letter of my brother's name, but the second-last in yours, Sary. He also learned that the chariot driver who stranded me in the desert was on your payroll for more than a year. My brother is innocent. You're the only one to blame.'

Ramses's old teacher, tight-lipped, avoided his eyes. Dolora appeared neither upset nor surprised.

'You don't have a case,' reasoned Sary 'No court will convict me without solid evidence.'

'Why do you hate me?' asked Ramses.

'You won't get out of our way,' cried his sister, wild-eyed. 'You're a strutting rooster, so sure of yourself, young and strong. My husband is a remarkable man, cultured, intelligent and capable. He should be the one to govern Egypt, and thanks to me, the pharaoh's daughter, he has a legitimate claim!'

Dolora took her husband's hand and pushed him forward.

'You've both gone mad with ambition,' Ramses told them. 'To spare my parents a painful ordeal, I won't bring charges. But I want you out of Memphis. Some provincial town will be your permanent residence. Cause any more trouble and you'll leave the country.'

'I'm your sister, Ramses.'

'That's why I'm letting you off so lightly. Against my better judgement, I may add.'

Despite the bodily harm he had suffered, Ahmeni agreed not to press charges, out of friendship for Ramses. His gesture went a long way towards healing the fresh wound of Dolora and Sary's betrayal. If Ahmeni had demanded vengeance, the prince would not have objected. At the moment, however, the young scribe seemed more concerned with the guest list for Ramses's wedding.

'Setau is just back from his last venom-gathering expedition, a big success, as usual. He and Lotus are going straight to Memphis. Moses should arrive day after tomorrow. That only leaves Ahsha. He's on his way, but you never know how long it may take.'

'We'll wait for him.'

'I'm happy for you. They say that Nefertari is the fairest in the land.'

'Don't you agree?'

'I can tell when a scroll is beautiful, or a poem, but a woman? Don't ask too much of me.'

'How has Homer been?'

'He can't wait to see you again.'

'He's on the list, isn't he?'

'Of course.' Ahmeni's eyes darted towards the door.

'Expecting someone?'

'No, but I'm afraid that you are. I don't know how much longer I can hold out. Iset the Fair has been demanding to see you.'

Iset the Fair had planned to give vent to her fury, bombard her lover with recriminations, call him names. Instead, he surprised her with a visit, and the moment she saw him she was helpless. Ramses had changed, really changed. More than the passionate young man she was so in love with, he was a reigning prince. He was coming into his own.

The young woman felt as if she were meeting someone new, someone she had no power to influence. Her bitter resentment gave way to a mixture of fear and respect.

'I'm so . . . I'm honoured to see you.'

'My mother told me you called on her.'

'I was worried, so worried you wouldn't come back!'

'And now that I have?'

'I've heard—'

'That tomorrow I'm marrying Nefertari.'

'She's gorgeous, and I . . . I'm pregnant.'

Ramses tenderly took her hand. 'Did you think I'd abandon you? The child will still be ours. If one day my destiny is to be king, Nefertari will be my consort, the Great Royal Wife. But if you still wish, and if she consents, you'll also live in the palace.'

She clung to him. 'Do you love me, Ramses?'

'Abydos and the wild bull I met there showed me my true nature. I can't be like everyone else. My father has given me a heavy burden to carry, and I may falter, but I need to try. You're my wild youth, Iset. You're passion and desire. Nefertari is a queen.'

'I'll grow old and you won't want me any more.'

'I'm head of a clan, and that means I take care of my own. Do you want to belong to my clan, Iset?'

She offered her lips to him in answer.

The wedding was a private affair, with no religious ceremony. Seti did not attend; while he gave the match his blessing, he never took a day off. Egypt did not allow it.

Nefertari had asked for a simple celebration in the country: a palm grove, wheat fields and bean blossoms, a sandy ditch where grazing animals stopped to drink.

In a short linen gown accented with lapis lazuli bracelets and a carnelian necklace, Nefertari had adopted Queen Tuya's manner of dress. The most elegant member of the party was Ahsha, back from Asia that very morning, and surprised at the outdoor setting for a gathering that included the pharaoh's principal wife, Moses, Ahmeni, Setau, a famous Greek poet, an oversized lion and a playful yellow dog. He would have preferred something slightly more formal, but kept his reservations to himself and shared the rustic meal as Setau looked on in amusement.

'You don't look very comfortable,' remarked the snake handler.

'A lovely spot.'

'But oh, my, the grass stains on that fine white linen! Life can be so unfair. Especially when there isn't a snake to be found.'

Homer was not too blind to be fascinated by Nefertari. He admitted, albeit reluctantly, that she was even lovelier than Helen.

'Thanks to you,' Moses told Ramses, 'I'm enjoying a real day of rest.'

'Your work at karnak is hard, then?'

'The scale of the project is so huge that the smallest miscalculation could lead to disaster. I have to keep a constant check on details to make sure everything goes according to plan.'

It was a relaxed and happy day. Back at his residence, Ramses carried Nefertari over the threshold. In the eyes of the law, they were man and wife.

48

Shaanar was a whirlwind of activity. He made contact after contact, courted key players at a round of lunches, dinners, public receptions, private meetings. He played the role of chief of protocol to the hilt, improving social relations in the top echelons of the kingdom.

In reality, Shaanar was capitalizing on his brother's monumental error: marrying a commoner, a *poor* commoner, and planning to make her his consort! Perhaps it was not without precedent, and there was no law against it, but in Shaanar's interpretation it became a slap in the face to the court, the Egyptian nobility – and he found a most receptive audience. It was anyone's guess how far this unconventional prince might go. The nobles had their name, their position to think of! And who knew how Nefertari would act? With her humble beginnings, power might turn her head. She would choose her own inner circle, without regard to old titles or new money.

Ramses's star was fading, fading fast.

'Your poor face!' exclaimed Shaanar. Dolora was a sight! 'Is anything wrong?'

'Everything's wrong,' she sobbed.

'My dear little sister . . . Do you mind telling me?'

'Sary and I have been banished from Memphis.'

'Is this a joke?'

'Ramses pressured us.'

'No! On what grounds?'

'His snivelling secretary claims . . . They're accusing my husband of the basest crimes. If we don't leave town, Ramses says he'll take us to court.'

'Does he have evidence?'

Dolora pouted. 'Not really. It's all circumstantial. But you know how trials are: it can go either way.'

'Are you saying that you and your husband really did try to plot against Ramses?' The princess hesitated. 'I'm not a judge. Tell me the truth, Dolora.'

'Well, we had *ideas*, yes. But what do you expect? Ramses is out to get us!'

'No need to shout. I understand completely.'

'You're not angry with me?' she asked, reverting to her usual listlessness.

'I'm only sorry your plans didn't work out.'

'Ramses thought you were to blame.'

'I think he's an impostor, and he knows it. He thinks I've given up the fight, and I haven't.'

'Sary and I could work with you.'

'I was going to suggest it.'

'We won't be able to do much where we end up!'

'I'm not so sure. I have a villa near Thebes I can let you use. You can make contacts there. I know there are government and religious leaders who are less than thrilled with our brother. They need convincing that his accession may not be a foregone conclusion.'

'You're too kind, and we appreciate your help.'

Shaanar's eyes narrowed. 'If you *had* got rid of Ramses, what was your next step?'

'We thought . . . we just wanted him out of the way.'

'You wanted your husband on the throne, didn't you? He could claim a connection through you, am I right? If we're going to work together, you'll have to forget that fantasy.

Back me and only me. I'm going to win the throne, and when I do, I'll take care of my friends.'

Ahsha did not return to Asia without first attending one of Shaanar's famous parties, featuring finest-quality food, excellent entertainment and the latest gossip. Acid comments about the crown prince and his bride were interspersed with fulsome praise for Seti. No one found it strange to see the king's older son conversing with the young diplomat who was making such a name for himself.

'Your promotion is all set,' Shaanar revealed. 'In less than a month you'll be chief interpreter with the Asian delegation. At your age, it's an accomplishment.'

'How can I express my gratitude?'

'Keep me supplied with information. By the way, did you attend Ramses's wedding?'

'Yes, with a handful of his closest friends.'

'Any leading questions?'

'None.'

'He still trusts you?'

'Beyond a doubt.'

'Did he ask what's happening in Asia?'

'No. He doesn't dare encroach on his father's territory. Besides, his mind is on his marriage.'

'Any progress in the field?'

'Significantly so. Several of the smaller principalities would gladly support you, with the right incentives.'

'Gold?'

'It's traditional.'

'And its use strictly limited to Pharaoh.'

'Nothing prevents you from making extravagant promises. Channel them through me, and no one will be the wiser.'

'Excellent idea.'

'Until you take power, our most important tactic is making

you sound like the answer to everyone's prayers. When the time comes, you'll hand-pick your cabinet.'

The court was astonished to learn that Ramses and Nefertari continued to live as before. The regent went on working in his father's shadow; his wife managed Tuya's household. Shaanar explained that this outwardly humble behaviour was a clever hoax. They were wolves in sheep's clothing, and neither the King nor the Queen sensed the danger.

The various elements of Shaanar's grand design were beginning to mesh. Moses had so far resisted his overtures, but if there was a way to persuade him, in time Shaanar would find it.

Another important defection might prove closer at hand. Tricky, but worth a try.

He went to Merur for the dedication of a huge artificial lake where the harem ladies could swim and go boating. Iset the Fair, now visibly with child, was one of the guests of honour.

'Feeling well, my dear?' he greeted her.

'Never better, thank you. My son will be Ramses's pride and joy.'

'Have you met Nefertari?'

'Yes, she's a lovely person. We've made friends.'

'She accepts—'

'We'll both be Ramses's wives. As long as he loves me, I don't mind not being the consort.'

'A noble attitude, but an awkward position.'

'You have no understanding of Ramses or those who love him.'

'I envy my brother's luck, but I doubt you'll be happy.'

'As mother of the next crown prince, I'll have glory to spare.'

'You're getting ahead of yourself. Ramses isn't on the throne yet.'

'Are you questioning Pharaoh's judgement?'

'Of course not. But there's no telling what might happen. My dear, you know how highly I regard you. The way Ramses treats you has been unspeakably cruel. Your grace, your intelligence, your noble lineage make you the perfect choice as Great Royal Wife.'

'That was a dream. I prefer reality.'

'Are you dreaming now? Because I'm prepared to offer you the chance my brother has robbed you of.'

'How dare you, when I'm carrying his child?'

'Think it over, Iset. Think hard.'

Despite discreet feelers and tantalizing third-party offers, Shaanar had been unable to buy one of Seti's personal physicians. Incorruptible? No, they were merely prudent. They had more to fear from Seti than from his older son. Pharaoh's physical condition was a state secret; breaches of confidentiality met with severe sanctions.

Since the doctors were out of reach, Shaanar changed his approach. Doctors prescribed medications, and temple laboratories controlled the manufacture of all pharmaceuticals. If only he knew which one . . .

The process was painstaking, but it finally paid off. Seti's pills and potions were all made to order at the temple of Sekhmet. Approaching the laboratory director, an elderly, well-to-do widower, would be too risky. However, checking on his assistants proved worthwhile. One, a man in his forties, complained that on his salary he could hardly afford to keep a new, younger wife in gowns, jewellry, cosmetics. He looked like the perfect candidate, and he was.

Studying the pharmacy records, Shaanar deduced that Seti suffered from a serious but lingering illness. Within three years, four at the most, the throne would be vacant.

* * *

At summer's end, Seti made an offering of wine to the harvest goddess, a benevolent cobra. Her basalt likeness could be found protecting the fields. The farmers gathered around the king; his presence was a blessing in itself. The ruler liked to mingle with these simple folk, whom he preferred to most of his courtiers.

When the ceremony was finished, there were speeches of thanks to the goddess of abundance, the god of grains and the Pharaoh who represented them on earth. Ramses became aware of his father's direct connection to his people, who loved him as much as his officials feared him.

Seti and Ramses sat down in a palm grove, by a well. A woman brought them grapes, dates, cool beer. The crown prince had the feeling that for the king was this was a respite, far from the court and affairs of state. His eyes were closed, his face glowing with a faint light.

'When you are pharaoh, Ramses, look deep into the souls of men. Look for advisers who are upright and firm, able to give an impartial opinion while ever mindful of their oath of obedience to you. Put them in the right positions, to make sure that Ma'at is respected. Be merciless with the corrupt as well as those who corrupt them.'

'But father, you have a long time left to reign. We haven't celebrated your jubilee yet.'

'Thirty years on the throne of Egypt? It's not to be.'

'You're solid as a block of granite, aren't you?'

'No, Ramses. Stone is eternal, my royal names will live through the ages, but my mortal form will disappear. I feel the time coming.'

The prince felt a searing pain in his chest.

'The country needs you too much.'

'My son, you have endured many trials. You are wise beyond your years, but still in the springtime of life. As you grow older, remember the look in the wild bull's eyes. Let it inspire you and give you the strength you need.'

'At your side, it all seems so easy. Fate may still grant you many more years as king.'

'The most important thing is to prepare yourself.'

'Do you think the court will accept me?'

'When I go, your opponents will create obstacles, undermine your path. Your first great battle will be one you fight all alone.'

'Without a single ally?'

'Not even your family. Where you were most generous, you will find ingratitude; where you were kindest, betrayal. Beware of your closest associates and friends. Rely only on yourself. On that fateful day, no one will be there to help you.'

49

Iset the Fair gave birth to a lusty boy. They named him Kha-em-Waset, 'He Who Appears in Thebes', where Iset now lived in the royal palace. Once Ramses had seen him, Kha was handed over to a wet nurse so that his beautiful mother could rest and recover. Ramses was proud of his first-born son. Touched by his happiness, Iset the Fair promised to give him more children if he would keep loving her.

When he left, she felt very much alone. Shaanar's words came back to haunt her. Ramses had gone home to Nefertari, so exasperatingly kind and thoughtful that it would have been simple to hate her. But Ramses's principal wife was beginning to win people over without even trying, just by being herself. Iset the Fair had also fallen under her spell, to the point of condoning Ramses's behaviour.

It was hard being on her own. She missed the glitter of court life in Memphis, the endless conversations with her childhood friends, boating on the Nile, poolside parties at splendid mansions. Thebes had its wealth and splendour, but it was not her home.

Perhaps Shaanar was right. Perhaps she should never have settled for the role of secondary wife.

Homer ground up dried sage leaves and poured the powder

inside a good-sized snail shell, inserted a hollow reed, lit the mixture, and inhaled hungrily.

'Strange custom,' remarked Ramses.

'Helps me write,' said the poet. 'How is that wonderful wife of yours?'

'In Egypt only the most hideous crimes carry the penalty of burning at the stake.'

'Still working for the Queen.'

'Your women are so independent. In Greece, they don't get out much.'

'And you think we're mistaken?'

'To tell the truth, I don't, at least not on that score, but you have plenty of other customs I disagree with.'

'Feel free to tell me.'

Ramses's receptiveness amazed him. 'You don't mind criticism from your guests?'

'If your comments can lead to improvements, they're more than welcome.'

'Strange country. In Greece, we spend hours debating, our orators are fiery, we argue with daggers drawn. Here, who questions a word that Pharaoh says?'

'He is the instrument of Ma'at, the goddess of truth. If Pharaoh falters, disorder will follow, man will revert to his natural state of misery.'

'Have you no faith in the individual?'

'None at all, for my part. When man fends for himself, cowardice and treachery are rampant.'

Homer drew another puff. 'In my *Iliad* you'll find an old acquaintance of mine, a soothsayer who could read the past, present and future. I feel a certain peace of mind for your country at present; your father is a wise man in the truest sense. But the future . . .'

'So you're a soothsayer too?'

'What poet isn't? Listen to these verses from my first book.'

"From the peaks of Olympus, Apollo descends, furious, carrying the bow on his shoulder and the quiver well closed: he is full of rage, and on his back, when he leaps, the arrows knock against each other. Like dark night he approaches, shooting men . . . innumerable pyres must light to burn the corpses."'

'In Egypt only the most hideous crimes carry the penalty of burning at the stake.'

Homer seemed irritated.

'Egypt is at peace – but for how long? I had a dream, Prince Ramses, a dream of arrows falling from the sky like rain, piercing the bodies of young men. There's war on the way, and no way out of it.'

In Thebes, Sary and Dolora were hard at work for Shaanar. After long discussions, they had decided to do as he asked and become his staunchest supporters. Not only would they be getting back at Ramses, they could also earn prominent positions in Shaanar's court – allies in war, allies in victory.

Dolora had no trouble establishing relations with the best families in town. She was, after all, a princess. She had moved south, she explained, to learn more about their marvellous province, enjoy the country life, and be closer to the great temple of Amon at Karnak, where she and her husband planned several long retreats.

At parties and in private conversations, Dolora dropped hints about Ramses. Who knew him better than she did? Seti was a great king, an irreproachable ruler; Ramses would be a tyrant, ignoring Thebes and its dignitaries. The temple of Amon would receive less support; commoners like Ahmeni would be put in positions usually reserved for aristocrats. She added detail after detail, adding up to a horrific picture. Opposition to Ramses solidified.

Sary's tack was to take the high moral ground. The head

of the *Kap* accepted a teaching position in the temple school at Karnak and volunteered to help design altar displays. His humility was much admired. Influential members of the religious hierarchy enjoyed his conversation and invited him to dine. Like his wife, he spread poison everywhere he went.

When he was allowed to view the construction site Moses directed, Sary congratulated his former student on Karnak's incomparable new hall of columns, truly in proportion to the greatness of the gods.

Bearded and weather-beaten, Moses had toughened physically. He was meditating in the shade of a giant pillar.

'It's so good to see you again! Another one of my students who's gone on to do great things.'

'Don't speak too soon. I won't rest easy until the last column is standing.'

'I hear over and over how hard you work.'

'Making sure the workers work hard, that's all.'

'You're brilliant, Moses, and you do me credit.'

'Are you here on business?'

'No, Dolora and I have taken a villa just outside Thebes; I'm teaching scribes in a temple school at Karnak.'

Moses raised an eyebrow. 'You left the *Kap*.'

'I was forced to.'

'What happened?'

'Do you want the truth?'

'If you want to tell me.'

'It's not easy to talk about.'

'Then don't.'

'All right. The fact is, Ramses had me dismissed. He made horrible accusations against his own sister and me.'

'Can he back them up?'

'He doesn't have one shred of evidence. You know that otherwise he'd insist on pressing charges.'

Yes, he would, thought Moses, momentarily stunned.

'Power has changed him,' Sary continued. 'My wife made the mistake of suggesting he take things more slowly. He's as headstrong and extreme as ever, unsuited to his new responsibilities. I'm sorry to say so, believe me. Like Dolora, I tried to reason with him: no use whatsoever.'

'Exile must be difficult.'

'Exile? I'd hardly call it that. The country is magnificent, the temple soothes my weary soul, and I'm satisfied passing my knowledge on to young scribes. I'm beyond the age of ambition.'

'Wouldn't you say that you've suffered an injustice?'

'Ramses is the prince regent.'

'Misuse of power is still a crime.'

'It's better this way, believe me. But take care with Ramses.'

'Why should I?'

'I'm convinced he plans to eliminate his oldest friends, one by one. He no longer has any use for us, and neither does Nefertari; it's the two of them against the world. She's a terrible influence. Be careful, Moses! It's too late for me, but look out for yourself.'

The Hebrew meditated longer than was his custom. He respected his former teacher, who showed no hostility towards Ramses. Had marriage changed his old friend?

The lion and the yellow dog had accepted Nefertari. Except for Ramses, she was the only one who could pet the huge beast without being cuffed or bitten. Every ten days the young couple and their pets would take a day off and go to the country. Invincible ran alongside the chariot, Wideawake wedged himself behind his master's legs. They picnicked at the edge of a field, watched ibises and pelicans soar and dive, chatted with village people. Nefertari charmed them with her beauty and ability to find the right tone for each person and every situation. More than once, she found an unobtrusive way to ease a villager's struggles with old age or infirmity.

Whether she was dealing with Tuya or a servant, Nefertari's manner was the same: attentive and calm. She possessed all the qualities Ramses lacked: patience, restraint, equanimity. Her every gesture bore the stamp of a queen. From the first, he knew she was irreplaceable.

The love that grew between them was quite different from his feelings for Iset the Fair. Nefertari also took joy in her lover's body and her own, but even in their moments of passion, a different light shone in her eyes. Unlike Iset the Fair, Nefertari implicitly shared Ramses's innermost thoughts.

When the twelfth year of his father's reign arrived, Ramses asked him for permission to take Nefertari to Abydos and introduce her to the mysteries of Osiris. The royal couple, the regent and his wife left together for the holy city, where Nefertari was initiated.

The morning after the ceremony, Queen Tuya gave her a golden bracelet to wear as she celebrated the daily rites at the Great Royal Wife's side. The young woman was moved to tears. She had not left the religious life behind after all.

'Not acceptable,' huffed Ahmeni.

Ramses was so used to his secretary's constant complaints that sometimes he only half listened.

'Not in the *least* acceptable,' he repeated.

'What? Are they selling you second-rate papyrus now?'

'You know that would never pass. No. What I mean is that I don't like the way things are going for you.'

'Why? Pharaoh is still going strong, my mother and my wife think the world of each other, the country is at peace, Homer is writing his epic . . . What more could we want? Oh, I know! You need a girlfriend.'

'I have no time for such foolishness. Seriously, don't you see anything strange?'

'Honestly, no.'

'You only have eyes for nefertari, and who can blame you? It's a good thing that I still look out for your interests.'

'It is. So out with it, man!'

'I've been hearing things. Someone is trying to ruin your reputation.'

'Shaanar?'

'Your older brother has been unusually quiet these last few months, but somehow the tide of opinion is turning against you.'

'It's only talk.'

'I don't agree.'

'Someday I'll get rid of those old busybodies at court!'

'They know it, too,' observed Ahmeni. 'That's why they'll fight you.'

'They may gossip in the palace and plot in their plush salons, but they're too scared to cross me out in the open.'

'I agree in theory, but I'm still afraid there's something brewing.'

'Seti has named his successor. Everything else is speculation.'

'Do you believe Shaanar has given up?'

'You just told me how well behaved he's been.'

'That's what bothers me. It's not at all like him!'

'You worry too much, old friend. Seti will protect us.'

As long as he's alive, thought Ahmeni, resolving somehow to make Ramses see the quicksand under their feet.

50

The tiny daughter born to Ramses and Nefertari lived only two months. Lacking an appetite, she faded back into the netherworld. The doctors fretted even more over the young mother. Seti had to channel his energy into her every day for three weeks before she could begin to overcome her grief.

The prince regent stayed at his wife's side constantly. Nefertari never complained. Death was notoriously fond of infants, whatever their station in life. Another child would be born of her love for Ramses.

Little Kha, on the other hand, was thriving. A wet nurse cared for him while Iset played an increasingly prominent role in Theban society. She listened sympathetically to Dolora and Sary's grievances, aghast at Ramses's unfairness. The southern capital shuddered at the thought of the regent's ascension: he was regarded as a potential despot, flaunting the law of Ma'at. Iset tried to protest, but was quickly shouted down. Was the man she loved really a power-hungry tyrant, an inhuman monster?

Little by little, Shaanar's proposal crept back into her mind.

Seti pushed himself harder than ever. When there was an opening in his schedule, he summoned Ramses. Deep in conversation, father and son would stroll in the palace gardens. Seti, who did not care at all for writing, transmitted

332

his knowledge orally. Other kings had composed maxims to prepare their successors; he preferred direct transmission, from old mouth to young ear.

'This knowledge will not be enough.' Seti cautioned. 'Think of it as a foot soldier's shield and sword, to aid in defence and attack. When things are going well for the country, everyone will take credit; when there's a turn for the worse, it's all your fault. If you make a mistake, blame no one but yourself and do your best to correct it. The just exercise of power is a constant series of corrections, seeking balance in thought and deed. The time has come, my son, for me to send you out on a mission alone.'

Ramses tried to feel pleased. He would have preferred to sit listening at his father's feet for years.

'A small town in Nubia is challenging the viceroy's authority. The reports that have reached me are unclear. I want you to go there and decide on a course of action – decide in the name of Pharaoh.'

Nubia was bewitching as ever, to the point that Ramses almost forgot this was not a pleasure trip. He felt a weight lift from his shoulders. The golden sands and blood-red rocks made him feel light as the warm breeze rustling the dum palms. He was tempted to send the soldiers with him back to Egypt and wander off alone through this sublime country.

But here was the Viceroy of Nubia bowing before him, verbose and servile.

'I trust my reports were informative?'

'Seti found them confusing.'

'The situation couldn't be clearer! There's a rebellion that must be put down at once.'

'Have you suffered any losses?'

'No, but only because I've been cautious. I was waiting for you to come.'

'Why didn't you make a move, if the matter's so urgent?'

The viceroy could only babble: No way of knowing . . .
Large numbers . . . Might be . . .'

'Take me there,' ordered Ramses.

'Some light refreshments first?'

'Let's go.'

'In this heat? I thought the end of the day would be
favourable . . .' Ramses's chariot was already off.

The village slumbered by the Nile, in the shade of a palm
grove. Men milked cows, women prepared food, naked
children splashed in the river. Underfed dogs were curled
up outside the huts.

The Egyptian forces were posted on the surrounding
hilltops, vastly outnumbering the villagers.

'This is the rebel stronghold?' Ramses asked the viceroy.

'Don't be deceived by appearances,' he warned.

The scouts were positive: no Nubian warriors anywhere
in sight.

'The village chief challenged my authority,' asserted the
viceroy. 'Without a forceful response, the unrest could spread.
Let's take them by surprise and wipe out the village. That will
keep things quiet for a while!'

A woman had just noticed the Egyptian soldiers. She
screamed. The children came running out of the water and
ducked back inside the huts with their mothers. The men
grabbed bows, arrows and spears and gathered in the centre
of the village.

'See!' exclaimed the Viceroy. 'Just as I predicted.'

The chief came forward, proud of bearing, with two ostrich
plumes in his nublly hair, a red sash across his chest, and in
his right hand a six-foot pike trimmed with streamers.

'He's going to attack,' the Viceroy warned. 'Our archers
can take him down!'

'I'm giving orders here,' Ramses reminded him. 'I want
nothing done that might be interpreted as a threat.'

'But . . . what do you have in mind?'

Ramses took off his helmet, leather vest and gaiters. Laying down his sword and dagger, he descended the rocky slope towards the village.

'Your Majesty!' yelled the viceroy. 'Come back, he'll kill you!'

The regent walked steadily, his eyes fast on the Nubian chief. He was a man of sixty, thin to the point of emaciation.

When he waved his pike, Ramses thought he might have miscalculated the risk. But how could a Nubian tribal chief pose any more danger than a wild bull?

'Who are you?'

'Ramses, son of Seti and Prince Regent of Egypt.'

The head man lowered his pike. 'I'm the chief here.'

'And you will be as long as you obey the law of Ma'at.'

'Your viceroy is the one who broke it.'

'That's a serious accusation.'

'What's fair is fair. I delivered on my promises; the viceroy should too.'

'Let me hear your grievances.'

'He promised us wheat in exchange for our tributes. Where is it?'

'Where are the tributes?'

'Come.'

The chief walked through the group of warriors. The prince followed. The viceroy, convinced the regent would be killed or taken hostage, covered his face. No one laid a hand on Ramses.

He inspected the sacks full of gold dust, the panther skins, plume fans and ostrich eggs so prized by noble families.

'If your man won't keep his word, we're bound to fight him, even if all of us die. No one can live in a world without honour.'

335

'There will be no fight,' Ramses assured him. 'The wheat you were promised will be delivered.'

Shaanar was tempted to accuse Ramses of weakness in dealing with the Nubian rebels, but the viceroy dissuaded him. In the course of a long secret meeting, the viceroy spoke of Ramses's growing popularity with the military. The soldiers admired his bravery, endurance and ability to think on his feet. With a leader like him, they feared no enemy. Calling Ramses a coward might reflect badly on Shaanar.

The Pharaoh's elder son yielded to this line of reasoning. Not controlling the army would be a drawback, of course, but when he became Lord of the Two Lands they would learn to obey him. Brute force alone would never govern Egypt. However, no ruler could take power without the consent of the court and the high priests.

It became increasingly clear that Ramses was an intrepid and dangerous warrior. As long as Seti held the reins of power, his aggressive nature was held in check. But afterward, it was anyone's guess. Impulsive attacks that would put the country in peril . . . Shaanar further stressed how Seti had reached a truce with the Hittites rather than pressing on and laying siege to their fortress at Kadesh. Would Ramses be so prudent? Shaanar's influential friends all hated war. Generals with dreams of glory threatened to upset their comfortable existence.

Egypt had no need of a conquering hero who might put the Near East to the fire and the sword. Ambassadors and returning couriers reported that the Hittites were pursuing peaceful goals and had given up their designs on Egypt. Consequently, a warrior prince like Ramses was unnecessary, if not downright harmful. If he kept posturing as a commander, he might need to be removed from the scene.

Shaanar's arguments were persuasive. He sounded so level-headed and realistic, and the facts backed him up.

During a trip to the Delta to clinch the future support of two provincial governors, Shaanar also met with Ahsha. The well-appointed cabin of his private boat was a perfect setting. His cook had prepared them delicacies, his steward had produced an exceptionally fruity vintage white wine.

As usual, the young diplomat's appearance was elegant, even a trifle haughty. His lively eyes were occasionally unsettling, but his smooth voice and calm, even manner were reassuring. If Ahsha proved trustworthy after they overthrew Ramses, he would make an excellent secretary of state. Today, however, he toyed with his food.

'Is anything wrong with your lunch?' Shaanar enquired.

'Forgive me. I'm rather preoccupied.'

'Personal problems?'

'Heavens, no.'

'Trouble at work?'

'Quite the contrary.'

'Ramses, then! Ramses is on to us.'

'I'm sure he isn't.'

'Then what has you so worried?'

'The Hittites.'

'Reports reaching us in Memphis show them quite thoroughly pacified.'

'That's the official story, yes.'

'And what do you think is wrong with it?

'Too naive, unless my superiors are simply trying not to trouble Seti with pessimistic forecasts.'

'Your version of the facts, then?'

'The Hittites are no simple-minded savages. They tried to achieve their goals through open confrontation; it didn't work, so they're switching strategies.'

'They'll buy up more disgruntled princelings and incite them to revolt, in other words.'

'That's what the Asia experts think, yes.'

'But you don't?'

'Not any more.'

'What are you afraid of?'

'That they're working from within to turn our own protectorates against us.'

'It's highly unlikely. Seti would crush any serious sedition in a flash.'

'Seti doesn't know about it.'

Shaanar did not take the young diplomat's warnings lightly, given his record for accuracy.

'This time the Hittites want to move carefully. In four or five years, they'll be ready to spring the trap.'

'Keep a close watch on the situation and don't breathe a word to anyone but me.'

'That's asking a lot.'

'You'll be getting a lot in return.'

51

Life was slow in the seaside fishing village. A naval police detachment of fewer than a dozen regulated shipping; fairly easy work, with only the occasional northbound Egyptian boat requiring the commander (potbellied and well past sixty) to log its passage. Ships returning from abroad used another branch of the Delta.

The shore patrol helped the fishermen pull in their nets and keep their boats in trim. They had all the fish they wanted, and on feast days the villagers would share the patrolmen's bi-weekly wine ration.

Dolphin-watching was the little community's favourite entertainment. They never tired of the graceful leaps and excited chases. In the evenings, one old fisherman told stories. In the nearby marshlands, the goddess Isis hid her newborn son in the rushes, to keep Horus safe from the avenging Set.

'A boat, sir.'

The commander was taking his afternoon nap and did not want to leave the comfort of his reed mat.

'Have them sign and record the name.'

'It's coming from the sea.'

'You must not have seen right. Look again.'

'It's coming this way, for sure.'

Intrigued, the commander got up. It wasn't a wine day.

Their usual weak beer would never produce such a wild hallucination.

From the beach, they clearly spied a large ship making straight for the village.

'It's not Egyptian . . .'

No Greek boat landed here. Their orders were strict: intercept intruders, order them to head west for escort by Pharaoh's navy.

'Into your armour – quickly,' the commander told his men, who had nearly forgotten how to handle spear, sword, bow and shield.

Aboard the strange vessel were swarthy men with curling moustaches, real horns set in their helmets, metal breastplates, pointed swords and round shields.

In the bow stood a giant.

The Egyptian patrolmen recoiled. 'A monster,' one of them whispered. 'Only a man,' replied the commander. 'Fire!'

Two arrows flew through the air. One went wide. The other was about to hit the giant's chest when he slashed it in half with his sword.

'Over there!' another patrolman shouted. 'Another boat!'

'An invasion,' the commander agreed. 'Retreat, men!'

Ramses was happy.

It was a daily happiness, strong as the south wind, mild as the north. Nefertari brought a fullness to each moment, eased his cares, guided his thoughts towards the light. With her at his side, the days were softly radiant. This woman knew how to soothe him without denying the fire that burned in him. She seemed to herald a strange, almost unsettling future – a new order.

Nefertari surprised him. Her new life might have spoiled her; instead, she assumed the stately elegance of a queen. What destiny would be hers to rule or to serve? Nefertari was a mystery. A mystery with an enchanting smile, so like the goddess Hathor's in the tomb of his grandfather, the first Ramses.

Iset the Fair was the earth, Nefertari the heavens. Ramses needed them both, though for Iset he felt only passion and desire.

Nefertari was love.

Seti contemplated the setting sun. When Ramses came in, the palace was growing dark. The king had not lit a single lamp.

'An alarming report from the Delta,' he told his son. 'My advisers think it's a minor incident, but I'm convinced they're wrong.'

'What happened?'

'Some pirates attacked a fishing village on the Mediterranean coast. The shore patrol had to retreat, but insist the situation is under control.'

'Could they be lying?'

'That's for you to find out.'

'Why the suspicion?'

'These pirates are fearsome pillagers. If they make their way inland, terror will follow in their wake.'

Ramses was indignant. 'Is that the kind of security our shore patrol provides?'

'Those in charge may have underestimated the danger.'

'I'll leave within the hour.'

The king once again looked out at the setting sun. He would have liked to go with his son, glide through the Delta again, sit in command of an army. In this fourteenth year of his reign, however, illness consumed him. Fortunately, the strength that was leaving him seeped into Ramses's young blood.

The shore patrol had regrouped about twenty miles inland, at a town on one of the Nile's lesser branches. Holed up in makeshift fortifications, they awaited aid. When the prince regent and his troops sailed in, they ran out to greet their rescuers.

Their portly commander was in the lead. He threw himself in front of Ramses's chariot.

'Our full complement is here, Your Majesty! None dead, none wounded.'

'On your feet.'

A chill fell over the joyous little gathering.

'We weren't . . . there weren't enough of us to resist. The pirates . . . We would have been slaughtered.'

'Tell me their whereabouts.'

'They're still on the coast and took another village.'

'Because of your cowardice!'

'Your Majesty . . . we were outnumbered.'

'Out of my way.'

The commander barely had time to jump aside. The dust obscured his view of the prince's chariot speeding towards the flagship of the imposing fleet he had brought from Memphis. Back on board, Ramses gave the order to sail due north.

Furious with the pirates, furious with the bumbling shore patrol, the prince drove his rowers mercilessly. The intensity spread rappidly through the fleet, eager to re-establish order on Egypt's maritime border.

Ramses went on at full speed.

The pirates, camping in their two captive villages, were debating how to proceed: whether to try to extend their control of the coast or sail away with their booty and plan their return.

Ramses surprised them as they grilled fish for lunch. Vastly outnumbered, the pirates still managed a spirited defence. The giant alone fought off twenty foot soldiers before he was finally captured.

More than half of the pirates were dead, their ship was burning, yet their enormous captain refused to bow his head to Ramses.

'Your name?'

'Serramanna.'

'Where do you come from?'

'Sardinia. You beat me, but other boats from my island will avenge me. They'll come by the dozen, and you won't be able to stop them. We want Egypt's riches, and we shall have them.'

'Your own country isn't enough for you?'

'The Sards live to conquer. Your miserable soldiers won't last long against us.'

Shocked by the pirate's insolence, one guard raised his hatchet above the giant's head.

'Back off!' ordered Ramses, turning towards his soldiers. 'Which one of you will face this barbarian single-handed?'

Not one volunteer came forward. Serramanna snorted with laughter.

'You're no warriors!'

'What are you after?' Ramses asked the giant. The question caught him off guard.

'Gold and jewels, of course! Then women, the finest wine, a house and land, and—'

'If I offer you all that and more, will you agree to become my personal bodyguard?'

The giant's eyes grew so wide they nearly engulfed his face.

'Kill me, but never laugh at me!'

'The true warrior thinks on his feet. What is it: serve me or die?'

'Untie me!' Two foot soldiers nervously freed his wrists.

Ramses was tall, but Serramanna stood a head taller. He strode forward. The archers took aim. If the giant rushed Ramses and overpowered him, would it be possible to shoot the pirate without harming Seti's son?

The Sard wanted to kill him – Ramses saw it in his eyes.

Yet he stood there, arms crossed, seemingly unconcerned. The giant sensed no trace of fear in the prince.

Serramanna bent one knee to the ground and bowed his head.

'At your command,' he said.

52

Memphis society was scandalized. Hadn't they given enough valiant sons to the army? Weren't their own men quite capable of protecting the regent's person? Seeing a veritable barbarian in charge of his royal guardsmen was a shocking insult to the nobility, even if it was generally agreed that Serramanna, in his Sardinian garb, made quite an effective deterrent. And yes, the rest of his crew had been convicted of piracy and sent to the mines, but did that mean their captain should hold a post of honour? If he stabbed Ramses in the back, it would only be what the regent had coming.

Shaanar rejoiced in this latest blunder. Ramses's outlandish decision proved he put might over right. What was more, he shunned banquets and receptions in favour of endless horseback rides in the desert, intensive training in archery and sword fighting, and dangerous play sessions with his lion.

Serramanna became his special partner. They traded fighting techniques, armed and unarmed, and found a middle course between strength and agility. The Egyptian guard troops placed under the giant's command issued no complaints. They also underwent the intensive training that made them part of the military elite, housed and fed in the best of conditions.

Ramses kept his promises. Serramanna became the proprietor of an eight-room villa with a well and a pleasure garden.

His cellar overflowed with amphorae of vintage wine, his bed with willing beauties from Libya and Nubia, fascinated by the foreigner's size.

Serramanna kept his helmet, breastplate, pointed sword and round shield, but surrendered his allegiance to Sardinia. At home he had been a poor outcast. Here he was rich and respected. He was infinitely grateful to Ramses, who first of all spared his life, then gave him the life he had always dreamed of. Anyone who tried to lay a hand on the regent would have to answer to his bodyguard.

In Year Fourteen of Seti's reign, the inundation did not look promising. The meagre rise in the Nile's water level might mean famine. As soon as the king received confirmation from the experts in Aswan, who measured the river and consulted their centuries of records, he summoned Ramses. Pharaoh ignored his growing fatigue and took his son to Gebel el-Silsila, where the riverbanks met; according to ancient tradition, that was where the flood arose, where the goddess Hapi's energy flowed from twin caves, giving rise to pure, life-giving water.

To restore harmony, Seti made an offering to the river: fifty-four jars of milk, three hundred loaves of white bread, seventy cakes, twenty-eight crocks of honey, twenty-eight baskets of grapes, twenty-four of figs, twenty-eight of dates, pomegranates, zizyphus and persea fruit, plus cucumbers, beans, ceramic figurines, forty-eight jars of incense, gold, silver, copper, alabaster and cakes shaped like a calf, goose, crocodile and hippopotamus.

Three days later, the water level rose, but remained inadequate. Now there was only the slimmest hope.

The House of Life in Heliopolis was the oldest in Egypt. It was a repository for scrolls that held the mysteries of heaven and earth, for secret rituals, maps of the heavens,

royal annals, for prophecy, mythology, medical and sur-
gical research, mathematical and geometric treatises, keys
to the interpretation of dreams, for hieroglyph dictionaries,
works on architecture, sculpture, painting, for inventories of
ritual objects used in religious ceremonies, calendars of feast
days, magic spell books, Books of Wisdom compiled by the
ancients, and texts on 'transforming into light' serving as
guidebooks to the netherworld.

'For a Pharaoh,' declared Seti to Ramses, 'no place is
more important. When you're assailed by doubts, come here
and consult the archives. The House of Life is Egypt's past,
present and future. Immerse yourself in its teachings and as
I have seen, you will see.'

Seti asked the director of the House of Life, an old priest
completely cloistered from the outside world, to bring him
the *Book of the Nile*. A younger priest carried out his order.
Ramses thought he looked familiar.

'Bakhen? Is that you?'

'At your service, Prince Regent.'

'What happened to the Royal Stables?'

'For many years I've been serving as a lay priest. When I
turned twenty-one, I gave up my secular role.'

Bakhen looked much the same, except that his square,
unprepossessing face, clean-shaven now, looked less harsh.
With his stocky build, bulging biceps and deep, husky voice,
Bakhen hardly resembled a classical scholar. He unrolled the
papyrus on the table in front of them and withdrew.

'Keep an eye on that man,' counselled Seti. 'In a few
weeks, he will leave for Thebes and serve in the Temple
of Amon at Karnak. Your paths will cross again.'

The king studied the venerable document, the work of a
Third Dynasty pharaoh more than thirteen hundred years earlier. In contact with the spirit of the Nile, he gave instructions
on how to appease the river when the waters were too low.

Seti found the solution: the ceremonial offering made at

Gebel el-Silsila must be repeated at Aswan, Thebes and Memphis.

On his return from this long journey, Seti was exhausted. When messengers arrived reporting that the inundation would be nearly normal, he ordered provincial governors to take special care in checking the dykes and reservoirs. A national disaster had been averted, but now it was essential to conserve every drop of river water.

Each morning the king, frail and hollow-cheeked, conferred with Ramses and spoke to him of Ma'at, the goddess of justice represented as a slender woman, sometimes as the Feather of Righteousness directing birds in flight. However fragile in appearance, Ma'at alone had the strength to hold the world together. Only if her Divine Rule was followed would the sun shine, the wheat grow, the weak be protected from the strong, cooperation and respect guide the daily life of Egypt. Of all a Pharaoh's accomplishments, first and foremost must be to live by the principle of Ma'at.

His words nourished Ramses's soul. The prince dared not enquire about his father's health, aware that he was moving towards another plane of existence and transmitting its energy to his son. Intent on absorbing all he could, Ramses deserted Nefertari, Ahmeni and their friends. Pharaoh's voice became his world.

His wife encouraged him. With the help of Ahmeni, she handled his daily affairs, freeing Ramses to be Seti's servant and heir to his inner strength.

The latest information left no room for doubt: Seti's illness was advancing quickly. Choking back his tears, Shaanar spread the dreadful news at court and sent messages to the high priest of Amon and the provincial governors. The doctors still hoped to prolong the king's life, but feared the final crisis was approaching. Worse than the prospect of Pharaoh's death was the catastrophe that would follow, namely Ramses's coronation.

Shaanar alerted his supporters. Naturally, he would try first to convince his brother that he was unfit to wield the sceptre, but would he listen to reason? If the country's safekeeping required, perhaps they would have to resort to other methods, steps that might be of questionable legality yet represented the only hope of keeping a young warlord from bringing Egypt to ruin.

His rationale was well received, moderate and realistic, the court thought. Everyone hoped that Pharaoh's reign would last for years, but braced themselves for the worst.

Menelaus's Greek soldiers, posing as shopkeepers, sharpened their swords. At their king's order, they would snap into action as a militia. The surprise would increase their effectiveness: no one expected these law-abiding, assimilated foreigners to take part in a coup. As the day grew nearer, Menelaus was itching for a fight. He could hardly wait to swing his heavy sword, puncture chests and bellies, hack off arms and legs, crush skulls, with the same abandon as on the battlefields of Troy. Then he would head for home with Helen and make her pay for her insolence and infidelity.

Shaanar was optimistic. His support was broad and deep, his strategy diversified. He saw only one possible hitch: Serramanna. When Ramses appointed the Sardinian giant as head of his royal bodyguard, he unwittingly parried one of his brother's master strokes. The Greek officer Shaanar had planted in the guard regiment would never be able to get past Serramanna. The solution was painfully obvious: Menelaus would murder the Sard. He would hardly be missed.

Everything was in place. All Shaanar had to do now was wait for Seti's passing and give the signal.

'Your father can't see you this morning,' Tuya said regretfully.

'Is he worse?'

'They've decided not to proceed with surgery. He's been given a strong sedative made from mandrake.' Tuya maintained her remarkable dignity, but the pain was evident in every word she spoke.

'Tell me the truth. Is there any hope left?'

'I don't think so. His system is too weak. Your father had so much energy but he should never have worked so hard. Still, how can you persuade a Pharaoh not to give his all for his people?'

Seeing the tears in his mother's eyes, Ramses hugged her tight.

'Seti does not fear death,' She assured her son. His eternal dwelling is finished. He is ready to appear before Osiris and his judges. When Seti's soul is weighed, he has nothing to fear from the monster that devours those who flout the law of Ma'at. In our earthly rites, that will be my verdict.'

'What can I do to help you?'

'Prepare yourself, my son. Prepare yourself to keep your father's name alive through all eternity, to follow in the footsteps of your ancestors, to confront the unknown forms your destiny will take.'

Setau and Lotus started work at nightfall. The flood waters had receded from the lowlands. The landscape looked the same as before. Poor as it was this year, the inundation still had a purifying effect, drowning countless rodents and reptiles in their burrows. The survivors were the toughest and most resourceful specimens, and late-summer venom was therefore the choicest.

The snake hunter had set his sights on a familiar area of the desert where huge and deadly cobras lived. Setau approached the den of the largest snake he had sighted before the flood – an imperturbable creature. Lotus walked barefoot behind him; despite her experience and cool head, he never let her take an unnecessary risk. His pretty young wife carried a forked stick, a cloth sack and a vial. Pinning a snake and milking its venom were her routine tasks.

A full moon shone on the desert. It agitated the snakes and made them stray to the limits of their territory. Setau chanted in a low voice, accentuating the low notes that attracted cobras. He spotted the entrance to the den, an opening between two flat rocks. Wavy tracks in the sand told him an enormous cobra had recently been here.

Setau sat down, still chanting under his breath. The cobra was late.

Lotus suddenly dived headlong to the ground. In a blur, Setau saw her wrestling the black cobra he had been planning to trap. The brief struggle ended when his bride stuffed the serpent into her sack.

'He was coming at you from behind,' she explained.

'Never heard of such a thing,' Setau asserted. 'If snakes are losing their senses, it's a bad sign. A very bad sign.'

53

' "For we will not have any respite, however short it may be, until the hour when the night comes to separate us and calm our zeal. Under the heavy shield which protects the body, our chest will be drenched in sweat; the hand will linger on the sword's hilt," ' declaimed Homer.

'Are these new verses another warning from you?' asked Ramses.

'My *Iliad* deals strictly with the past.'

'It doesn't foretell the future?'

'Egypt has grown on me. I'd hate to see it heading for destruction.'

'Why are you so concerned?'

'I keep up with my fellow Greeks here, and lately they seem on edge. You'd swear they were about to storm Troy again.'

'Do you know anything more?'

'I'm only a blind old poet, son.'

Helen thanked Tuya for granting her an audience at such a difficult time. Yet the Great Royal Wife's face bore no trace of suffering beneath its subtle make-up.

'I don't know how—'

'Words are useless, Helen.'

'I am sincerely sorry, and I pray to the gods for your husband's recovery.'

'Many thanks. I, too, have called on the unseen.'

'I also pray because I'm worried, Majesty.'

'What troubles you, my dear?'

'The change in my husband's spirits. He's been so discontent until lately. Now he's acting smug. He must think he's taking me home soon.'

'Even if Seti leaves us, you will be protected.'

'I'm afraid I won't be.'

'Menelaus is my guest. He has no power over you.'

'I want to stay here, in this palace, working with you!'

'Calm down, Helen. Nothing can harm you.'

Despite the Queen's reassurances, Helen feared her vindictive husband. He must have thought of some way to spirit her out of Egypt. Seti's imminent death would provide the perfect occasion. Helen decided to follow her husband's movements. Why, Tuya's life might even be in danger! When Menelaus failed to get what he wanted, he turned violent. His anger had been held in check too long.

Ahmeni read the letter Dolora had written to Ramses.

Beloved brother,

My husband and I are concerned for your health, even more than for that of our revered father, Pharaoh Seti, whom we understand to be gravely ill. Is this not the time for forgiveness? My place is in Memphis. I know you can find it in the goodness of your heart to pardon my husband's offence and allow him to stand by my side as we pay our respects to Seti and Tuya. Let us comfort one another in our hour of need. Let our family heal. Let us put the past behind us. Sary joins me in hoping for a prompt and merciful reply.

'Read it once more to me, slowly,' requested the Prince Regent.

Nervously, Ahmeni complied. 'It doesn't deserve an answer,' he muttered.

'Take a new papyrus.'

'Should we give in?'

'Dolora is my sister, Ahmeni.'

'She wasn't so upset when I nearly died, but then I'm not a member of the royal family.'

'You're awfully bitter.'

'And you're too soft-hearted. Those two will only try to double-cross you.'

'I want you to take a letter, Ahmeni.'

'My wrist is sore. Wouldn't it be more personal in your own handwriting?'

'Please take this down.'

Livid, Ahmeni gripped his reed pen.

'It will be short, I promise. "*Under no circumstances may you return to Memphis, unless you intend to appear in court. Further, refrain from any contact whatsoever with the Pharaoh,*"' he dictated.

The scribe's pen flew across the clean papyrus.

Iset the Fair spent hours consoling Dolora. Ramses's reply to her plea for mercy was scathing. In his sister's opinion, the prince's stubbornness, hot temper and hard heart did not bode well for his lesser wife and infant son.

It was painfully clear that Shaanar had been right: Ramses was power-hungry, spreading misery in his wake. Despite her deep affection for him, Iset had no choice but to align herself with the opposing camp. So must his own sister.

Egypt's future lay with Shaanar. Iset the Fair would forget Ramses, wed the new master of the country and start a legitimate family.

Sary added that Shaanar also had the backing of the high

priest of Amon and many other influential figures who would bolster his claim to the throne after Seti's passing. Duly informed, Iset the Fair could take her destiny in hand.

When Moses arrived at the construction site, shortly after dawn, not one stone-cutter was there to meet him. Yet it was an ordinary work day, and his elite crew were conscientious to a fault; their professional company held them accountable for every absence.

Still, Karnak's new hall of columns, planned as the largest in Egypt, was deserted. For the first time, Moses experienced its grandeur untroubled by the ring of mallets and chisels. He contemplated the sacred images carved into the columns and admired the offertory scenes showing Pharaoh at one with the gods. This hugely powerful expression of the sacred transcended the human soul.

Moses remained there alone for hours, as if he possessed this magic place, a future home for the creative forces essential to Egypt's survival. But were they the true expression of the divine, he wondered? Finally, he noticed a foreman coming in to pick up some misplaced tools. He greeted the workman at the foot of a column.

'Why isn't anyone working today?'

'Didn't they tell you?'

'I've just come back from Gebel el-Silsila.'

'The project supervisor told us this morning that we're off until further notice.'

'What reason did he give?'

'Pharaoh needs to give his final approval in person, but he's been held up in Memphis. We can't go on until he comes to Thebes again.'

It sounded like an incomplete explanation. Nothing would keep Seti from an important project like Karnak – nothing but a serious illness. Seti dying? It was almost inconceivable. Ramses must be in despair.

Moses was on the next boat to Memphis.

'Come closer, Ramses.'

Seti lay on a gilded wooden bed by a window. The setting sun illuminated the room. Ramses was amazed at the serene glow on his father's face.

There was still hope! He was strong enough to have visitors. He looked so much better. Seti could battle death and win, he knew it!

'Pharaoh is the image of the Creator who created all things,' Seti instructed. 'He acts in the name of Ma'at, the Goddess of Truth. Honour the gods, Ramses, be the shepherd of your people, watch over the great and the small, let your every action serve a worthwhile purpose.'

'*You* are Pharaoh, Father.'

'I see death coming for me, young and smiling, with the face of the goddess of the West. It is not a defeat, Ramses, but a journey. A journey into the vastness of the universe for which I have prepared myself, for which you must prepare from the first day of your reign.'

'Don't go, Father, I beg you.'

'You were born to command, not to beg. The time has come for me to live my death and be judged at the entrance to the netherworld. If my life has been righteous, my being will move to a higher plane.'

'We need you here.'

'Since the time of the gods, Egypt is the only daughter of the sun, and the son of Egypt sits on the throne of light. You must succeed me, Ramses, carry on my work and surpass it. You were named for the sun – "Ra-Begot-Him". Live up to your name, Son of Light.'

'I have so many questions to ask you, so much to learn.'

'Since that first encounter with the wild bull, I have been teaching you, for no one knows what unexpected twists his

356

destiny may have in store. You must now master that destiny. Your fate is to guide a great nation.'

'I'm not ready, Father.'

'No one is ever ready. When your grandfather Ramses, the founder of our dynasty, left this earth for his home in the sun, I was as anxious and confused as you are today. Anyone seeking to rule is a fool or a madman. The hand of God alone can choose the one to walk down this path of sacrifice. As Pharaoh, you are your people's first servant, a servant no longer permitted to rest or enjoy life's simple pleasures. You will be alone – not desperately alone like a lost soul, but alone like the captain of a ship who must find the right course and discern the truth among all the mysterious forces surrounding him. Love Egypt more than yourself, and your course will be clear.'

The sunset bathed Seti's peaceful face in gold; his body glowed with an aura, as if he were a source of light.

'There will be many obstacles in your path,' he predicted. 'You will have to face powerful enemies, for man is too fond of evil. Look deep into yourself and you will find the courage to prevail. Nefertari's magic will protect you. She has the heart of a Great Royal Wife. Be the falcon soaring in the sky, my son. See with the falcon's eyes.'

Seti's voice trailed off. His eyes looked beyond the sun, towards another world, a world he alone could see.

Shaanar was not quite ready to set his plans in motion. Seti was on his deathbed, that much was certain, but no official announcement had yet been made. A premature move would jeopardize everything; as long as Pharaoh was still alive, any rebellion would be unpardonable. He must move when the throne lay vacant for the sixty-six days of the mummification process. Then he would clearly be attacking Ramses, not his father. And Seti would not be around to uphold his choice of successor.

Menelaus and his soldiers were itching for a fight. Dolora and Sary had enlisted Iset the Fair, persuaded the High Priest of Amon to maintain strict neutrality and garnered the support of the Theban upper crust. Meba, the secretary of state, had deftly manoeuvred in Shaanar's favour at court.

Ramses was walking straight into a trap. The twenty-three-year-old crown prince was naive enough to think that his father's word was all it took to put him on the throne.

How should Shaanar dispose of him? If Ramses surrendered gracefully, a token position in Nubia or a desert oasis would be appropriate. Even then, he might still be able to stir up some opposition, however feeble. He was too impetuous to adjust to exile. No, Ramses required a permanent solution. Death was the logical answer, but Shaanar balked at eliminating his own brother.

The easy way out would be sending him to Greece with Menelaus, with the official explanation that Ramses renounced his claim to the throne and preferred to travel. The King of Sparta would hold him prisoner until he died, far from home and utterly forgotten. Nefertari could become a priestess in some distant provincial temple, her childhood dream.

Shaanar called for his hairdresser, manicurist, keeper of the wardrobe: the future ruler of Egypt must appear flawlessly groomed.

The Great Royal Wife personally announced Seti's death to the court. In Year Fifteen of his reign, Pharaoh had turned his face towards the great beyond. Each night he would be reborn from his heavenly mother, appearing anew at the break of day. His fellow gods would welcome him to the netherworld, where he would live for ever, at one with Ma'at.

The period of mourning began immediately.

The temples were closed and religious rites were discontinued, except for prayers for the dead each morning and evening. For sixty-six days, men refrained from shaving, women wore their hair down, no meat or wine was eaten; scribes stopped working, the government shut down.

Pharaoh was dead, the throne sat empty, and Egypt was in flux. It was a fearsome time, when Ma'at was in mortal danger. The Queen Mother and Prince Regent were close at hand, but still, the throne was vacant. The powers of darkness were rampant, eager to hold the country in their sway.

The border patrols were put on highest alert. The news of Seti's death would spread quickly and excite an unhealthy interest. The Hittites and other hostile nations might attack the fringes of the Delta or launch a massive invasion. Seafaring pirates and Bedouin marauders also had their designs on Egypt. Seti had thwarted them. With Seti gone, would the country's defences crumble?

The very day of his passing, Seti's corpse was transported to the hall of purification on the West Bank of the Nile. The Great Royal Wife presided over the tribunal called to judge the dead king. She, her sons, the vizier, the members of his council, religious and government leaders all testified under oath that Seti had been a just king and they had no complaint to lodge against him.

The living had reached their verdict. Seti's soul could go to meet the ferryman, cross the river to the netherworld, and sail towards the stars. His mortal remains, however, must still be transformed into Osiris and mummified according to royal rituals.

Embalmers would remove the viscera, desiccate the flesh with natron and exposure to sunlight. Then other mortuary priests would swathe the late pharaoh's body in strips of linen and he would depart for his eternal dwelling in the Valley of the Kings.

Ahmeni, Setau and Moses were concerned. Ramses would

see no one. After thanking his friends for their sympathy, he retreated to his private chambers. He spoke to Nefertari, but only barely, and even she failed to bring him comfort.

Adding to Ahmeni's worries was Shaanar. Once he had made a proper display of his grief, he seemed to be everywhere, contacting the heads of various agencies and generally taking matters in hand. He called on the vizier, insisting he merely hoped to be of service and help provide a smooth transition of power, with due respect to the period of mourning.

Tuya would soon have set him straight, except that her duty still lay with her husband. As the incarnation of the goddess Isis, she played a magical role in the mortuary rituals essential for his resurrection. Until the moment when Seti-Osiris was laid in his sarcophagus, or 'master of life', the Great Royal Wife would take no part in worldly affairs.

Nothing and no one stood in Shaanar's way.

The lion and yellow dog stuck close to their master, as if to console him.

His future had seemed so full of promise. He only had to listen to his father's advice, obey him, follow his example. With Seti at his side, ascending to the throne would have been so simple. Ramses had never realized how alone he would be without his father's all-seeing eyes to guide him.

Fifteen years' reign. Much too short! Abydos, Karnak, Memphis, Heliopolis, Gurnah – so many temples proclaimed the glory of this great builder, in the mould of the Old Kingdom pharaohs. But he was gone, and Ramses felt his twenty-three years acutely: he was bent with sorrow, but still too young to be king.

Could he bear the weight of his name, the Son of Light?